ARIS & PHILLIPS HISPANIC CLASSICS

PEDRO CALDERÓN DE LA BARCA

Life's a Dream

La vida es sueño

A Prose Translation and Critical Introduction
by

Michael Kidd

Aris & Phillips
is an imprint of
Oxbow Books, Oxford, UK

ISBN cloth 978-0-85668-896-6
ISBN paper 978-0-85668-895-9

A CIP record for this book is available from the British Library.

This book is available direct from

Oxbow Books, Oxford, UK
Phone: 01865-241249; Fax: 01865-794449

or from our website
www.oxbowbooks.com

*Cover image (paperback only): A traveller peeks through the firmament
and discovers the cosmic machinery that moves the universe.
First published by Camille Flammarion in
L'Atmosphère: météorologie populaire (Paris, 1888).*

For my father

CONTENTS

PREFACE

This prose translation of Pedro Calderón de la Barca's *La vida es sueño* is envisioned as both a classroom text and a script for performance, and the accompanying materials reflect that dual function. The Introduction and Glossary are written especially for students encountering the play for the first time, while the Suggestions for Directors are intended primarily for those interested in taking the play to the stage. The Translator's Notes will appeal to specialists, translators, and others with an interest in Spanish language and poetry or in the details of textual criticism. The Bibliography provides a starting point for anyone who wishes to pursue in greater depth the issues raised in the introductory materials.

The Spanish text used as the basis of the translation is that of J. M. Ruano de la Haza (Castalia, 2nd. ed., 2000), for reasons explained in section 7 of the Translator's Notes. To permit an unencumbered encounter with the play, no footnotes have been used in the body of the translation itself; all issues of interpretation and necessary clarifications are dealt with in the supplementary materials (see especially Introduction, section 4; Translator's Notes, sections 5–7; and the Glossary.)

This translation was first published by the University Press of Colorado with American high school and college students in mind. I am delighted to have the opportunity to present it to UK students, and I have used the occasion to review and, where appropriate, revise my renderings as well as to update the introductory materials and bibliography. I am grateful to Dr. Jonathan Thacker of Merton College, Oxford for his generous assistance in the adaptation to British English, and I wish to thank my former editor at Colorado, Darrin Pratt, for his permission to republish the manuscript in the Aris and Phillips series.

INTRODUCTION

1. Spain in the Seventeenth Century

When Calderón was born in the year 1600, Spain was the most powerful country in the world, but the seeds were already planted of a decline that would take it, by the time of his death in 1681, to the humiliating status of a second-tier power. The story of Spain's rise and fall is the sobering tale of a country that collapsed under the burden of its own achievements. Rather than chronicle that process in detail, which would occupy more space than this Introduction will allow, I will begin with three salient general features of early modern Spanish society: religious intensity, inequality before the law, and a deep sense of national pride that nevertheless suffered serious blows throughout the seventeenth century. These three characteristics are important because they forcefully underpin the ideology of Calderonian Spain and, more broadly, of what is known as the Old Regime, that is, the set of social and political norms that held sway across Europe prior to the French Revolution in 1789. Although none of the characteristics is unique to Spain, they all imply a series of assumptions about the world strikingly different from those that inform modern liberal democracies (including present-day Spain), and their examination will provide an essential preface to the survey of Spanish literature and culture with which I end section 1 of the Introduction.

***

Calderón was born in an age of deep religious conviction. It may be difficult for westerners of the early twenty-first century, anaesthetized by the freedom of worship that all liberal democracies guarantee, to grasp the significance of this fact. Especially in Spain, whose Middle Ages were defined by a long struggle to reunite the peninsula under Christian rule, religious belief was not a matter of choice, and Catholicism permeated all aspects of life and determined the course of history. Even language reflects the omnipresence of religion: to speak Spanish became (and remains) synonymous with speaking "Christian" (*hablar cristiano*), while official correspondence of the period refers to "both Majesties" (*ambas majestades*) in deference to God as well as the king. Early modern Spanish identity, to the extent that one can generalize about it, was forged in a crucible of religiosity that never wavered.

Many of the major events and institutions associated with this period came about as a result of that religiosity. The Spanish Inquisition was founded in 1478 with the purpose of rooting out heresy, especially among Jewish (and later Muslim) converts to Christianity. Unlike the Papal Inquisition, which had been in place in other parts of Europe since 1233, the Inquisition in Spain was placed under nearly exclusive control of the monarchy; the Pope's power was limited to naming the Inquisitor General. Because its jurisdiction was restricted to baptized Christians, its power was considerably extended when all unbaptized Jews were forced to convert or leave the peninsula in 1492.[1] Also in 1492, King Ferdinand and Queen Isabella were honoured by the Pope with the title of Catholic Monarchs *(los Reyes Católicos)* upon their reconquest of Granada, the last independent Muslim kingdom on the peninsula; in 1609 the Moriscos (Moorish converts to Christianity) suffered the same fate that the Jews had in 1492. In 1540, Ignatius of Loyola founded the Jesuit Order, dedicated to an active (rather than speculative) pursuit of faith. The Jesuits provided great impetus to the Counter Reformation, which by then had come into full swing as Spain united with Rome to stay the rising tide of Protestantism. Costly wars of religion between Catholics and Protestants ensued across Europe, exhausting the Spanish treasury in its struggle against countries like England (which it tried to invade) and the Low Countries (part of its Hapsburg patrimony, which it was able to hold only by force) in addition to its traditional Mediterranean rival, France. There was, finally, great cost in manpower and wealth imposed by the subjugation and evangelization of the indigenous peoples of the Americas.

***

Modern readers may also be accustomed to take for granted the legal axioms of political representation and equality before the law, two products of enlightenment thought that form the cornerstone of liberal democracy. But no such principles existed in early modern Europe, as several examples from Calderón's Spain will demonstrate.

First, the distribution of power in society was far from equitable. At the top, of course, reigned the king and his court. The powerful nobility, concentrated in the countryside, had its own estate in parliament, as did the clergy, which, along with the military orders (religious in character),

---

[1] One estimate is that 175,000 Jews fled Spain in the spring and summer of 1492 and another 100,000 converted by the August deadline (Gerber 1992, p. 140 [Bibliography, section 7]). The total population of Castile and Aragón at the time was somewhere between eight and nine million (O'Callaghan 1975, pp. 604–05 [Bibliography, section 7]).

wielded considerable influence. A third parliamentary estate was occupied by the major municipalities, which were of considerable diversity in structure and tended to represent a democratising force. Above the municipal level, however, citizens had no political representation; nor was there trial by a jury of peers, for the king was the ultimate arbiter in cases of injustice. Private property was held primarily by the monarchy and the first two parliamentary estates, although the municipalities were allowed to lease land from the crown for public use. Taxation was regressive, with the poor shouldering the burden of contributions to the state treasury. The inferiority of women, peasants, slaves, Indians, and the unbaptized was routinely (though not universally) asserted, and discrimination against such groups not only prevailed but was legally sanctioned. For example, in the wake of the expulsion of the Jews, as those who chose to convert rather than leave the country began to occupy civil and clerical positions of authority, promulgation began of the infamous "pure-blood" statutes – analogous to English anti-Catholic laws of the same period – which excluded those of Jewish or Muslim lineage from occupying positions of power. The anguish subsequently felt by many writers and intellectuals of Jewish descent became, according to the twentieth-century Spanish historian Américo Castro, a defining feature of early modern Spanish literature.[2]

Despite all these factors, the term "absolute monarchy" gives an inaccurate impression of sixteenth- and seventeenth-century Spain, which was actually "one of the freest nations in Europe, with active political institutions at all levels. Remarkably free discussion of political affairs was tolerated, and public controversy occurred on a scale paralleled in few other countries."[3] The fact that the system was inequitable does not mean that its inequities went unperceived, and the literature of the period amply documents many diverse perspectives regarding justice and equality. As far back as the thirteenth century, St. Thomas Aquinas had argued for the radical equality of all human souls, and his arguments were now invoked in Spain to defend the rights of Indians and women. Typically, however, such arguments were directed against abuses of the system rather than the system itself. This is an important distinction. Men like Bartolomé de las Casas (1474–1566) and Francisco de Vitoria (1492–1546) argued for a humane treatment of the Indians, but they firmly supported the effort to convert them to the Catholic faith. Hence the New Laws of 1542 – promulgated largely in response to Las Casas's unpublished manuscript, *A Brief Account of the Destruction of*

---

[2] See especially Castro 1954 and 1972 (Bibliography, section 7).

[3] Kamen 1985, p. 99 (Bibliography, section 7).

the Indies (*Brevísima relación de la destrucción de las Indias*) – abolished the encomienda system, the abuse of which had made de facto slaves of the Indians.[4] Teresa of Ávila (a.k.a. Saint Teresa, 1515–1582), for her part, notes in the second paragraph of her autobiography that her father's caring nature led him to pity the plight of slaves (whose bondage was legally sanctioned throughout most of sixteenth- and seventeenth-century Europe); yet, rather than question the system that permitted slavery to exist, he simply refused to own them himself and made sure to treat those owned by others with kindness.[5] Similarly, the lesson that María de Zayas apparently intends to teach women readers in her *Eye-Opening Love Stories* (*Desengaños amorosos*, 1647) is not to rebel against male authority but simply to dissociate from men altogether, as does the character Lisis upon entering the convent at the end of the last story.[6] Finally, regarding the inherent inequality that was believed to exist between lords and vassals, it is telling that when the peasants of Lope de Vega's *Sheep's Fount* (*Fuente Ovejuna*, 1619) rise up to overthrow and murder their tyrannical master, literally tearing him to pieces, they do so with shouts of "Long live King Ferdinand! Death to evil Christians and traitors!"[7]

Lest there be any doubt, however, the occasional *real* threat to the values of the Old Regime was met with a severity intended to discourage future disturbances: such was the case with the Comuneros Revolt of 1520, the Morisco uprising of 1568, the Catalonian insurrection of the 1640s (in which Calderón himself fought on the side of the king), the Pueblo rebellion of 1680, and so on.

***

---

[4] The lax enforcement of the New Laws, however, led Las Casas to denounce the situation in 1552 by publishing his manuscript, which he dedicated to Prince Philip (soon to be King Philip II) in order to assure his awareness of the abuses.

[5] "Era mi padre hombre de mucha caridad con los pobres y piadad con los enfermos, y aun con los criados; tanta, que jamás se pudo con él tuviese esclavos, porque los había gran piadad y estando una de un su hermano, la regalaba como a sus hijos: decía que, de que no era libre, no lo podía sufrir de piadad." Teresa of Ávila 1990, p. 120 (Bibliography, section 7).

[6] "Estoy tan cobarde, que, como el que ha cometido algún delito, me acojo a sagrado y tomo por amparo el retiro de un convento, desde donde pienso (como en talanquera) ver lo que sucede a los demás. Y así, con mi querida doña Isabel, a quien pienso acompañar mientras viviere, me voy a salvar de los engaños de los hombres." Zayas 1993, p. 509 (Bibliography, section 7).

[7] "¡Viva el Rey Fernando! / ¡Mueran malos cristianos y traidores!" (*Fuente Ovejuna*, ed. Juan María Marín, 9th ed., Madrid: Cátedra, 1988, vv. 1882–83).

Historians may lament the fact that Columbus's maiden voyage to the Indies in 1492 tends to eclipse other events of that remarkable year, but few would deny the magnitude of his achievement. Although Columbus died insisting that he had reached India, it soon became apparent that he had come upon two great continents previously unknown to Europeans.[8] Spain's primary claim to those continents and to whatever riches they contained catapulted it almost immediately from its traditional, Mediterranean sphere of influence onto the centre stage of European politics, forever changing the course of history. Eventually, Spain's pretensions in the New World would put it at odds not only with its traditional Mediterranean rival, France, but also with two rising Atlantic powers, Holland and England, toward whom its animosity only grew with the success of the Protestant Reformation.

Columbus's voyage, together with the other momentous events of 1492[9] and several that soon followed,[10] cemented in the identity of Spaniards a proud nationalism bound to a profound sense of manifest destiny. By the seventeenth century, however, national pride was coming under increasing strain. An ominous portent was the catastrophic defeat of the Invincible Armada by the English Navy in 1588. More importantly, the shiploads of gold and silver that flooded into the country from the New World, much to the envy of Spain's European enemies (and subject to relentless pirate attacks on their part), were not nearly enough to finance the staggering military expenditures of the Spanish crown against those same European enemies on the continent, and the treasury was forced to declare bankruptcy at least eight times between 1557 and 1680. At the same time, the influx of American bullion into the peninsula came about without a corresponding rise in productivity, creating a galloping inflation that necessitated a seemingly endless series of currency devaluations throughout the seventeenth century,

[8] It is worth noting that Columbus (1451–1506), though he was financed by the Spanish crown and wrote his diary in Spanish, was probably not Spanish by birth. His obscure origins have become the subject of intense speculation, and while nothing has been proved, the most credible theories point to Genoa, Italy as his birthplace.

[9] For example: the reconquest of Granada (January); the expulsion of the Jews (authorized in March and carried out in July); the election of the Valencian Rodrigo Borgia as Pope Alexander VI (August); the publication of Antonio de Nebrija's Spanish grammar; and the performance of Juan del Encina's nativity plays (December). Nebrija's and Encina's achievements are discussed in the following section.

[10] For example: Spain's defeat of France and the consequent consolidation of its Italian possessions, confirmed in the Battle of Pavia (1525); and, upon the inheritance of the Spanish throne by Charles of Ghent (Charles I of Spain, Charles V of the Holy Roman Empire) in 1516, the addition of the German lands and the Low Countries to its European possessions.

popularly known as the "currency dance" *(baile del vellón)*. Intelligent observers saw such events as a dire warning of the country's political decline, which was confirmed in 1648 when the Peace of Westphalia (which ended the Thirty Years' War) formalized Spain's surrender of European hegemony to France. By the time of Calderón's death in 1681, Spaniards could look back to the time of the Catholic Monarchs only with nostalgia, a golden age of their country's history from which they had been forever expelled.

***

Spain's literary golden age also took root in the time of Ferdinand and Isabella, although it did not reach fruition until much later. In this sense, the year 1492 is yet another milestone. Antonio de Nebrija (1444–1522), a renowned humanist and professor at the University of Salamanca, published in 1492 his *Grammar of the Castilian Language (Gramática de la lengua castellana)*, the first grammar of a modern vernacular language, which prophetically argued for the use of Spanish as an instrument of empire. In December of the same year, Juan del Encina (1468–1529), a student of Nebrija's, composed and performed several short nativity sketches, which he called eclogues after the Virgilian model, in the palace of the Duke and Duchess of Alba outside Salamanca. In the history of Spanish drama, which had no significant medieval tradition upon which to build, these unrefined plays are of tremendous importance and can be seen as the starting point of an unbroken dramatic tradition that eventually culminates in Calderón and *Life's a Dream*. (More detail on the evolution of Spanish theatre is offered in section 2 of this Introduction.)

Spanish poetry and prose also flourished during this period. In 1496, Encina published his eclogues together with a treatise titled *Art of Spanish Poetry (Arte de poesía castellana)*, the first manual of poetry written in Spanish, in which he argues for the beauty and poetic potential of the Spanish language. He was proved right only a few decades later: through the incorporation of traditional Italian Renaissance metres, Garcilaso de la Vega (1501–1536) conferred on Spanish poetry a prestige previously unknown to it. A hundred years later, Luis de Góngora (1561–1627), though much maligned during his life, gave seventeenth-century poetry its most unique voice with his sixty-three-stanza *Myth of Polyphemous and Galatea (Fábula de Polifemo y Galatea,* 1613*)*. In narrative, landmarks include the anonymous picaresque novel *Lazarillo de Tormes* (1558), a devastating critique of laxity and corruption at all levels of society; and, of course, the two volumes of Cervantes's masterpiece *Don Quixote* (1605,

1615). Straddling both poetry and prose are the sublime writings of three of sixteenth-century Spain's most intensely spiritual authors: Saint Teresa (1515–1582), Fray Luis de León (1527–1591), and Saint John of the Cross (1542–1591) – all of them, significantly, from families of Jewish origin (as were Nebrija, Encina, Góngora, and possibly Cervantes). Of great importance for historiography, finally, is the first generation of New World chroniclers to follow in Columbus's footsteps: Las Casas (1474–1566), Fernández de Oviedo (1478–1557), Cortés (1485–1547), Cabeza de Vaca (*c.* 1490–*c.* 1557), and Díaz del Castillo (*c.* 1495–1584) .

By Calderón's time, Spanish literature had assumed a set of characteristics that later critics, borrowing from art history, termed *baroque*. Formally speaking, the Spanish baroque, in all literary genres, employed elaborate or highly stylized syntax, frequent use of Latin- and Italian-based neologisms, and a heavy dependence on greatly exaggerated metaphors and wordplay. The first two of these characteristics are usually associated with the term *culteranismo* and the latter with *conceptismo*. Rather than opposed, as many critics tend to view them, these two phenomena are intricately connected and represent two sides of the coin that is baroque language, of which the poetry of Góngora is perhaps the prime example. Thematically, baroque writers came to terms with their disappointment over Spain's political decline by emphasizing the deception and uncertainty of earthly existence, harking back to the biblical view of life as a walk through "the valley of the shadow of death,"[11] a mirage that could be shattered only through the liberating embrace of death. To emphasize the illusory nature of earthly existence, the Spanish baroque relied on three central metaphors: life as art, life as a stage, and, most important for students of Calderón, life as a dream.

Apart from literature, Spain's contribution to written culture (I leave aside painting and music) in this period can be grouped into three main areas: theology, philosophy, and science. To begin with, it is instructive to point out that this distinction is not one that would have been maintained in Calderón's time, which considered philosophy and science as two sides (one theoretical, the other practical) of the same coin of knowledge. Theology, furthermore, given its perceived relationship to truth, had been thought of in the Middle Ages as the "Queen of the Sciences" and is still referred to that way in Cervantes's *Don Quixote*, although its popularity as a course of study notably declined in the Renaissance.[12]

---

[11] Psalms 23.4.

[12] By the seventeenth century, law students outnumbered theologians by over twenty to one in Salamanca and Valladolid (Kamen 1991, p. 154 [Bibliography, section 7]). Hence, in the

In Spain, as in the rest of Europe prior to the Protestant Reformation, theology owes its existence to scholasticism, the peculiarly medieval attempt to imbue faith with rational content. Scholasticism was perfected in the thirteenth century by Thomas Aquinas through a harmonization of Christian dogma with the philosophical principles of Aristotle, whose entire corpus, thanks in large part to scholars working in Spain, had been translated into Latin from the Arabic (previously, only the early works of Aristotle had been available in Latin). In Spain, the scholastic method continued to be the basis of important writings in theology throughout the Renaissance, and the universities of Salamanca and Alcalá were major centres of scholastic thought. The rational subtleties and nuanced details characteristic of Calderonian drama, in fact, owe much to scholasticism's influence.

Scholastic-based theology was given new impetus in Spain by the Council of Trent (1545–63), which convened to deal with Protestantism at a theological level and which was dominated by Spaniards in its closing years. The Council's pronouncements, which had been reached through classic scholastic debate, neatly summarize the essence of Catholic theology and elucidate its major points of conflict with Protestantism. Of particular importance for the interpretation of *Life's a Dream*, the Council reaffirmed the traditional view of *justificatio* (the transformation of the sinner from a state of unrighteousness to one of holiness) through the exercise of individual free will; this view stood in sharp contrast to Protestantism's – and especially Calvinism's – emphasis on salvation by predestination. Predictably, the Council also upheld the authority of popes and councils in the determination of doctrine, whereas Protestantism gave sole authority to the Bible. The Council reaffirmed the number of sacraments at seven, which Protestants had reduced to two; and it reiterated that the sacrament of communion implies the transubstantiation of the body of Christ in the communal bread and wine. The Council also upheld belief in purgatory, the use of indulgences (although it called for an end to obvious abuses), the worship of saints, and the veneration of relics and icons.[13] All these dogmatic points surface in Calderonian drama.

Because scholasticism always subjects reason to faith, it is not philosophy in the sense that we know it today. For many years, however, philosophy

---

passage from the *Quixote* alluded to, Don Diego laments the fact that his son, a student at the University of Salamanca, refuses to study theology (part 2, chapter 16).
[13] See Ozment 1980, pp. 407–08 (Bibliography, section 8) for more detail on the Council of Trent's pronouncements.

and theology were considered complementary and compatible in their conclusions, one focused on the natural order and the other on the supernatural order. Yet, by the time of the Renaissance, a new metaphysics permitted a break between theology and philosophy, a major result of which was political philosophy, best exemplified by Machiavelli's *The Prince* (1513). In its exclusive concern with the history and government of human affairs, Machiavelli's treatise represented a radical departure from the theocentrism of medieval thought.

In Spain, where Machiavelli never took deep root (despite the fact that, in *The Prince,* he based his model of the ideal ruler on the shrewd policies of King Ferdinand), an interesting blend of traditional scholasticism and the daring new political philosophy is found in the writings of Francisco Suárez (1548–1617). Considered the last of the great scholastic thinkers, Suárez was also at the forefront of political thought in his defence of the concept of national sovereignty. In his book *On the Defence of Faith* (*De defensio fidei,* 1613), he rejected the divine right of kings and insisted that political power resided in the people. Even more radical is the position of Juan Mariana (1536–1624), whose book *On Kings and Kingship* (*De rege et regis institutione,* 1599) defended the right of the people to murder despotic kings. The response to both Suárez's and Mariana's works, especially abroad, was dramatic. *On the Defence of Faith* was burned in London; *On Kings and Kingship* suffered the same fate in Paris. Neither book was banned in Spain, however; the crown tolerated such writings presumably because it considered them aimed at the Protestant monarchies of northern Europe, which it had an interest in undermining. In any case, because the authors of both treatises were Jesuits, it is almost certain that Calderón was familiar with their ideas and, moreover, that he addressed them in *Life's a Dream.*

Another branch of thought that had a profound impact on early modern society, if not on philosophy itself, was humanism, the educational program initiated by Petrarch and based on the rigorous study of ancient Greek and Latin texts. Because humanist approaches to ancient texts required a thorough knowledge of Greek and Latin, it was only a matter of time before they were applied to the New Testament, originally written in Greek but transmitted throughout the Middle Ages in Latin, as well as to theology and canon law, written exclusively in Latin. In a momentous treatise from 1440, for instance, the Italian scholar Lorenzo Valla, relying on a knowledge of Latin that humanism had taught him, demonstrated that the document known as the Donation of Constantine, on which the Church based its rich patrimony and territorial claims to Italy, was a forgery. Valla was only the first of many humanists who would inevitably bring to the surface the many errors and contradictions buried in Christianity's long stewardship of textual transmission. As the Spanish humanist Hernán Núñez so aptly explained over a century later (1566): "when a humanist corrects an error in Cicero, for example, the same error has to be corrected in Scripture."[14]

Such methods represented a serious threat to the Church's authority, and thus the tools of humanism – in a way that many of its practitioners would never have wished – precipitated and bolstered the claims of the Protestant Reformation. Nowhere is this contradiction more evident than in the remarkable life and work of Thomas More (1478–1535). More's early association with prominent humanist and reform-minded circles in England earned him a recognition that would ultimately gain him entry into the inner circle of King Henry VIII. But More, always a faithful Catholic, refused to support Henry's divorce from Catherine of Aragon and the resulting break with Rome, and the king had him beheaded for his opposition.

In Spain, humanism flowered in the late fifteenth and early sixteenth centuries in figures such as Antonio de Nebrija and Juan del Encina. Before the Protestant Reformation, the Church supported the goals of humanism and even sponsored the University of Alcalá's publication of the Polyglot Bible (1514–17), which contained the first New Testament printed in Greek. After the Reformation, however, as Spanish authorities watched with chagrin the rapid advance of Protestantism across Europe, humanism came to be identified with the Reformation, and the position of humanists became untenable. This was especially the case with the brand of humanism associated with the great Dutch scholar Erasmus (*c.* 1466–1536), who had made a particularly profound impact in Spain. In 1530, an outstanding Spanish humanist, Juan de Valdés (*c.* 1510–1542), fled the country for Italy to avoid arrest related to his *Dialogue of Christian Doctrine (Diálogo de doctrina cristiana)*, which smacked of Erasmian influence. Three years later, in a chilling letter written to Juan Luis Vives[15] from Paris, Rodrigo Manrique, son of the Inquisitor General, commented on the state of the country from which both now lived in exile:

---

[14] Quoted in Kamen 1991, p. 188 (Bibliography, section 7).
[15] Another outstanding Spanish humanist, 1492–1540, friend of Erasmus and tutor to Princess Mary of England, who was forced to flee Spain at the age of seventeen when the Inquisition burned his parents for being Judaizers (his mother, already dead, was disinterred for the occasion). The entirety of his works was written in exile between England, France, and Flanders.

You are right. Our country is a land of pride and envy; you may add, of barbarism. For now it is clear that down there one cannot possess any culture without being suspected of heresy, error and Judaism. Thus silence has been imposed on the learned. As for those who have resorted to erudition, they have been filled, as you say, with great terror.... At Alcalá they are trying to uproot the study of Greek completely.[16]

Manrique's letter is uncannily prophetic. The Council of Trent, among its other rulings, soon reaffirmed the sole authority of the Vulgate (the Latin Bible) in an attempt to insulate it from the tools of classical philology that humanism espoused; it also rejected humanist education for priests even though clerical education was widely acknowledged to be desperately in need of reform. From this point on, to be a humanist in Spain almost certainly meant rousing the ire of the Holy Office. This was the case of Fray Luis de León, who, besides authoring some of the sixteenth century's most beautiful poetry, was also an excellent scholar of Hebrew at the University of Salamanca. Ignoring the Council's wishes regarding the Vulgate, he insisted in his classes on the authority of the Hebrew Bible, for which he was ultimately denounced and imprisoned. By the time Calderón wrote *Life's a Dream*, humanism was virtually extinguished in Spain, having been eclipsed by its ideological opposite: neostoicism. Best represented in the brilliantly sardonic writings of Francisco de Quevedo (1580–1645) and in striking contrast to the optimism and engagement of humanism, neostoicism counselled detachment and resignation in answer to the disillusioned reality of seventeenth-century Spain.

Regarding the early modern scientific tradition in Spain – or lack thereof, for Spain produced no equivalent to Copernicus (1473–1543), Galileo (1564–1642), Kepler (1571–1630), or Newton (1642–1727) – one must bear in mind two important points. First, Spanish science was dominated early on by Jews and Jewish converts to Christianity; their persecution, consequently, was one of the factors that negatively impacted the scientific tradition in Spain.[17] Second, a series of restrictive measures taken in 1558–59 as part of the Counter Reformation, while not intended to impede scientific development, could not but negatively impact it. The measures included a formalization of censorship procedures, leading to the publication of the first Index of Prohibited Books; a ban on the importation of foreign books;

---

16 Quoted in Kamen 1991, p. 117 (Bibliography, section 7).
17 López Piñero 1979, p. 77 (Bibliography, section 7).

and a prohibition against teaching or studying at foreign universities.[18] The last measure was particularly harmful considering that twenty-five percent of the 228 scientific authors who flourished in Spain at the beginning of the sixteenth century (prior to the ban) had studied abroad.[19] With these facts in mind, we may now turn to the individual disciplines.

Spain was never at the vanguard of original work in theoretical mathematics. Its most important contribution of the sixteenth-century, Juan Pérez de Moya's *Practical and Speculative Arithmetic* (*Aritmética práctica y especulativa*, 1562), is entirely derivative. The situation did not change in the seventeenth century, which was, in the rest of Europe, the age of coordinate geometry (Descartes), differential calculus (Newton), and integral calculus (Leibniz). Whether the poverty of the Spanish mathematical tradition was a consequence of the association that, as Américo Castro has suggested, early modern Spaniards made between the exercise of the intellect and the impurity of blood (*i.e.*, intellectuals were identified with Jews) matters little.[20] Whatever the cause, the result was far reaching: "without a basis in mathematics there can be no astronomy or physics with a scientific grounding, and thus the physics that was taught in [Spanish] universities continued to be Aristotelian, a mass of philosophical abstractions not only without relationship to reality but also, in many occasions, closed to reality and experimentation."[21]

These attitudes explain why the works of key figures such as Copernicus, Galileo, Kepler, and Newton were not widely understood in Spain even though they were available. Copernicus, in fact, was on the reading list at the University of Salamanca when Calderón studied there in the early seventeenth century. And yet the Spanish view of the universe, as seen in Vasily's astrological predictions in *Life's a Dream*, continued to follow the one outlined by Ptolemy in the second century AD. At its centre lay the Earth: fixed, immobile, and immediately surrounded by the three other primal elements (water, air, and fire). At a greater distance were suspended eight concentric spheres. The first seven spheres contained, respectively (in

---

[18] There is some dispute as to the extent of the university ban. One historian notes that exceptions were made for certain colleges in Bologna, Rome, Naples, and Coimbra (Kamen 1985, p. 78 [Bibliography, section 7]). Another asserts that, in the second half of the sixteenth century, distinguished Spaniards were to be found in universities throughout Italy, Flanders, and France (Elliott 1963, pp. 223–24 [Bibliography, section 7]).

[19] López Piñero 1979, p. 141 (Bibliography, section 7).

[20] See especially Castro 1972 (Bibliography, section 7).

[21] Domínguez Ortiz 1973, p. 389 (Bibliography, section 7).

order of proximity to Earth): the Moon, Mercury, Venus, the Sun, Mars, Jupiter, and Saturn. The eighth sphere, called the firmament, contained the fixed stars and constellations. Beyond it, an unseen prime mover (*primum mobile*), to which all the spheres were tethered, revolved once every twenty-four hours around the earth, dragging everything along with it.

In addition to the stagnating effect it produced on astronomy, the lacuna in theoretical math helps explain why modern philosophy never flowered in Spain. Descartes's work in geometry, for example, was crucial to his revolutionary epistemology. In contrast, Spaniards were at the forefront of applied math and science. Driven by the imperative to explore and conquer the New World, cartography achieved great distinction in the peninsula, and Pedro de Medina's *Art of Navigation* (*Arte de navegar*, 1545) is a key text in which the Atlantic Ocean assumes an outline very close to reality. Cartography was complemented by work in natural history, that is, the cataloguing of the flora and fauna of the Americas, as evidenced in early chroniclers such as Fernández de Oviedo and in later ones such as Francisco Hernández, a physician who was appointed by Philip II in 1570 to lead the first modern, scientific expedition to the New World. Spain also led the way in reforming the old Julian calendar. A Spaniard, Pedro Chacón, was among the three authors of the final document that Pope Gregory XIII approved in 1582 – the import of which, judging by the jokes made in *Life's a Dream*, was still remembered in the time of Calderón. The charter that Philip II granted in 1583 to Madrid's Academy of Mathematics – whose mission was entirely practical in nature – confirmed the Spanish preference for the applied sciences.

An important fruit of this preference was medicine, which flourished in the first half of the sixteenth century in figures such as Pedro Jimeno, who in 1549 published his discovery of the third bone of the inner ear. The enigmatic figure of Miguel Serveto (a.k.a. Michael Servetus, 1511–53) is also worthy of mention. Born in Navarre, Serveto seems to have fled Spain some time after the publication of his heretical theological treatise, *On the Errors of the Trinity (De Trinitatis erroribus*, 1531), which disputed the nature of the Trinity. He resettled in France, studying medicine in Paris and Montpellier, and became quite distinguished in anatomy. Convinced that the soul resided in blood, he was the first to discover the principles of pulmonary circulation. Serveto's theological views, despised by Catholics and Protestants alike, eventually caught up with him, and he was arrested in Switzerland and burned at the stake by order of Calvin.

Even with the restrictive measures of 1558–59, the end of the century produced several Spanish figures worthy of note, such as the surgeon Francisco Díaz, whose treatise on kidney disease in 1588 is considered a foundation of modern urology. In 1575, Huarte de San Juan published his monumental *Examination of Scientific Aptitude (Examen de ingenio para las ciencias)*. An intriguing, multifaceted work that confirms the pre-enlightenment permeability of the disciplinary boundaries now imposed between medicine, philosophy, and political science, Huarte's work was based on the idea that the faculties of the soul are influenced by the four bodily humours. It had an enormous impact on the psychological development of literary characters in the following century, and Calderón was almost certainly familiar with it.

The theory of the four humours popularized in Huarte's treatise provides an excellent opportunity to examine the state of scientific knowledge and the modes of rational thought current in the seventeenth century. Like the Ptolemaic view of the universe, the theory of the bodily humours dates back to ancient world, specifically, to the Greek physician Galen in the second century AD. It posits a body composed of four basic humours, each of which is associated with a certain temperament. In the healthy individual, blood predominates, but a disproportionate rise in one of the other humours brings about an ailment related to the characteristics associated with that humour. By the Renaissance, each humour had become linked through analogy to a series of other paradigms such as the four elements of which all matter was believed to be composed, as shown in the diagram below.[22]

Humour	Temperament	Primary Qualities	Element	Age	Season	Planet
blood	sanguine	hot, moist	air	childhood	Spring	Jupiter
phlegm	phlegmatic	cold, moist	water	middle age	Autumn	Moon
choler	choleric	hot, dry	fire	youth	Summer	Mars
melancholy	melancholic	cold, dry	earth	old age	Winter	Saturn

The connections between the different parts of this elaborate system served as a guide to interpreting man's relation to the cosmos, which was viewed as an organic, meaningful whole: hence Sigismund's reference to man as "a world writ small" in act 2 of *Life's a Dream*. The theory is thus important not only because of its prevalence but also because it demonstrates the great gap between a rational process predisposed to drawing connections based on analogies and surface similarities and that of the modern scientific method,

---

[22] The diagram is adapted from Murillo 1990, p. 22 (Bibliography, section 7).

which seeks to break down and classify on the basis of natural physical laws and inherent characteristics.

The intellectual background of Calderón's play is living testament to the period in which these two fundamentally opposed scientific approaches were engaged in an active contest for legitimacy. Indeed, the play's reliance on the Ptolemaic universe and the theory of the four humours shows that, while certain intellectual fields undoubtedly suffered in Spain as a result of the Counter Reformation, what we now call the pseudo-sciences – alchemy, astrology, chronology, the study of emblems – all flourished. It is almost as if, along with literature, which reached its maximum brilliance *after* the restrictive measures of 1558–59, the pseudo-sciences became the prime expression of creative energies that no longer found an outlet in philosophy, the natural sciences, or even theology (for after the Council of Trent's pronouncements, which were considered definitive, the Church preferred to consider closed any discussions of dogma). The only thing left to do with received knowledge was to popularize it, and this was the role now assumed by the public theatre, whose greatest representatives – Lope de Vega, Tirso de Molina, and Calderón – were all men of the cloth. We may now consider their dramatic formula in some detail.

2. The Spanish Comedia

Comedia is a generic term used to refer to Spanish secular drama – whether tragic or comic – in the sixteenth and seventeenth centuries, the most prolific national theatre in world literature. Its history dates back to Juan del Encina, who performed his first eclogues in the palace of the Duke of Alba in December 1492. Encina's early eclogues were nativity pieces, but his extensive visits to Italy brought about a gradual secularization of his theatre, culminating in a veritable apotheosis of classical mythology in the *Eclogue of Plácida and Vitoriano* (*Égloga de Plácida y Vitoriano,* 1513), which was placed on the Index of Prohibited Books in 1558. Encina's contemporaries, Bartolomé de Torres Naharro, who spent a significant amount of time in Italy as well, and Gil Vicente, a Portuguese national who often wrote in Spanish, also contributed to the secularization of the theatre.

Encina's generation of playwrights is characterized by its courtly performance venues and aristocratic spectators. By the middle of the century, following the successful tours of several Italian theatre companies through the peninsula, a bourgeois audience began to develop. A key figure during this period was Lope de Rueda (d. 1565/66), whose success as an actor and owner of a theatre company led him to write his own plays. In the 1570s, immediately prior to the success of Lope de Vega's new dramatic formula, there was a brief experimentation with tragedy (especially Senecan tragedy) in figures such as Juan de la Cueva and Cristóbal de Virués. By this time, however, popular tastes had completely overrun the early aristocratic framework of Spanish theatre, and the narrow precepts of classical tragedy did not find the reception in Spain that they had in Italy and France.

At this point, Calderón's immediate predecessor, Lope de Vega (1562–1635, often referred to simply as "Lope"), enters the scene and consolidates the tradition into a fixed formula that, insofar as the public theatre is concerned, forever vindicates popular over aristocratic sentiment. In his *New Art of Writing Plays in Our Time* (*Arte nuevo de escribir comedias en nuestro tiempo,* 1609), presumably written as a defence against those who would attack his populism, de Vega outlines the general formula of his dramaturgy, which by then was already assiduously followed throughout Spain: plays are divided into three acts and written exclusively in verse; they assign primacy to plot, which is dizzying in detail; they freely mix serious and comic elements; they disregard the so-called classical unities[23] and frequently employ subplots; finally, they tend to eschew tragic dénouements in favour of happy and often moralizing endings. Thematically, de Vega's formula draws from history and legend, Italian drama and novellas, classical mythology, the Bible, and the lives of saints; the subject matter is generally presented as realistically as the highly condensed plots will allow. The themes of love and honour are particularly privileged, and tension between the two often gives rise to the plays' basic conflicts. Honour, in particular, seems to have had something of a cathartic effect on audiences, as de Vega's own words in the *New Art* attest: "Instances of honour work best because they move everyone deeply."[24]

By the time that Calderón began writing plays, the immense success of de Vega's formula had assured its supremacy, although it can be argued that Calderón perfected the formula by introducing more economical plots, greater subtlety of thought, and, in some cases, deeper character development. As is the case with *Life's a Dream*, his plays often include an important allegorical or preternatural dimension designed to test moral

---

[23] Time, place, and action. Thought in the Renaissance to have been mandated in Aristotle's *Poetics*, strict observation of the unities is actually a product of postclassical criticism.

[24] "Los casos de la honra son mejores, / porque mueven con fuerza a toda gente." Vega 1989, vv. 327–28 (Bibliography, section 3).

and philosophical premises, and thus they are not always best served by rigorously realistic or literal interpretations.

The ideology of the Comedia tends to be conservative by contemporary standards, as it naturally reflects the values of the Old Regime outlined in section 1 of this Introduction. However, I believe it is a mistake to go as far as those who, like José Antonio Maravall, see it merely as a tool used by the State to solidify its interests.[25] Such views ignore the fundamental power of the artist to resist authority. In Counter-Reformation Spain, of course, few writers would have risked open critique of royal power, although such a stance was tolerated to some extent in the Jesuit treatises of Suárez and Mariana. Calderón had to be particularly careful because his livelihood was intimately connected to and dependent on the court of Philip IV. But the best writers of any period state their cases subtly rather than overtly, and I firmly believe that *Life's a Dream*, on one level, represents a subtle critique of certain practices of the Hapsburg monarchy (see section 4 below for more detail).

The language of the Comedia is a product of the exclusive verse format in which it is written. Tellingly, playwrights of Calderón's period were known as poets rather than dramatists; consequently, all poetic figures, including many of the excesses of baroque poetry, were incorporated into drama. Metaphor, in particular, was stretched to the limit through the use of *conceptismo*. Many verse forms were cultivated, but the conventional eight-syllable verse in assonant rhyme, a favourite of the traditional ballad, predominated. When read aloud, this form does not stray far from the rhythms of prose and was easily understandable in the oral context of performance. Audiences, at any rate, were accomplished listeners and spoke of going to "hear a play" rather than to see it, demonstrating the great gulf that separates them from present-day patrons of theatre (not to mention those of film).

In the primary importance it assigned to plot and to the spectator's ability to listen, classical Spanish drama was closer to the principles of Aristotelian theory than the lack of tragic elements would first lead one to believe. Aristotle noted that plots "ought to be so constructed that, *even without the aid of the eye*, he who hears the tale told will thrill with horror and melt to pity at what takes place."[26] While Lope de Vega and Calderón were not as concerned with provoking horror and pity in the spectator – although it is significant that Rossaura mentions precisely these two elements after

---

[25] See Maravall 1990 (Bibliography, section 8).

[26] Aristotle 1961, p. 78 (Bibliography, section 3). My emphasis.

overhearing Sigismund's first monologue – it is clear that for them, as for Aristotle, elements such as costume, scenery, and special effects (what Aristotle called "spectacle") were secondary. As a consequence, staging techniques were, as in Shakespeare's England, extraordinarily simple. By the 1560s – the period associated with Lope de Rueda and the beginnings of a middle-class dramatic ethos – public plays were being performed in the courtyards (*corrales*) of hospitals run by charitable institutions (*cofradía*s), where space and mobility were extremely limited. The first permanent public theatres arose around 1580, just as Lope de Vega's formula was taking hold. Similar in blueprint to the hospital courtyards, the permanent theatres were built in the inner patios of pre-existing buildings; hence they continued to be known as *corrales*.[27] They attracted rowdy, heterogeneous audiences that were segregated by class and sex. (Actresses, by contrast, were from the beginning allowed onstage alongside actors.) While more advanced than the hospital courtyards, they still did not favour elaborate staging techniques; and, being open-air like the courtyards, they were at the mercy of the elements.

Over the past twenty years, the outstanding work of three theatre historians in particular – J. E. Varey, J. M. Ruano de la Haza, and John J. Allen – has considerably advanced our understanding of the seventeenth-century Spanish stage and allowed us to reconstruct its details. A platform stage, about six feet high and roughly twice as long as it was deep (a common ratio was 12 feet by 24), projected into the audience. On the two ends were lateral platforms that could be used for seating in more conventional productions or as additional staging areas if required. Across the back of the central stage, and perhaps extending along the lateral platforms, ran a permanent, five-story structure commonly referred to as the *vestuario* (dressing room) because the basement level, hidden from the view of the audience, served as the men's dressing area (as well as a space for managing special effects) while the stage level provided access to the women's dressing room. Balconies with detachable railings projected from the second and third levels and were supported by two sets of columns that rose from the stage. The top level, hidden in an attic area, housed stage machinery. Each of the three exposed tiers, which measured about eight feet tall and several feet deep, was curtained off and divided horizontally (superficially by the columns and internally by thin partitions) into three separate sections. This arrangement created a total of

---

[27] The first permanent public theater was the Corral de la Cruz, built in Madrid in 1579. The Corral del Príncipe followed in 1582, also in Madrid.

nine independent, recessed cells that could be used for a variety of scenic effects. The left and right curtains of the bottom tier generally served as the main entrances and exits, while the middle curtain (but sometimes the left or right one) could be drawn back to reveal a "discovery space" such as an allegorical setting, a cave, or a prison. The second tier of the *vestuario* could be used to play balcony or window scenes; the third tier might represent additional windows, the top of a castle wall, or a mountain peak. Mountains could be simulated, with varying degrees of realism, by a ramp leading from one of the balconies onto the lateral platforms or, alternatively, onto the centre stage providing it did not block access to the lower-tier entrance and exit curtains. In principle, any of the nine niches could be used as a discovery space or "inner stage," creating a dynamic, multidimensional flexibility that often led to an inversion of natural spatial relationships.

Because the plays were performed in broad daylight (local statutes prohibited night shows), the recessed niches of the *vestuario* would have provided a distinct lighting contrast to the brighter surroundings of the main stage. Costumes, gestures, and textual cues were used to compensate for the general lack of scenery, requiring a strong suspension of disbelief on the part of the audience in order to complete the theatrical illusion. Although Italian innovations in set design had made possible more elaborate staging techniques by the time Calderón wrote *Life's a Dream*, the limited stage directions of the text do not appear to call for much beyond the description just offered. As Ruano de la Haza concludes in his excellent reconstruction, "with the help of the curtains, a simple background décor and one spatial inversion, *La vida es sueño* was probably staged [...] simply, efficiently, with a minimum of disruption and without unduly straining either the imagination or the credulity of the audience."[28] (More details regarding the staging of *Life's a Dream* are offered in the Suggestions for Directors.)

In conclusion, it is worth noting that the formulaic structure of the Comedia favoured prodigious output. De Vega's biographer, Juan Pérez de Montalbán, claims that he wrote an astonishing two thousand plays, of which "only" some five hundred have survived (in contrast to the thirty-eight that we possess of Shakespeare). Tirso de Molina (1583-1648), author of the original Don Juan play, claimed over four hundred dramatic works, of which about eighty are known today. Calderón's complete works, in one modern edition,[29] total 108 full-length secular plays and seventy-five

---

[28] Ruano de la Haza 1987, p. 58 (Bibliography, section 8).

[29] Valbuena Briones 1952–62 (Bibliography, section 2).

short allegorical plays *(autos sacramentales)* – very close to the count that the playwright himself made the year of his death. Although the formulaic structure of the genre led to quite a few ill-conceived plots and some very tenuously developed characters, many of the plays are still worthy of study, and the best of them rank with the best of Shakespeare. Among the latter, Calderón's *Life's a Dream* is the undisputed gem.

3. Calderón the Man: A Brief Chronology

1598   The Spanish throne passes from Philip II to Philip III, who will become the first of the Hapsburg kings to actively patronize the theatre. The golden age of Spain's dramatic tradition, under the leadership of Lope de Vega, is in full swing.

1600–06   Calderón is born on January 17, 1600 to noble parents in Madrid, the third child of six. In 1601 his family moves to Valladolid, where the Spanish court has briefly relocated. By 1606 both he and the court are back in Madrid to stay.

1608–13   Following his father's wishes that he become a priest, Calderón receives an excellent Jesuit education at the Colegio Imperial of Madrid, where he masters Latin and learns the rudiments of New Testament Greek.

1610   Calderón's mother dies giving birth to her last child, which also dies. The mother's death may be behind the horrific description of Sigismund's birth in *Life's a Dream*.

1611   Francisco, an illegitimate son of Calderón's father, who has lived with the family with no one but the father aware of the blood relationship, is banished from the household and disinherited; at the same time, Calderón's sister Dorotea (thirteen years old) is sent to a convent in Toledo, and his brother Diego (sixteen) is entrusted to the care of a relative in Mexico. Upon the father's death four years later, Francisco's biological relationship to the family is revealed and his banishment is explained as punishment for an act of violence. One critic has seen in these events an attempted rape of Dorotea by Francisco with the possible collusion of Diego, instilling in Pedro a horror of incest that haunts several of his works including *Life's a Dream*.[30]

1614   Calderón enrols in the University of Alcalá. His father remarries.

---

[30]   Parker 1982 (Bibliography, section 8).

1615–20   Calderón's father dies in 1615; his will reveals an authoritarian character that may inform the troubled relationship between Vasily and Sigismund in *Life's a Dream*. His father's death prompts Pedro to interrupt his studies at Alcalá in a fight with his stepmother over the inheritance, which is finally settled in 1618. Calderón abandons his plans of becoming a priest and continues his education at the University of Salamanca, where he studies law, history, theology, and philosophy, receiving his degree in canon law. In 1620 he composes a sonnet for a literary contest and is mentioned favourably by Lope de Vega.

1621   In the spring, Philip IV ascends to the throne, initiating a lavish patronage of the theatre that will ultimately shower Calderón with attention. In the summer, Calderón and his brothers are accused of murdering a servant of the High Constable of Castile; seeking refuge in the house of the German ambassador, they are eventually convicted and forced to pay a crippling fine to the victim's father.

1622   Calderón again composes poems for various literary contests.

1623   Calderón writes his first play: *Love, Honour, and Power (Amor, honor y poder)*. Some biographers suggest that he may have spent several years around this time in the service of the king in Milan and Flanders, but it has proved impossible to document such assertions.

1629   An enraged Calderón pursues the assailant of one of his brothers (it is not known which) into the Convent of the Trinitarians in Madrid, where he joins several ministers of justice in irreverently stripping the nuns of their veils and searching their cells in a futile hunt for the aggressor. Lope de Vega, whose daughter Marcela is a member of the convent, complains of the incident in a letter to the Duke of Sessa. The famous court chaplain, Father Hortensio Félix Paravicino de Arteaga, delivers a sermon in which he uses the incident as a pretext to attack playwrights. Calderón is later placed under brief house arrest for poking fun at Paravicino in a passage from his play *The Steadfast Prince (El príncipe constante)*. According to Ruano de la Haza, an early version of *Life's a Dream* was underway by this point.

1633   Calderón writes *Devotion to the Cross (Devoción de la Cruz)*, an unsettling and highly influential play that centres on the incestuous desire of a brother and sister who are unaware of their relationship, recalling the events of 1611.

1635   On St. John's Eve (June 23), Calderón stages an elaborate production of *Love, the Greatest Enchantment (El mayor encanto, amor)*. The play is performed before the king on a floating stage, designed by the Florentine engineer Cosme Lotti, in the pond of the Retiro Park in Madrid. Calderón also writes *Secret Affront, Secret Vengeance (A secreto agravio, secreta venganza)* and *The Doctor of Honour (El médico de su honra)*, two deeply disturbing works about jealous, honour-driven husbands who murder their wives on the basis of suspicion and innuendo, recalling Shakespeare's *Othello*. Lope de Vega's death in August confirms Calderón's supremacy in the theatre.

1636   Calderón publishes, with significant personal involvement, many of his most important works in *Comedies, Part One (Primera parte de comedias)*, in which *Life's a Dream* is assigned an important first place in the order of plays. He is named Knight of the Order of Santiago by Philip IV. Documentation suggests that an allegorical version of *Life's a Dream* was performed in the village of Fuente el Saz for the Feast of Corpus Christi.[31]

1637   Calderón writes *The Wonder-Working Magician (El mágico prodigioso)*, the chilling tale of a student of metaphysics who sells his soul to the devil in order to win the woman he desires.

1640s   A difficult period for the playwright on all levels. The uprising in Catalonia, in which Calderón participates in 1641–42, continues unabated, creating a sombre mood in Madrid. The moralists, long enemies of the theatre, succeed in severely restricting performances. The queen's death in October 1644 furthers their cause, and public theatres are closed (as was customary) in an act of mourning. The Prince's death almost exactly two years later (October 1646) extends the closure until the king remarries in 1649; theatres are then reopened but never recover the sprit of the twenties and thirties. In stark contrast to the more than forty plays he penned during the previous ten years, Calderón's literary production throughout the forties amounts to less than ten works. One of his most important, however, is probably from this period: *The Mayor of Zalamea (El alcalde de Zalamea)*, a

---

[31] Pérez Pastor 1905, pp. 98-99 (Bibliography, section 6).

searing indictment of the abuse of power and the resulting erosion of boundaries between public and private life. Also during this period, Calderón fathers an illegitimate child, Pedro José (the mother's identity remains unknown), who dies by the age of 10. Calderón initially calls the boy his nephew but confesses the real relationship when he is ordained; he makes almost no reference to the child in his writings.

1651   Turning point in Calderón's life. He suffers a serious illness, witnesses the death of both his brothers as well as his mistress, and decides to be ordained a priest, belatedly fulfilling his father's wishes. From this point until his death on May 25, 1681, Calderón devotes his energies to composing short allegorical plays based on Catholic theology (*autos sacramentales*) and extravagant mythological pieces for the court. In 1673, only eight years before his death, he writes an allegorical version of *Life's a Dream* (perhaps a revision of the one performed in 1636).

4. Life's a Dream: *Analysis and Interpretation*

(Those who are not already familiar with *Life's a Dream* are encouraged to postpone their reading of the following section until finishing the play itself.)

Love, dishonour, vengeance. Kingship, loyalty, rebellion. Knowledge, control, choice. Dreams, illusion, reality. These are the themes that haunt *Life's a Dream* and make it the peer of such plays as *Oedipus* and *Hamlet*. That Calderón's play belongs with Sophocles' and Shakespeare's atop the dramatic canon is also reflected in the sheer volume and diversity of the critical response it has inspired, as documented by Jesús A. Ara Sánchez's superb annotated bibliography (to which I am heavily indebted in the preparation of these pages). The immensity of the secondary literature and its heterogeneous, often conflicting content prevent any exhaustive treatment in this Introduction. Instead, I have limited myself to a brief survey of three levels of analysis that I consider crucial to the play's interpretation – the human, the political, and the philosophical – along with a sampling of the bibliography most relevant to each area (whether or not the references cited corroborate my own readings).

***

The human level of *Life's a Dream* informs the play's basic dramatic structure through an intense interrogation of the boundaries of traditional social and familial roles, giving pride of place to the themes of love, honour, and vengeance that so thrilled audiences of the Comedia. As king, Vasily has sought to rob Sigismund of his birthright to the throne; as father, he acts toward him in a way that has "denied me my humanity," as the prince furiously exclaims in act 2. The first action is unlawful, for kings have a duty to educate princes in a manner that prepares them for governing. The second act is immoral, for Christians have a duty to raise their children with compassion and understanding. Sigismund is consequently consumed with rage and a desire for revenge, expressed in a remarkable passage at the end of act 2 in which he dreams out loud that "Clothold shall die by my hands! My father shall kiss my feet!" This passage emphasizes the archetypal similarities between the story of Sigismund and the myth of Oedipus, popularized in antiquity by the Greek playwright Sophocles and the Roman dramatist Seneca (the latter, a favourite of Calderón, is mentioned by Vasily at the end of his long speech at court in act 1). In both stories, a father, in attempting to avoid fulfilment of a prophecy that predicts his overthrow by his own son, ends up precipitating precisely the events he wishes to avoid. In the Greco-Roman plays, Oedipus unknowingly kills his father and, again unknowingly, marries his mother. In *Life's a Dream*, Sigismund symbolically kills his mother when she dies giving birth to him, and, as the passage quoted above demonstrates, he desires to humiliate his father.[32] A disastrous outcome is averted only when the king, recognizing his own error, decides to confront his fate rather than run from it. This act enables – without requiring – Sigismund's conversion and points the play toward a happy end.

Like Sigismund, Rossaura has never known her father, Clothold, who abandoned her mother Viola and violated his secret marriage vow to her. Rossaura now faces an eerily similar situation, as she finds herself abandoned by her lover, Aistulf, Duke of Muscovy, who has left her to claim the Polish throne. Unlike Sigismund, Rossaura is hindered by biology. With no known male guardian to avenge her dishonour, she must disguise herself as a man and seek justice on her own. Her arrival in Poland brings her into contact with the prince, who is spellbound by her beauty even as she is dressed as a man. She also meets Clothold, and, probably suspecting that he is her father, speaks in a series of double-entendres that, as Ruano de la Haza suggests,[33]

---

[32] On the Oedipal resonances of *Life's a Dream*, see especially Valbuena Prat 1956, Parker 1966, Rozik 1989, and Molho 1993, pp. 240–48 (Bibliography, section 8).
[33] Ruano de la Haza 2000, pp. 49–57 (Bibliography, section 2).

seems aimed at forcing a confession from him: "You have given me, sire, my life," she tells him after he frees her and Bugle at the end of act 1. When this approach fails, she reveals her gender to him, a move that places a particular obligation on him as her father, as she appears to have calculated. Indeed, Clothold recognizes his debt to Rossaura in an aside but refuses to admit it to her directly. Furthermore, he is unwilling to act publicly on her behalf because the Spanish honour code dictates that the dishonour of an unmarried daughter also disgraces her closest male guardian. He is further handicapped when he becomes indebted to the duke for saving him from the wrathful Sigismund, and, ultimately, all he can offer Rossaura is life in a convent. She rejects his offer and pleads to the prince. At this point the two threads of the plot are united as the symbolically orphaned protagonists come together in their struggle for justice, both fighting against their fathers in the chaos that envelops the country in act 3.

As one of the more complex characters of the play, it is surprising that Rossaura has not generated more critical interest.[34] Her male disguise in act 1 along with her strong will and independent streak throughout the play recall several of Shakespeare's more famous heroines. Like Viola in *Twelfth Night* and Rosalind in *As You Like It*, Rossaura proves attractive to the opposite sex even while dressed as one of them; like them, and like Portia in *Merchant of Venice* (another cross-dresser), she also displays great ingenuity and wit in her manoeuvrings through a male-dominated world, particularly in her bold confrontations with Clothold and Aistulf. Such actions certainly make for highly captivating drama and might even be interpreted as a sign that Calderón believed in some degree of equivalency between the sexes; but any such reading must take into account several important points. First, Rossaura leaves Poland to search for Aistulf only at the suggestion of her mother Viola, who gives her Clothold's sword – a symbol of male authority – knowing that he, as Rossaura's closest male guardian, is the only one who can legitimately restore her honour; the masculine disguise is simply a means of ensuring safe passage to Poland so that the plan can be put in motion. Second, when Clothold proves unable to assist Rossaura in the way she desires (by killing the duke), she admits that her plan to take matters into her own hands is "madness" and "self-destruction." Third, what ultimately convinces Aistulf to marry Rossaura is not the latter's feminine independence but rather the male authority of Sigismund and Clothold. Finally, Rossaura

---

[34] Among the few studies focused on Rossaura, those of Whitby 1960, Lavroff 1976, and Bueno 1999 deserve special mention (Bibliography, section 8).

accepts a solution that reunites her with the very man who abandoned her and whom, just one scene earlier, she had threatened to kill.[35] None of these points, however, need detract from the sympathy and depth of Rossaura's characterization.

Rossaura's sidekick Bugle is a less complex figure, governed by many of the traits commonly associated with servants of the period: self-interest, an intolerance for physical hardship, loquaciousness (hence his name), quick wit, and a certain intuition that appears to have allowed him to deduce the real relationship between Rossaura and Clothold, as he suggests in act 3. Though it is unclear precisely when or how he makes this connection, he hints at it when, at the beginning of act 2, he blackmails his way into the service of Clothold, who evidently perceives him as enough of a threat to order his imprisonment along with Sigismund at the end of act 2. Officially, Clothold might justify Bugle's incarceration as a reason of state: to prevent him from exposing Aistulf's role in Rossaura's dishonour and thus spoiling the king's plans for the duke. Unofficially, if Clothold suspects that Bugle has inferred his relationship to Rossaura, jailing him also becomes a convenient way to silence him and thus protect Clothold from the dishonour that would stain him as Rossaura's closest male guardian. At any rate, Bugle's syllogistic conclusion that he is being punished for having kept quiet – in contrast, he insists, to the typical servant – rings a bit hollow and perhaps serves to pre-empt sympathy over his sudden and unexpected death two scenes later, which proves useful in confirming the king's recognition that he has caused the current chaos precisely by attempting to avoid it.[36]

The other relationship of note in the play is that of Aistulf and Stella. First cousins who have never met, they harbour competing claims to the Polish throne, and their initial exchange, far from following the protocol of the period, is charged with sly innuendoes and double-entendres. Aistulf, for example, compares Stella's gaze to a comet that lights the night sky: regal and spectacular but also whimsical and fleeting (not to mention that comets in antiquity were frequently associated with calamity and especially with the fall of kings).[37] They agree to marry as a peaceful solution to

---

[35] The great gulf that separates Rossaura's attitude from modern feminist sensibilities becomes apparent in Laird Williamson's recent adaptation of the play (Bibliography, section 1b), which rewrites the ending to have Rossaura refuse Aistulf's hand and offer it instead to Sigismund.

[36] For more on Clarín see Bandera 1971 (Bibliography, section 8).

[37] Ruano de la Haza 2000, p. 66 (Bibliography, section 2).

their conflicting claims to the throne, revealing the importance of arranged marriage among royal families and also, perhaps, hinting at the Hapsburg propensity toward intermarriage. The revelation of Sigismund's existence throws the plan into doubt, however, and Rossaura destroys it for good when, employed as Stella's lady-in-waiting, she makes a fool out of Aistulf in front of the princess. The matter is settled only when Sigismund restores Rossaura's honour by forcing Aistulf to marry her. Thus the duke is punished for his arrogance, losing the crown he has so relentlessly pursued. In a final insult, Sigismund offers his own hand in marriage to Stella, whom Aistulf must now watch inherit the throne without him. This final act of poetic justice, which ostensibly cements the play's happy end, nevertheless leaves a nagging suspicion regarding a marriage between relatives (Sigismund and Stella). A discussion of the work's political and historical dimensions will serve to clarify this point.

***

On a political level, *Life's a Dream* demonstrates the vulnerability of the institution of monarchy in the early modern era, especially in transitional periods when there was no clear heir apparent or when, as in the play, there were several competing claims to the throne. By laying bare this Achilles heel of monarchy, Calderón raises important questions about the role of kingship and about the limits of knowledge and power. Aistulf's observation in act 1 that Vasily is "more inclined to academic pursuits than to women" is not to be taken lightly. The pursuit of academic questions is fine for academics, but in a king, who should be concentrating on the affairs of state – which include ensuring and properly raising a legitimate heir – it is a serious error. When, moreover, the academic pursuit comes to dictate the affairs of state, as when Vasily's astrological predictions determine the prince's barbaric education, the results prove catastrophic.

Vasily is punished for his foolishness with a civil war that divides the country. On one side is the mob that liberates Sigismund from prison, described by the king as "defiant and reckless" and by Clothold as a "reckless and blind." Perhaps because of the historical rivalry between Russia and Poland, or perhaps because of the common people's traditional role in monarchy – as guarantor of legitimate succession – the mob strongly prefers the natural heir to the throne, the Polish Sigismund (despite his obvious incompetence), to the foreign-born Duke of Muscovy. Against the mob stands the aristocracy, which supports the king's brokered solution. Even though the Jesuit treatise of Father Mariana authorized popular rebellions against tyrannical kings (or against more benign kings who, like Vasily, made tyrannical decisions), Calderón must have been aware that he was dealing with an explosive issue given his close connections to the court of Philip IV. His dilemma was how to use a popular rebellion to punish the king's error without appearing to justify popular rebellion *per se*.

At the centre of the problem is the extent to which monarchy can be considered "absolute." The issue is concisely summarized in Sigismund's exchange at court with Servant 2: "When the law isn't just, the king needn't be obeyed," the prince insists. "It wasn't for him to decide whether it was just or not," the servant replies. Later, in his dream at the end of act 2, Sigismund goes even further when he praises "the prince who punishes tyrants." Sigismund's revolutionary formula clearly reflects the treatise of Father Mariana, while the servant's words imply an unswerving loyalty that is best embodied in Clothold, who prefers to die rather than betray the crown: "You would wage war against your father; I cannot counsel you or come to your aid against my king. I am at your mercy; kill me," he tells the prince upon the latter's liberation from the tower in act 3. It matters not that Clothold disagrees with the king's tyrannical act; as a vassal, he considers himself bound by the laws of fealty and, for the same reason, is prepared in act 1 to kill Rossaura even knowing that she is his offspring. It is a conflict similar to the one that Shakespeare develops between John of Gaunt, Duke of Lancaster, and his son Harry Bolingbroke, Duke of Hereford. Lancaster, even with the knowledge that the king is guilty of murder, refuses to accuse him openly: "God's is the quarrel; for God's substitute, / His deputy anointed in his sight, / Hath caused his death; the which if wrongfully, / Let heaven revenge, for I may never lift / An angry arm against his minister."[38] Harry, by contrast, ends up overthrowing Richard and proclaiming himself Henry IV. That a legitimate monarch should be thus overthrown provoked such controversy in Shakespeare's time that the lines in which Richard loses his crown were omitted in all sixteenth-century printings of the play (and perhaps in performance).[39]

Calderón attempts to contain the controversy in several ways. First, the instigators of the rebellion are described disparagingly as "outlaws and peasants," as the soldier tells Sigismund at the beginning of act 3. Second, Sigismund asks his father's forgiveness at the end of the play and even

---

[38] *Richard II* 1.3.37–41
[39] Greenblatt 943–44 (Bibliography, section 3).

offers him his life. Finally, the soldier who led the rebellion and liberated Sigismund from prison is punished with life imprisonment by Sigismund himself. This final act has struck many critics as excessively cruel and ungrateful, but to leave the rebel soldier unpunished or, worse, to reward him for his rebellion (as he requests), would be to strike openly at the very foundation of monarchy: the notion of the king as "God's substitute" and the related idea that his word is unquestionable. While Calderón may have been critical of royal power, he could not have risked such a brazen affront to royal authority.

Another way that Calderón attempts to contain the potential impact of the theme of rebellion is by setting the play in Poland. If the plot could be interpreted, at least partially, as unique to a remote country that lay, in the mind of most Spaniards, at the margin of the civilized world, then there was less chance that it would be seen as applicable at home. While any quasi-exotic setting might seem to satisfy this condition, the choice of Poland in particular is not a gratuitous one. The fact that there were three Polish kings named Sigismund (see Translator's Notes) suggests a closer connection. Sigismund I fought intermittently with Vasily III of Moscow, while Sigismund III invaded Russia and held Moscow for two years. These events, while not paralleled explicitly, are echoed in the play in the prince's rivalry with his father Vasily (Basilio in Spanish), a common Russian name, and with the duke, a Muscovite. Furthermore, Poland's reconversion to Catholicism was one of the great successes of the Counter Reformation, thanks in no small part to Sigismund II, who, among other measures, introduced the Society of Jesus (the Jesuits) in 1565. What better country in which to set Sigismund's ostensible triumph of free will (Catholicism) over Vasily's foolish belief in predestination (Protestantism)?

From a Counter-Reformation perspective, however, the prince's triumph is somewhat vitiated by the fact that the king, whose obsession with "subtle mathematics" is based on the Ptolemaic system, represents the old order of knowledge that Spain wished to preserve: and this, no less, in the homeland of Copernicus. In this way the play foregrounds the clash between the two approaches to science outlined above (Introduction, section 1). Vasily's defeat at the hands of Sigismund, who in some sense represents the new philosophy of Descartes as explained below, parallels the threat that the Copernican system represented to the old order – a threat made resoundingly clear by the Church's public condemnation of Galileo (a follower of Copernicus) in 1633. Calderón's excellent university education almost certainly would have provided him with enough background to draw these connections, and one critic suggests that he could have become aware of further historical details through contact with ambassadors at the court of Philip IV.[40] At any rate, his gift for subtlety allows him to emphasize the more evocative contours of history without forcing them toward facile resolution or bogging the play down in detail.

Although Calderón makes few specific references to Poland's geography, at least two critics have identified the mountainous setting of the prince's tower with the hilly, forested terrain around Krakow.[41] One passage that has caused some confusion is the scene in act 2 in which Sigismund throws the servant "from the balcony to the sea below." Some editors, following a footnote in Hartzenbusch's Spanish edition of *Life's a Dream*,[42] have asked whether Poland bordered the sea in Calderón's time. In fact, prior to the partitioning of the country at the end of the eighteenth century, Poland had always possessed a port on the Baltic Sea; moreover, during the reign of Sigismund II, Poland formed a commonwealth with Lithuania (1569) that effectively pushed its boundaries to the Black Sea. Hartzenbusch's misunderstanding may stem from that fact that, at the time he was writing (1848), Poland was a landlocked country. The real question, however, is how the Polish royal palace, which before 1596 was located in Krakow and afterwards in Warsaw – neither a seaport – could have been conceived of as bordering the ocean. One critic suggests that Calderón's baroque fondness for exaggeration led him to magnify the River Vistula into the sea in the same way that he turned the hills around Krakow into mountains;[43] another points out that the reference to the sea would not have struck readers of the period as odd because many of them associated the seventeenth-century Polish state with the naval policies that King Wladislaus IV pursued from 1632 until his death in 1648.[44] Some of the play's Spanish-language editors feel that Calderón should not be held to strict geographical accuracy and that natural features such as the mountains of act 1 and the sea of act 2 are more literary than real.[45] I believe that the truth lies at an intersection of all these opinions: Calderón intends the play's geographical references to

---

[40] Ginard de la Rosa 1881, pp. 296–97 (Bibliography, section 8).

[41] Brody 1969, p. 43; Ziomek 1983, p. 992 (Bibliography, section 8).

[42] Hartzenbusch 1918, p. 8n (Bibliography, section 2).

[43] Brody 1969, p. 43 (Bibliography, section 8).

[44] Strzalko 1959, p. 644 (Bibliography, section 8).

[45] Morón Arroyo 2000, p. 137n; Ruano de la Haza 2000, p. 169n (Bibliography, section 2).

represent Poland; but, in the same way that he subtly employs references to Polish history, he is interested in broad, evocative allusions with some basis in reality rather than letter-of-the-law accuracy.

In addition to its Polish echoes, *Life's a Dream* may reflect Spain's own past. At the beginning of the reign of Philip II (1556–98), there was a considerable amount of uncertainty regarding the issue of succession. Philip's first wife, the Portuguese Infanta Maria, gave birth to a son, Charles, who early on showed signs of mental instability and had to be excluded from affairs of state or any position of authority. The prince "had several violent fits, engineered bizarre plans to escape, and even plotted against his father. Finally in January 1568 Philip ordered him to be arrested and confined; an action taken, as he explained to the pope, 'with sorrow and grief, since he is my only son and first born.' Six months later [Prince Charles] died in confinement."[46] Are we to see in Sigismund a reminder of this sad episode? A limited but steady stream of critics has said yes.[47] But would Calderón have been drawn to the event for any reason other than its inherent dramatic appeal?

The question becomes all the more intriguing when one considers that Prince Charles, like many Hapsburg offspring, was the product of a poor mixing of the gene pool, for Maria was Philip's first cousin. Although such marriages were not considered incestuous and were actually quite common among all social classes of Calderón's time, they were (and still are) considered by the Catholic Church to be a diriment impediment to marriage as far as the fourth degree of kinship (*i.e.*, first cousins), and special dispensation is required to perform them. Furthermore, astute observers such as Calderón may have intuited what modern genetics has confirmed: that close inbreeding tends to produce offspring who, like Prince Charles, are mentally or physically unfit.[48] For his fourth wife, in fact, Philip II went on

---

[46] Kamen 1991, p. 123 (Bibliography, section 7).

[47] Schevill 1903, Cotarelo y Mori 1914, Levi 1920, Millé y Giménez 1925, Leider 1930, Ferdinandy 1961, Alcalá Zamora 1978 (Bibliography, section 8).

[48] That a knowledge of modern genetics (*i.e.*, since the discovery of the structure of DNA in 1953) would not have been necessary for Calderón to intuit the negative consequences of inbreeding is clear from the following statement, which appears in the article titled "Consanguinity" published by the *Catholic Encyclopedia* in 1908 (Bibliography, section 5): "Nature itself seemed to abhor the marriage of close kin, since such unions are often childless and their offspring seem subject to grave physical and mental weakness (epilepsy, deaf-muteness, weak eyes, nervous diseases), and incur easily and transmit the defects, physical or moral, of their parents, especially when the interbreeding of blood-relations is repeated" (qtd. from the on-line version). As evidence, the article cites multiple sources including an Encyclical of Pope Gregory XVI from 1836.

to choose his niece, Ana of Austria, twenty-two years younger than he: a union that produced the incompetent Philip III, whose reign coincided with the playwright's youth. As both a faithful Catholic and a court insider with a vested interest in the institution of monarchy, Calderón may have felt a very strong opposition to such marriages on both religious and political grounds; furthermore, he appears to have had an unusually strong revulsion to incest based on an obscure event from his childhood that has been plausibly reconstructed (see the entry for the year 1611 in section 3 above).

In light of such facts, I believe that Calderón's peculiar choice of the name Clorilyn for both the king's sister and wife is more than an error or oversight, although that is the way many editors and translators have preferred to view it (see Translator's Notes, section 7). On the contrary, the repetition of the name is significant whether it is interpreted to mean that Vasily married his actual sister or not. If he did, then the intertextuality of the story of Oedipus as well as the allusions to the myths of Prometheus and Uranus, all of which involve incest and end in tragedy, could be interpreted as a sinister reflection of the king's own actions and as a warning of the consequences.[49] Are these the "details that have no place here" to which Aistulf obliquely refers in act 1? If the two Clorilyns are one and the same, furthermore, then Sigismund and Stella, who end up marrying at the end of the play, are half-siblings, possibly even full siblings given that we are never told who Stella's father is and must at least entertain the possibility that it is Vasily. Finally, even if the name Clorilyn is understood to refer to two separate women, the uncanny repetition could be taken as an indication that the king, in true Freudian fashion, married someone who *reminded* him of his sister, that is, a substitute. In this case, the dark omens that foreshadow the prince's birth and the latter's repeated identification with monstrosity would take on new meaning, as a sign of the king's suppressed incestuous desire.[50]

Interestingly, the Prince Charles legend has inspired a long line of literary works, perhaps the most famous being Friedrich Schiller's *Don Carlos*, in which another pseudo-incestuous desire is manifested: in this case, between the prince and his stepmother, Elizabeth of Valois. Do such works somehow

---

[49] On the Prometheus myth in *Life's a Dream* see, for example, Ginard de la Rosa 1881, Morales San Martín 1918, Valbuena Prat 1956, and Navarro González 1977 (Bibliography, section 8). On Uranus, see Ruiz Ramón 1990 (Bibliography, section 8).

[50] On Clorilyn and the issue of incest, see especially Vida Nájera 1944, Feal and Feal-Deibe 1974, García Barroso 1974, Rodríguez López Vázquez 1978, De Armas 1986, pp. 111–13, Molho 1993, pp. 240–48, Soufas 1993, and Sullivan 1993 (Bibliography, section 8).

confirm or build upon Calderón's apparent transformation of the first-cousin kinship between Philip and Maria into the mysterious relation between Vasily and Clorilyn?[51] In any case, the coincidences between Sigismund and Prince Charles – both the product of an incestuous or symbolically incestuous marriage, both judged unfit to govern, both locked away in prison, both conspirators against the king – are too numerous to overlook, and I believe that *Life's a Dream* represents, at least on one level, a veiled critique of the deleterious effects of endogamy, which the Hapsburg monarchy (like all European monarchies of the period) routinely practiced.[52] The fact that the "happy ending" of *Life's a Dream* is cemented by a marriage between first cousins (Sigismund and Stella) – perhaps between siblings – comes as a final confirmation of this interpretation. Like the traces of Polish history in the play, those that point to Spain's own past deserve more attention than they have received at the hands of commentators, who have generally been more interested in the work's philosophical and religious implications.

***

Yet the focus on the intellectual content of *Life's a Dream* is not misplaced, for the play represents the fruit of a mature mind's wrestling with the deep philosophical and religious issues of its time. The play's very title echoes a profoundly unsettling question that has often preoccupied Western philosophy and that, even today, has no satisfactory answer. As Sigismund asks in act 3, "Are delights so akin to dreams that the real ones are taken for lies and the fake ones for genuine? Is there so little difference between one and the other that it's debatable whether what's seen and enjoyed is real or made up? Is the copy so close to the original that the mind doubts which is which?" Might we be simply the figments of someone else's imagination or the characters of someone else's dreams? In Calderón's time, the question was a favourite among baroque writers, having been emphasized by the advance of science, the spread of Protestantism, and the rapid decline of Spain's European hegemony, all of which seemed to represent a threat to previously accepted truths. In considering Calderón's response to this question, embodied in

---

[51] Rank 1992 (Bibliography, section 8) offers a fascinating study of the incest motif in world literature including a significant discussion of the Prince Charles theme: see especially pp. 33–50, 99–118.

[52] Another interesting parallel occurs in Shakespeare's *Hamlet*, where Claudius, upon murdering his brother the king and inheriting his crown, marries his widow, to whom he refers as "our sometime sister, now our queen" (1.2.8), meaning, of course, "sister in law."

Life's a Dream, it is instructive to compare it to René Descartes's *Discourse on Method*, published only a year later.

In investigating the nature of reality, Descartes formulated a sceptical approach that began with the mind as the basis of existence; hence his famous axiom "I think, therefore I am," which would become the cornerstone of modern philosophy. Descartes's approach is revolutionary because, at least in its first step, it rejects everything outside the self including God. Although Descartes later affirms God's existence through classic scholastic arguments, he does so as a *second* step. This may seem like a distinction without a difference, but it is crucial to understanding the conservative character of Calderón's philosophical approach, which, in *beginning* with a sure knowledge of God's existence and a firm conviction regarding all the doctrinal points of Catholicism, remains essentially medieval and scholastic.

In making this point, however, one must be careful to distinguish Calderón's perspective as creator of *Life's a Dream* from that of Sigismund as its main character. The process that Sigismund employs to arrive at a knowledge of reality may, in fact, be compared to the Cartesian method precisely because it depends on a radical doubt that deeply marks the prince's character. "What is life? A frenzy. What is life? An illusion, a shadow, a fiction; and the greatest good is fleeting, for all life is a dream, and even dreams are but dreams," declares Sigismund in his famous soliloquy at the end of act 2. This Cartesian doubt has an interesting parallel in Shakespeare's *Hamlet*, as when the protagonist finds himself paralyzed by scepticism regarding the legitimacy of his father's ghost:

> *Yet I,*
> *A dull and muddy-mettled rascal, peak*
> *Like John-a-dreams, unpregnant of my cause,*
> *And can say nothing – no, not for a king*
> *Upon whose property and most dear life*
> *A damned defeat was made. Am I a coward?*
> *[...] The spirit I have seen*
> *May be the devil, and the devil hath power*
> *T'assume a pleasing shape; yea, and perhaps,*
> *Out of my weakness and my melancholy –*
> *And he is very potent with such spirits –*
> *Abuses me to damn me."*[53]

---

[53] *Hamlet* 2.2.543–48, 575–80. On the Cartesian parallels of *Life's a Dream* see, for example, Ginard de la Rosa 1895, p. 130; Riquer and Valverde 1958, pp. 375–76; García Bacca 1964;

Whereas Hamlet ultimately resolves his doubts by staging a play "Wherein [to] catch the conscience of the King",[54] even at the very end of *Life's a Dream*, Sigismund harbours the sinking feeling that one day he will "wake up and find myself locked away again in my dark prison."

Such gnawing doubt is inconceivable in the mind of Calderón's spectators because the play's fundamental dramatic irony makes them privy to a perspective that is beyond Sigismund's reach. And while the prince's doubts about reality are almost certainly meant to parallel the audience's own experience in the real world, in the audience's case such doubts are more literary than real, reflecting an old, popular metaphor that becomes central to the Spanish baroque and that again finds a parallel in Shakespeare: "We are such stuff / As dreams are made on, and our little life / Is rounded with a sleep."[55] Life is a dream, a pitiful imitation of eternity, filled with confusion and despair, from which we must awaken (that is, die) in order to experience things as they really are (*i.e.*, eternity); this is the basic meaning of the contrast between the Spanish terms *engaño* (deception) and *desengaño* (revelation of that deception) that was so dear to Calderón and his contemporaries. Moreover, because we may awaken at any moment – for death can come when we least expect it – we must always live according to Christian principles and be on guard against temptation lest we risk condemnation. Before such truths as these, the play offers no doubt of the Cartesian type for the spectators, who, while they may compare the confusion experienced by the prince to the uncertainty of their world, remain certain of their uncertainty; that is, they remain certain of the essential dividing line between dreams (this life) and reality (the eternal). The protagonist, by contrast, doubting to the very end, remains something of a Cartesian, and this curious tension between the inner and outer perspectives on the action of the play goes unresolved. Thus, while Calderón hints at a radical new epistemology that is confirmed by Descartes the following year, he takes care to do so in a character whose perspective is severely limited. The medieval marriage of philosophy and theology is strained but not broken.

Sullivan 1979; Resina 1983; Bradburn-Ruster 1997 (Bibliography, section 8). Comparisons between *Life's a Dream* and *Hamlet* (though not from a Cartesian perspective) are drawn by Blanco Asenjo 1870, Abel 1963, and Morón Arroyo 1990 (Bibliography, section 8).

[54] *Hamlet* 2.2.582.

[55] *The Tempest* 4.1.155–57. See Rupp 1990 and Zaidi 1996 for recent comparisons of *Life's a Dream* and *The Tempest* (Bibliography, section 8). On the sources of the life-is-a-dream fable (Middle Eastern in origin), see Thomas 1910, Farinelli 1916, Olmedo 1928, Frenzel 1970, Richthofen 1970, and Galmés de Fuentes 1986 (Bibliography, section 8).

What is the role of the stars in this picture? Far from an arcane theological matter, the thrust of this question is one that, in slightly different terms, continues to spark fierce debate today and whose definitive answer, at least as of yet, continues to elude us. Simply put, to what extent is human choice mediated: whether by genetics, environmental factors, or, yes, even the stars (the widespread existence of astrology columns in the twenty-first century necessitates the inclusion of the latter term)? In short, to what extent is free will *free*?

By Calderón's time, the Catholic Church had long recognized that astrology could predict events and measure one's inclinations, and it is noteworthy that all of Vasily's predictions in *Life's a Dream* are ultimately fulfilled. But two crucial points must accompany this observation. First, as in the many misinterpretations of oracle in Greek tragedy including the Oedipus cycle, Vasily accurately foresees the outcome or *effect* of history but misinterprets the *cause* – a scholastic distinction – failing to see that he himself, in the barbaric way he has brought up the prince, precipitates precisely what he has attempted to avoid. Sigismund points this out in act 3 when he asks: "If any man were told, 'One day you will be killed by an inhuman beast,' would it be a good solution for him to wake one up while it was sleeping?" In the second place, the Church categorically refuted and prohibited what was called "judiciary" astrology, which counselled remedies that could be taken in order to avoid the fulfilment of prophecy, because such measures undermined the concept of free will so important to Catholic dogma. This is precisely Vasily's error, which Sigismund again clarifies: "He who foresees a danger can't remove himself from its path; yes, he can take a few humble measures to guard against it, but not until the moment is upon him, for there's no way of forestalling its arrival." In short, the stars can influence the future but cannot determine it outright. The point is brought home when Sigismund, contrary to all expectations, apparently repents at the final moment, affirming Catholicism's emphasis on the redemptory power of individual free will.[56]

One may, however, question the sincerity of Sigismund's sudden "conversion," viewing it as the product of a cynical *desengaño* or the culmination of a calculated quest for power in the spirit of Machiavelli's *Prince*. This is the play's last major unresolved question and – together with

---

[56] For more detail on astrology and Catholic theology in the play see, for example, Carrera Artau 1927, Febrer 1934, Lorenz 1961, Valbuena Briones 1961, May 1972, Howe 1977, Hurtado Torres 1983, and De Armas 1986, 1987, and 2001 (Bibliography, section 8).

the related issue of Sigismund's incarceration of the rebel soldier – the one that has most divided critics.[57] On the one hand, a sincere conversion would foreground the legitimacy of Catholic doctrine. On the other, a cynical grab for power, while it would not *negate* the legitimacy of Catholic doctrine, would be more in line with the critique of the Hapsburgs suggested above. Yet, just as in the question of Clorilyn (is she or is she not Vasily's sister?); in that of Vasily's defeat (positive – from a Catholic perspective – because it refutes judiciary astrology, negative because it marks a threat to the old order); and in that of the difference between dreams and reality (clear to the spectators, hazy to the prince even at the end of the play), Calderón rejects a facile solution to this problem and leaves all doors open. The issue of Sigismund's conversion has no easy answer and, in truth, leaves much to the discretion of the director, for there are no stage directions to indicate the prince's manner or gestures at this crucial moment (see the Suggestions for Directors for ideas on staging this scene). That *Life's a Dream* resists final closure in this way is one mark of its enduring vitality; that it leaves the question in the hands of directors is a sign of its inherent dramatic value; that it does so within the formulaic structure of the Comedia, where happy ends are the norm, is final proof of the subtlety of the author's genius.

***

Any interpretation of *Life's a Dream*, however brief, would be incomplete without a reference to the image of the hippogriff, a crucial symbol not only because it is the first word in the Spanish original but also because it unites so many of the play's themes. Rossaura uses the word to allude to the swiftness of the horse that has just thrown her, for the hippogriff is, among other things, a horse with wings. But its symbolism comprises more than just speed. As the unlikely product of a horse (*hippos* in Greek) and a griffin (itself a combination of an eagle and a lion) the hippogriff is "monstrous" in the strict sense of the word: a chaotic union of naturally irreconcilable elements, a blurring of boundaries that many of the play's characters incarnate in a way that parallels the three basic themes studied above. On a personal level,

---

[57] The essence of the polemical debate over the rebel soldier may be gleaned from the initial dialogue between Hall 1968, who maintains that Sigismund's punishment of the soldier is unjust; Parker 1969, who defends the punishment as an example of poetic justice; and Hall 1969, who reaffirms his original stance (Bibliography, section 8). More or less in line with Parker's view are Connolly 1972, Halkhoree 1972, Heiple 1973, Rull 1975, McGrady 1985, and Fox 1989 (Bibliography, section 8). In opposition stand May 1970, Hesse 1977, Alcalá Zamora 1978, and Homstad 1989 (Bibliography, section 8).

the dishonoured Rossaura, forced to take vengeance into her own hands, is half man, half woman, as her disguise in act 1 suggests. Sigismund, because of the savage conditions of his upbringing (and also, perhaps, because he is the product of incest), is half man, half beast. On a political level, the civil war that engulfs the country stems partially from Vasily's status as half king, half astrologer, and Aistulf's as half Pole, half Muscovite. Even at the philosophical level, the blurring of boundaries between dreams and reality reaffirms the omnipresent symbolism of the hippogriff. It is altogether fitting, then, that some semblance of order is restored in the last scene of the play only after the king, rejecting Aistulf's advice, refuses to flee upon the "swift miscarriage of the wind" that catapulted Rossaura onto the stage in scene 1.[58]

---

[58] For detailed studies of the hippogriff, see Valbuena Briones 1962, Maurin 1967, Cilveti 1973, León 1983, and De Armas 1990 (Bibliography, section 8).

TRANSLATOR'S NOTES

Rendering Calderón's *La vida es sueño* into English presents the translator with a series of difficult but unavoidable questions. Which dialect is desirable? Should archaisms be modernized or rendered into analogous English structures? Which is the most appropriate medium, verse or prose? What constitutes a scene change? How should proper names be handled? What about wordplay? And finally, what should be done with enigmatic or disputed passages? My dissatisfaction with the various answers given to these questions by previous translators has provided the primary impetus behind this translation of the crown jewel of classical Spanish theatre.

1. Dialect

My original intention in translating Calderón's masterpiece was to make it accessible to the current generation of American high school and college students. After the translation was published in the States by the University Press of Colorado, I was asked by the editors at Oxbow Books to consider reprinting it in bilingual format in the Aris and Phillips series. Accepting their kind offer necessitated turning my original premise on its head and re-imagining the translation, this time with a British public in mind; and I am very grateful to Professor Jonathan Thacker of Merton College, Oxford for his generous assistance in this regard. It is worth noting, furthermore, that the number of changes introduced as a result of this "reverse adaptation" was – apart from spelling differences – fairly minimal, which leads me to the happy conclusion that the standard written English of the States poses few challenges for contemporary British actors and audiences.

2. Historicity

Languages vary not only geographically, as between Ireland, Britain, America, and Australia, but also chronologically. Standard contemporary British English is quite different from the English of Shakespeare – whose life ran roughly parallel to Calderón's (the latter was sixteen years old when his English contemporary died) – which is, in turn, very different from the English of Chaucer some two centuries earlier. And while the evolution of the Spanish language is not nearly as pronounced as that of English, and Castilian texts from the time of Calderón are still accessible to contemporary readers with little or no specialized training, there are nevertheless some significant differences. Modern translators of Calderón are thus faced with a decision regarding not only dialect but also historicity. While the former question is generally resolved without much fanfare, in accordance with the translator's native dialect, and with little consequence for reception, the second question is one that all translators must consciously face and consistently wrestle with, for it is likely to have a strong impact on the play's reception and interpretation.

Because Calderón's Spanish is roughly contemporary to the English of Shakespeare, some translators have sought to render him into an Elizabethan-sounding idiom. William Colford, for instance, translates the opening lines of the play as follows:

> *Wild hippogriff, that matched the wind in flight,*
> *Dark lightning, dull-plumed bird, unscalèd fish,*
> *Brute beast that makes a mock of nature's laws,*
> *Now wherefore art thou come in headlong plunge*
> *Through twisting trails to reach this barren brink?*   5
> *Remain upon this crag so beasts may have*
> *Their Phaëthon; for I, with no more course*
> *Than destiny decrees, in blind despair*
> *Descend the tangled slope of this harsh hill*
> *That wrinkles to the sun its scowling brow.*   10
> *A poor reception, Poland, does thou give*
> *A stranger, since with blood her welcome's writ*
> *Upon thy sands, and hardly here, she fares*
> *So hardly. Yet my fate ordains it so.*
> *But where was pity e'er found for one in woe?*   15

While such translations may convey an archaic feel somewhat akin to the sensation produced in a contemporary Spanish speaker upon reading Calderón in the original, whatever correspondences thus achieved are based upon a poor analogy. It is true that Elizabethan English was the predominant dialect in England at the time Calderón wrote *Life's a Dream*, but Colford and those who follow similar approaches are not translating the play for audiences of Elizabethan England; only a seventeenth-century translator could meaningfully undertake such a task. [59] If the goal of translation is to bring texts to life for audiences unable to read the original, then the translator

---

[59] Other translators who adopt an Elizabethan-sounding idiom include Oxenford 1842, Trench 1856, Mac-Carthy 1873, Stirling 1942, and FitzGerald 2000 (Bibliography, sections 1a, 1b).

should use the language and dialect of the audience he or she wishes to reach, realizing that readers and spectators are a product of *time* as well as space. By reconstructing a historical English dialect in order to translate a play from classical Spanish, Colford and others end up producing works that are no more faithful to the original than a contemporary translation would have been and that, additionally, risk alienating their potential audiences.

In contrast to such approaches, I have chosen to render Calderón into a relatively transparent, contemporary idiom. As an example, I do not translate the Spanish *tú*, the familiar form of address in both classical and contemporary Spanish, with its Elizabethan equivalent *thou* as Colford does, because the latter form has since dropped out of the language and its presence throughout the play, I believe, would be overly jarring.

At the same time, I have preserved certain anachronisms that reflect the flavour of the time without clouding the play's reception. For example, in Sigismund's first encounter with the beautiful Rossaura, he refers to his eyes as *hidrópicos*, that is, as suffering from dropsy. Some translators paraphrase this passage so as to eliminate the reference altogether, as in Stanley Appelbaum's "my eyes must be / morbidly thirsty."[60] Yet there is something lost in this move, for the belief in dropsy (today called edema) as an illness rather than a symptom says a great deal about the state of scientific knowledge in Calderón's time (see Introduction, section 1). It is, furthermore, an unnecessary loss, for Calderón provides, in the same passage, enough of an explanation for audiences to grasp the basic metaphor even without specific knowledge of the condition.

Other lexical oddities that I have preserved for similar reasons include *henbane* and *halberd* in act 2 as well as the many historical and mythological references that form such an important part of Calderón's imagery. A prime example is the famous image of the hippogriff with which the play opens. It is lamentable, indeed, that readers of certain translations are barred from capturing this crucial metaphor, so central to the development of the play's meaning, because the translators either dilute it through periphrasis or leave it out altogether.[61] While it is true that not all contemporary spectators are

---

[60] Appelbaum 2002, p. 7. Similarly, Clifford 1998 translates as "My eyes must have a kind of rabies" (p. 10), whereas Raine and Nadal 1968 render "There is a fever in my eyes" (p. 7); Edwards 1991 translates the passage even more periphrastically: "... my eyes are so / Entranced, they long to see you more, / And hunger for the sight of you, / As if they were a man to whom / Drink is forbidden..." (p. 109). See Bibliography, section 1a.

[61] For example: "This headstrong horse must think itself / An eagle or some fabulous beast..." (Edwards 1991); "Where have you thrown me, mad horse, / half griffin?" (Honig

likely to capture such allusions, I would venture to say the same about Calderón's peers, and the playwright himself occasionally mixes up some of the more obscure references.[62] Yet, as in the case of *dropsy*, Calderón almost always provides enough of a context in which to grasp the meaning of the reference. In the few instances where he does not – as in the allusions to Timanthes, Lysippus, and Atlas – I provide a minimal degree of clarification that will serve to orient uninformed spectators. For *readers* of my translation who desire further information, I provide a full explanation of such terms in the glossary, where I also include acceptable substitutions for performance, although I would generally recommend against using them.

Rendering dialect and historicity is, without a doubt, a delicate balancing act. I can sum up my approach best by stating that my ultimate goal would be to have my readers exclaim, as Wendy Lesser does of Alfred Birnbaum's translations of Japanese novelist Haruki Murakami: "How, in short, could he make a Japanese writer sound so remarkably American [or British!] without losing any of his alien allure?"[63]

3. Medium: Verse vs. Prose

One of the more difficult questions that a translator of Calderón and of classical Spanish drama in general must face is whether to imitate the plays' exclusively poetic form or, by contrast, to render into prose. If verse translations are taken to mean, minimally, line breaks that correspond more or less to those of the original, then the overwhelming preference of previous translators of Calderón (including all those published in the past three decades) is for verse. This choice undoubtedly reflects a sincere desire to be as faithful as possible to Calderonian form, a desire that would be betrayed – so the reasoning goes – by a prose rendition. I am convinced, however, that verse translations are highly problematic, on both a practical and theoretical level, because of the vast differences in the conventions of rhyme, metre, and rhythm that exist between English and Spanish poetry.

Regarding perhaps the most obvious element of poetry – rhyme – it is

---

1993); and "There, four-footed / Fury, blast- / -engender'd Brute" (FitzGerald 2000). See Bibliography, sections 1a, 1b.

[62] Indeed, even some of Calderón's translators misspell *Phaethon*, failing to restore the *h* that drops out in the passage from classical Greek to modern Spanish. See Oxenford 1842, Mac-Carthy 1873, Clifford 1998, Edwards 1991, and FitzGerald 2000 (Bibliography, sections 1a, 1b).

[63] Lesser 2002, p. B5 (Bibliography, section 4).

instructive to begin with Rossaura's widely admired opening speech, which presents a relatively simple rhyme scheme in the original Spanish, consisting of eleven pairs of rhymed *silvas* of the pattern *aA-bB-cC...* (where the lower case indicates verses of seven syllables and the upper case, eleven). If any pattern should be imitated, it is this one, because of both the simplicity of the form and the importance of the play's opening speech. Yet, of the many translations to date (see section 1 of the bibliography below), only one reveals a true attempt to do so: that of the nineteenth-century Irish lawyer, Denis Florence Mac-Carthy. His translation has long since been out of print, but it deserves special mention for attempting such a Herculean task. Here is how Mac-Carthy renders Rossaura's opening speech:

Wild hippogriff swift speeding,
Thou that dost run, the wingèd winds exceeding,
Bolt which no flash illumes,
Fish without scales, bird without shifting plumes,
And brute awhile bereft   5
Of natural instinct, why to this wild cleft,
This labyrinth of naked rocks, dost sweep
Unreined, uncurbed, to plunge thee down the steep?
Stay in this mountain wold,
And let the beasts their Phaëton behold.   10
For I, without a guide,
Save what the laws of destiny decide,
Benighted, desperate, blind,
Take any path whatever that doth wind
Down this rough mountain to its base,   15
Whose wrinkled brow in heaven frowns in the sun's bright face.
Ah, Poland! in ill mood
Hast thou received a stranger, since in blood
The name thou writest on thy sands
Of her who hardly here fares hardly at thy hands.   20
My fate may well say so: –
But where shall one poor wretch find pity in her woe?

Mac-Carthy's faithful reproduction of Calderonian rhyme, even though it briefly breaks down at various points later in the translation, is a splendid achievement that remains without peer.[64] This particular passage, furthermore,

---

[64]   This observation is from 2003. In updating my introduction for Oxbow, I discovered G. J.

is one of the more clearly rendered of the entire translation and thus represents a best-case scenario. Even so, the perfectly executed rhyme of Rossaura's speech comes at a high cost. The forced English syntax is at times difficult to follow, especially in a reception context. Moreover, to maintain even a semblance of the original metre, Mac-Carthy must insert meaningless words, such as "awhile" in line 5 and "benighted" in line 13, that do not exist in the original. And yet, even with such efforts, the metre runs off course as in the impossibly wordy line 16.

Mac-Carthy's technique may seem extreme, but is there any other logical approach to translating rhyme? If one aims to reproduce a given structure, shouldn't one do so in a consistent and faithful manner? A tall order, no doubt, further complicated by the fact that the conventions of rhyme are quite different in Spanish and English. Spanish, for example, permits an assonant form of end rhyme, in which only the vowels coincide (as occurs, in fact, in verses 600–1223, 1724–2017, 2188–2427, and 3094–3315 of *Life's a Dream*). How is one to translate a structure that has no real equivalent in English? In such cases, even Mac-Carthy gives up and renders into loose blank verse.

Faced with such difficulties, verse translators have two choices with respect to rhyme. First, they can settle for something like the approach of Gwynne Edwards, that is, "a judicious mixture of end and internal rhymes, used in a way which does not distort syntax and rhythm."[65] This is, in fact, the approach that most verse translators have adopted even though they may not describe it in those terms. Unfortunately, it cannot come close to reproducing Calderonian rhyme. To make matters worse, Edwards and others tend to concentrate their rhymes in the mouth of the clownish Bugle, a move that creates the lamentable and incorrect impression that rhyme in Calderón is associated with foolishness and frivolity. The second approach, which has been employed by Appelbaum on the one hand and Raine and Nadal on the other, is to jettison rhyme altogether. But such a move only brings them, despite themselves, one step closer to prose.

The second formal element of poetry, metre, is equally problematic for translators of Calderón who insist on verse renditions. The metrical system of Spanish poetry is syllabic, in which the basic unit is the syllable, and

---

Racz's translation, published in 2009 in *The Norton Anthology of Drama* (Bibliography, section 1a). Like Mac-Carthy, Racz closely follows Calderón's rhyme scheme; and his translation, like Mac-Carthy's, presents many of the same problems of rhythm and oral comprehension.

[65] Edwards 1991, p. xxxi (Bibliography, section 1a).

the overwhelming majority of the 3319 verses of *Life's a Dream* consist of either seven, eight, or eleven *metrical* syllables.[66] As in the case of rhyme, it seems only logical for verse translators to imitate as closely as possible the metrical structure of the play. Yet here, even more than with rhyme, the practical impossibility looms large, as linguistic theory shows. With few exceptions, traditional English verse since the time of Chaucer has been of the accentual-syllabic variety, in which the basic unit is not the syllable but the foot, that is, a group of syllables with a defined stress pattern of varying length.[67] Although syllabic metre has been occasionally employed in English verse, it is considered experimental, the province of poets such as Auden, Pound, and Dylan Thomas; it is thus not the most appropriate choice for translating Calderón's more traditional metrical forms. What, then, would be the English metrical equivalent of a traditional eight-syllable Spanish verse, for instance? In answer to that question, many translators settle on "a syllabic line patterned on the octosyllabic *romance*."[68] Yet this solution ignores not only the fundamental metrical difference between traditional English and Spanish poetry but also the fact that, as mentioned above, the metre of *Life's a Dream* is not only octosyllabic but also includes a substantial number of heptasyllabic and hendacasyllabic verses.

With great clarity and detail, Victor Dixon has studied this rich "polymetry," or varied verse forms, of the Comedia, with special attention to the work of Lope de Vega. A translator himself, Dixon goes on to declare his strong preference for verse translations and for blank verse (unrhymed iambic pentameter) in particular, "convinced that performers and spectators accustomed to our own classic drama would most readily accept the *Comedia* in that familiar metre."[69] It is a preference that other verse translators have also expressed.[70] Tellingly, while Dixon suggests that my own adoption of prose "fails," presumably because it cannot represent the metrical variety

---

[66] One must distinguish between *metrical* and *phonetic* syllables because Spanish poets make use of certain licenses that allow for the combination, addition, or deletion of syllables for the purposes of meter; when any such license is employed (which happens fairly regularly), the total number of poetic syllables will differ from the total number of actual (phonetic) syllables. For a brief summary of versification in Spanish poetry, see Rivers 1988, pp. 23–24. More detailed treatment is offered in Baehr 1970 and Navarro Tomás 1991 (Bibliography, section 3).

[67] See Kinzie 1999 (Bibliography, section 3), especially pp. 215–16, for more detail on the history of English prosody.

[68] Honig 1993, p. x (Bibliography, section 1a).

[69] Dixon 2008, p. 64 (Bibliography, section 4).

[70] See, for example, MacKenzie 1989 (Bibliography, section 4).

he understandably admires, he does not explain how the blank verse he himself champions *is* a sufficient vehicle for capturing such variety.[71] Indeed, apart from being virtually unknown to Spanish poets of the seventeenth century, blank verse is characterized by a metrical regularity that necessarily introduces a levelling effect onto the formal richness rightly admired by Dixon. It is, furthermore, a form that disappeared from English drama in the nineteenth century, as Robert Shaw explains:

> Blank verse, for the would-be playwright, offered some specialized challenges. The most obvious was the break in the chain of tradition. Because theatrical blank verse had ceased to be a living medium in the mid-seventeenth century, it had not evolved as it otherwise likely would have done, adapting itself to changes in idiom over time. Because the finest models were frozen in time, later poets had either to ape an antiquated style or somehow find an equal eloquence in the language of their own time.[72]

Shaw demonstrates that, although it was once a popular form, by the nineteenth century blank verse had become characteristic of "endeavors that were academic or recherché."[73] These "frozen" and "recherché" associations of blank verse, which cannot but influence its reception in today's audiences, further undermine the case for using it to reproduce the rich verse forms and popular registers of the Comedia.

The problem is only compounded by the third formal element of poetry: rhythm. In the words of the great French Modernist poet Stéphane Mallarmé, poetry is human language "ramené à son rythme essentiel" 'restored to its essential rhythm.' Rhythm is the most defining feature of poetry, whether classical or contemporary. This observation is easily confirmed in the Spanish poetry of Calderón's time. For example, the typical eleven-syllable verse, obligatory in sonnets and *silvas* (the latter a staple of *Life's a Dream*), presents a fixed accent on the tenth syllable and hovering accents that tend to converge over the fourth, sixth, and/or eighth. The effect varies greatly depending on the particular combination of stressed syllables, which can be used to emphasize certain words or, alternatively, to create very peculiar, offbeat verses. In a brilliant study, the twentieth-century Spanish poet Dámaso Alonso shows just how well Spanish poets of the sixteenth and seventeenth centuries exploited the natural rhythm of their language in all its complexity,

---

[71] Dixon 2008, pp. 62–64 (Bibliography, section 4).

[72] Shaw 2007, p. 114 (Bibliography, section 3).

[73] Ibid., p. 113.

with profound consequences for the meaning and interpretation of their poems. Alonso's concluding remarks on Garcilaso de la Vega (1501–1536), Spain's most admired Renaissance poet, illustrate the idea:

> We have seen how the exquisite sensibility of Garcilaso uses all the expressive possibilities of rhythm as an agitator to awaken the word on the page. We have seen how this word, effectively swept away in a creative trance, thrusts itself into sudden movements and strange affinities that do not affect it, or do so only minimally, in everyday language. With what skill the rhythmic accents come to fall over exactly those words of greatest conceptual or affective expressiveness! Words enhance their aesthetic representation upon receiving the powerful light of the accent. Yes: the word, beneath the push of the accent, sometimes reinforces itself but, more frequently, as if sensually, absorbs new meaning and, increasing its phonetic expressiveness, that is, mysteriously motivating in itself the link between signifier and signified, grows in strength, richness, or colour.[74]

The shadow cast by Garcilaso de la Vega was enormous: in one way or another, all subsequent Spanish poets up through the time of Calderón were indebted to him. As a consequence, any attempts at verse translations of classical Spanish poetry (whether lyric or dramatic) that do not take seriously the centrality of rhythm seem destined to miss the mark.

Rhythm is not unique to poetry, moreover. It is among the first elements that human infants process and one of the last that second language learners master. It is, in short, one of the most deep-seated and defining features of language. The fact that the basic unit of English poetry is the foot and that of Spanish, the syllable, is, in fact, a result of the great difference between the natural rhythms of the two languages. The importance of this concept for translation theory together with the fact that few translators of Calderón seem to have given it much consideration justifies the length of the following citation:

> Languages tend to sort out into two main rhythmic types. One type, called *syllable-timed*, has a rhythm ticked off by even syllables, each syllable receiving one quick beat called a *mora*. The general acoustic effect is a distinctive staccato 'dot-dot-dot-dot-dot'. The other type, stress-timed, has a rhythm based on stress groups. Syllables are organized into feet, each foot containing one strongly stressed syllable plus unstressed and lesser stressed

---

[74] Alonso 1993, p. 105 (Bibliography, section 3).

satellites. Instead of each syllable taking one mora, each foot occupies about the same measure of time regardless of its number of syllables, and to equalize the feet requires that the unstressed syllables be shortened and squeezed in around the stressed ones. This yields a strikingly galloping effect, 'di-DUM-di-di-DUM-di-DUM.'

English, like other Germanic languages, is stress-timed; Spanish, like most other Romance languages, is syllable-timed. Native speakers hear the difference, though they may not be able to identify precisely what is happening. Spanish strikes the English speaker as fast and machine gun-like; English, to the Spanish speaker, can seem jerky, with alternate drawling and obliteration of syllables.[75]

More recent linguistic studies, while questioning the universality of this opposition, nevertheless confirm that English and Spanish fall on opposite sides of any continuum that contrasts syllable timing and stress timing.[76] This seemingly simple difference has, in fact, radical implications that effectively pre-empt any attempt to carry into English the great rhythmic richness of classical Spanish verse as studied by Dámaso Alonso. When combined with the differences already noted regarding rhyme and metre in Spanish and English, those involving rhythm would seem to suggest that while translators who insist on verse may end up producing very beautiful translations – assuming they are poets as well as translators – they cannot possibly reproduce the original form to any degree of faithfulness or consistency.[77]

Finally, verse renditions are problematic because their desire to mimic the formal similarity of the original necessarily exacts a heavy toll on the translation. When a translator willingly ties his hands with the complex constraints of rhyme, metre, and rhythm, it becomes impossible to reproduce the meaning of the text to any degree of faithfulness. When Edwards, for

---

[75] Whitley 1986, pp. 65–66 (Bibliography, section 4).

[76] See, for example, Frota and Vigário 2001; Grabe and Ling Low 2002 (Bibliography, section 4). My thanks to Professor José Ignacio Hualde for these references.

[77] See the articles by Dixon, Edwards, Gitlitz, MacKenzie, McGaha, Muir, and Paterson (Bibliography, section 4), all leaders in the field of Comedia translation. With the lone exception of McGaha, all vehemently defend verse translations. While they demonstrate an often keen awareness of some of the problems explored in this section, especially those regarding rhyme and meter, these critics tend to see the difficulty not as a theoretical impasse but rather as a practical stumbling block that can be overcome through patience and ingenuity. Significantly, none shows any knowledge of those studies in linguistics that demonstrate the great, irreconcilable differences between the natural rhythms of English and Spanish as discussed above.

example, has Bugle (whom he calls Clarion) quip to the royal servant in act 2, "In other words, old friend, old cock, / The prince means put a sock in it!"[78] the imperfect end-rhyme *cock / sock in it* is accomplished only through a gross distortion of the original "Dice el príncipe muy bien, / y vos hicistes muy mal" 'What the prince says is very right, and what you did was very wrong.' Such examples abound in the many verse renderings of *Life's a Dream*. In their attempt to reproduce both form and content, verse translators often end up achieving neither: in the first case, because it is impossible; in the latter, because the focus on form inevitably brings about a distortion of meaning.

My solution is to abandon verse in a quest for as accurate and accessible a meaning as possible. I believe the dramatic theory of Calderón's day supports my approach. In his humorous manifesto *The New Art of Writing Plays in Our Time*, Calderón's predecessor Lope de Vega spends over half the 390 total verses of the treatise explaining how to pick a topic, turn it into a riveting plot, and distribute the tension across the three acts of classical Spanish drama's conventional structure. He spends a total of only six lines[79] on the differing verse forms available, which he prefaces with the general caveat that "Verse forms should be prudently accommodated to the subjects that they describe."[80] In other words, de Vega's manifesto establishes a clear hierarchy that privileges plot and characterization (that is, content) over the more formal elements of poetry like rhyme, metre, and rhythm. Recognizing the impossibility of reproducing both form and content in the same translation, I have aimed to preserve as strictly as possible the favoured term in de Vega's hierarchy, confident that an accurate content will convey the exceptional beauty of Calderón's poetic imagery and mitigate to some extent the loss of poetic form.

4. Scene Boundaries

One point on which both translations and Spanish-language editions of classical Spanish drama differ widely is the interpretation and placement of scene boundaries. While the playwrights themselves almost always indicated the divisions between the play's three main acts (called *actos* or *jornadas*), they never indicated scene divisions as do modern dramatists, that is, with the labels Scene 1, Scene 2, *etc*. Calderón is no exception to this rule, and

---

[78] Edwards 1991, p. 140 (Bibliography, section 1a).
[79] Vega 1989, vv. 307–12 (Bibliography, section 3).
[80] Ibid., vv. 305–06.

several translators of *Life's a Dream*, following his cue, also decline to mark explicit scene boundaries.[81] Two questions arise from this practice. First, is it useful to introduce into the translation a nomenclature that is absent in the original? If the answer is yes, then what method should be used to measure scenes and mark their boundaries?

In the English-speaking world, it is standard practice to divide the main acts of plays into scenes. If the playwright does not do so, editors often will. This is the case in Shakespeare, where scene divisions, not consistently indicated in the earliest available versions of his plays, were inserted by later editors, often amid disagreement.[82] Basic scene division is important for modern directors because it offers a rough index to the complexity of the performance: the more scenes there are, the more scene changes will be necessary (and thus the equipment necessary to produce them). Marking scene boundaries also provides a helpful cue to the contemporary reader of drama, often unaccustomed to visualizing the mechanics of performance. Additionally, it serves as a convenient point of reference for class discussion. It seems logical, then, in translating a play for English-speaking readers, to follow the conventions with which they would be most familiar.

The question of how to mark scene boundaries is more complicated and depends on what is understood by the word "scene." The *Diccionario de Autoridades*, the first dictionary of the Royal Academy of the Spanish Language (published in the early eighteenth century and based on citations from the "authorities," that is, writers from the time of Calderón), gives two definitions of *escena*:

1. Location or place where playwrights perform their works, commonly called the Stage or the boards. Taken from the Greek *Scena*, which means a military tent or barracks, or a cover constructed from the branches of trees to offer shelter in the open field; by virtue of this [etymology], the Scene includes or signifies the place or stage with all the decorations, stage machinery, and set changes necessary for the execution of the play that is being performed.

---

[81] Campbell 1959, Edwards 1991, Clifford 1998, Appelbaum 2002 (Bibliography, section 1a).

[82] The editors of *The Norton Shakespeare*, for example, justify their particular reckoning of scenes in *Henry the Sixth, Part One* as follows: "Generally, additional scenes are marked at all points during a battle when the stage appears momentarily to be clear of all characters, the traditional indication in the Renaissance theater that one scene has ended and another begun" (Greenblatt 1997, p. 442 [Bibliography, section 3]).

2. A unit of the play that lasts the entire time that there are people on the stage; and thus when the stage is completely emptied and other characters enter again, it is said that another Scene begins.

The first definition, which basically means "stage," is a spatial one that implies the idea of a set; the second, which suggests that scene changes were determined by the movements of characters, is sequential or temporally based. Ideally, the two definitions coincided and reinforced one another: when all actors exited the stage, audiences imagined a *place* or *scene change* even when the meagre stagecraft of Calderón's period did not make a *set change* feasible.

The Academy's definitions, however, were not always completely borne out by the highly irregular theatrical practice of Spanish playwrights in the early modern period. A Latin source from Calderón's time notes that Spanish audiences "considered changes of scene superfluous, as neither the exactness of the thought, nor the elegance of the diction, nor the splendour of the production, depended upon them."[83] Another historian of Spanish theatre adds: "In the public theatre in the time of Lope and Calderón scene divisions were unknown, and on the big platform stage on which these plays were performed one scene flowed naturally into another without break in the action, or visible change. Only in the court theatre was scene change important, and here it is indicated by the relevant texts in their own way."[84] Sometimes a scene change could be implied by an actor's exit on the opposite side of the stage from which he entered or, alternatively, by re-entry through a different door than that through which the exit was made.[85] In other instances no exit at all was required, and the scene change was simply implied in the dialogue or in the unveiling of one of the nine niches that formed the backdrop of the stage (see Introduction, section 2). In Lope de Vega's *The Wiles of Favia (Los embustes de Fabia)*, for example, the playwright, always eager to poke fun at dramatic convention, has his character Aurelio state, without exiting the stage during a scene that takes place in the bedroom of his mistress: "Here is the palace and there Nero, our Emperor, appears, for the poet has permitted this expedient to be employed, since, if the Emperor should not enter now, the narrative would be so vague that nobody would understand it."[86]

---

[83] Quoted in Rennert 1963, p. 86n (Bibliography, section 8).

[84] Shergold 1967, pp. xxiv–xxv (Bibliography, section 8).

[85] Rennert 1963, pp. 87–88; Shergold 1967, p. 361 (Bibliography, section 8).

[86] Quoted in Rennert 1963, p. 87 (Bibliography, section 8).

Given the confusion regarding scene divisions, nineteenth-century Spanish editors began to mark scenes whenever there was *any* new entry or exit by a character. Juan Eugenio Hartzenbusch (1806–80), one of the founders of the classic *Library of Spanish Authors (Biblioteca de Autores Españoles)*, writes in the introduction to a volume on Tirso de Molina:

> To remind the reader, upon each entry or exit of a speaking character, the names of those who were speaking before he entered or who continue to speak after he exits, is good for the memory, facilitates the understanding of the drama, gives beauty to the book as well as a rest and a break to the eyes of he who reads; thus, following the example offered by the *Standard Collection of Selected Plays (Colección general de Comedias escogidas)*, which began publication in the year 1826, we have subdivided the dramas of Tirso into scenes.[87]

The practice of measuring scenes by the entrances and exits of characters, which may have its origin in eighteenth-century France,[88] was defended by Wolfgang Kayser in twentieth-century Germany on the grounds that it is useful for directors to know that each scene will have a fixed number of actors.[89] Perhaps resting on the authority of people like Kayser and Hartzenbusch (who was an accomplished playwright as well as an editor), many modern editors of the Spanish Comedia still follow a similar practice. In the Cátedra edition of *La vida es sueño*, for instance, Ciriaco Morón Arroyo indicates a total of eight scenes in act 1, nineteen in act 2, and fourteen in act 3 even though each act has only two or three settings. Several of the play's English-language translators reckon scenes in the same way.[90]

While Kayser may be right that it is helpful to directors to have the play's basic units associated with a fixed numbers of actors, it is equally helpful, in questions of setting and staging, to see the play broken down into unities of place, a perspective that is not possible in his scheme. Moreover, Kayser's approach may mislead or disorient general readers more accustomed to English-language conventions. Finally, it is not followed by contemporary Spanish playwrights.

It does not seem justified, then, to imitate a practice that is employed

---

[87] Hartzenbusch 1924, p. ix (Bibliography, section 8).
[88] I am grateful to Michael McGaha for this insight, although I have been unable to document it.
[89] Kayser 1954, pp. 268–69 (Bibliography, section 3).
[90] Mac-Carthy 1873, Stirling 1942, Colford 1958, Raine and Nadal 1968 (Bibliography, section 1a).

neither in the English-speaking world nor the contemporary Spanish-speaking world and, at best, only inconsistently in classical Spanish theatre. Some editors suggest a different approach, as J. E. Varey explains:

> Evidently, an act is usually conceived by the dramatist as divided into sections, which Ribbans has suggested should be called *cuadros*, a word less evocative of "scenery" than *escena*. A *cuadro* ends when all the characters leave the stage, and another set of characters appear, thus indicating to the audience a change of location, also indicated to the audience by direct textual references, by the costumes worn by the actors, and by their method of acting.[91]

Varey's suggestion, which follows Ribbans and has been endorsed by others as well,[92] streamlines the unwieldy approach of nineteenth-century editors; at the same time, it remains remarkably close to the eighteenth-century Academy definition of *escena*. Because I attempt to strike a balance in my own translation between the requirements of modern readers and faithfulness to the original, I have adopted this method of scene-reckoning in my version of the play.[93]

5. Proper Names

Calderón almost certainly took some of the character names in *Life's a Dream* from a tedious and little-known Byzantine novel, *Eustorgio y Clorilene, historia Moscovica*, published in 1629 by Enrique Suárez de Mendoza y Figueroa.[94] Others may have been inspired by his readings in history and mythology or were simply the result of pure invention or fancy. The handling of this diverse gallery of names is another point on which translators diverge rather broadly. Most have opted for a limited approach, selectively translating certain names while leaving others as is. Following is a summary of all character names from the play that have been rendered into English (translators are listed in parentheses):

Astolfo: Astolof (Mandel)
Astrea: Astraea (Appelbaum, Birch and Trend, Mitchell and Barton, Oxenford).

---

[91] Varey 1985a, p. 158 (Bibliography, section 8).
[92] Ruano de la Haza and Allen 1994; Allen 1996 (Bibliography, section 8).
[93] A similar approach to scene divisions is followed by Oxenford 1842; Birch and Trend 1925; Huberman and Huberman 1962; Mitchell and Barton 1990; Honig 1993; and FitzGerald 2000 (Bibliography, sections 1a, 1b).
[94] See Praag 1936 (Bibliography, section 8) for a summary.

Basilio: Basil (Campbell, Stirling), Basilius (Mac-Carthy), Bazylic (Mandel), King (Trench).

Clarín: Bocazas (Williamson), Clarion (Birch and Trend, Campbell, Edwards, Mitchell and Barton, Stirling), Fife (FitzGerald), Piper (Raine and Nadal).

Clorilene: Chlorylene (Stirling), Clorilena (Oxenford), Clorileña (FitzGerald).

Estrella: Stella (Campbell).

Eustorgio: Alfonso (FitzGerald), Eustorgius (Campbell, Mac-Carthy, Edwards, Stirling).

Recisunda: Recsunde (Stirling), Rosamunda (Mac-Carthy), Ruscinda (Edwards).

Rosaura: Rosanka (Mandel).

Segismundo: Segismund (Campbell, FitzGerald), Sigismund (Birch and Trend, Mac-Carthy, Mandel, Mitchell and Barton, Oxenford, Trench), Sigmund (Stirling).

As this list makes clear, there appears to be little rhyme or reason behind the names most frequently selected for translation or the ways in which they have been translated. Perhaps this fact explains why, in recent years, the tendency has been toward not translating character names at all.[95] Yet the seeming consistency of such an approach is belied by the fact that the same translators routinely translate proper geographic names; few would think of not translating *Polonia* as *Poland*, for example.[96] But if geographic names are to be translated, why not character names?

The simple answer is that there are pre-existing, standardized translations for most major geographic names: Italy for Italia, Pyrenees for Pirineos, Thames for Támesis, *etc.* While this is also the case with many common personal names, especially those with a Latin or Greek root, there are others that have no standard translation. But to translate only those names that have an obvious counterpart in the other language is to erect a boundary between the domestic and the alien that does not necessarily exist in the original. Some personal names, furthermore, have special meanings in Spanish that

---

[95] This is the case with Colford 1958; Huberman and Huberman 1962; Honig 1993; and Clifford 1998. Appelbaum 2002 maintains all the original Spanish names but for the restoration of the Latin spelling of Astraea. See Bibliography, section 1a.

[96] After writing this sentence I came across Laird Williamson's adaptation (Bibliography, section 1b), which indeed leaves *Polonia* untranslated. Nevertheless, I believe my point remains valid for serious translations.

often serve as the basis for wordplay; if left untranslated, those meanings are bound to be lost on an English-speaking audience.

At a bare minimum, I have sought to achieve the consistency that is lacking in my predecessors by translating or modifying all character names of the original. I have aimed to produce names that are faithful to the spirit of Calderón's play but that also facilitate pronunciation by monolingual actors as well as comprehension by monolingual audiences. These goals required different approaches depending on the name. With those that seem to allude to historical figures, I have employed the most suggestive English equivalents. Sometimes a literal or close to literal translation was called for, as in the case of Bugle or Stella. Other names are no doubt intended to bear a foreign or exotic feel to them, even in Spanish, in which case an obvious translation does not immediately suggest itself. In such cases, I have attempted to preserve the alien quality of the name while still adapting the roots of the original to a more intuitively English phonetic system.

Detailed explanations of each name are provided below; when necessary, pronunciation keys are offered in brackets at the end the entry. Directors should feel free to restore the originals (provided in parentheses) for the purpose of performance, but they must realize that, in doing so, they will neutralize the intentional puns made possible by translations such as *Bugle* for *Clarín* and *Stella* for *Estrella.*

> **Aistulf** (Astolfo). Originally the name of an eighth-century Lombard king who threatened the Papal States and was defeated by the Pepin the Short (Charlemagne's father) in 754 and again in 756. Also a character in Ariosto's *Orlando furioso* (based on the legends of Charlemagne), where he is cousin to the hero Orlando. The latter source may have lead Calderón to the historical figure. If this is the case, he may have chosen the name as an allusion to the duke's naked grab for power and a foreshadowing of his ultimate defeat by Sigismund. Balachov 1969 and Ziomek 1975 associate Aistulf with Wladislaus IV, son of Sigismund III and king of Poland from 1595–1648, but Strzalko 1959 and Baczynska 1991 link Wladislaus to Sigismund. [EYE-stulf]
>
> **Astraea** (Astrea). An archaic Greek divinity that coexisted on earth with mortals during the Golden Age, fostering justice and virtue; upon the degeneration of the Golden Age, she fled and was eventually transformed into the constellation Virgo. The astral connotations of her name link her to Stella, whom she (that is, Rossaura in disguise) serves as lady-in-waiting. [Ah-STRAY-ah]

Bugle (Clarín). A direct translation. Sidekicks in early modern Spanish theatre often had comic-sounding names indicative of a particular vice or other character flaw (in Bugle's case, his inability to keep his mouth shut). The name is subject to various puns throughout the course of the play.

Clorilyn (Clorilene). Curiously named both as Vasily's older sister (and Stella's mother) in Aistulf's first encounter with Stella and as Vasily's wife in the king's long, confessional soliloquy at court (see section 7 of the Translator's Notes for a discussion of this "coincidence"). She is one of the protagonists of Mendoza's novel, albeit in a very different role (Eustorgio's beloved). [KLOR-ih-lin]

Clothold (Clotaldo). Perhaps suggestive of the Greek fate Clotho, who spun the web of life that animated souls (Molho 1993, p. 250). As Sigismund's only contact with the outside world, Clothold has control over the prince's life in a similar fashion. Additionally, he is Rossaura's biological father as well as her protector, leading her to proclaim him her life-giver on several occasions. Ziomek 1983 relates the character to the Polish minister Jan Zamoyski. [KLOW-thold]

Eustorgius (Eustorgio). Vasily's father, his name comes from the Greek *eu* (good) + *storge* (familial love). He is the protagonist of Mendoza's novel, where he is the son of Basilio and the lover of Clorilene. [you-STORE-ghee-us. The *g*-sound should be pronounced as in *girl*.]

Grethissunda (Recisunda). A strange name that was probably invented for its exotic feel, perhaps on analogy with Segismundo. [Greh-thi-SOON-duh]

Rossaura (Rosaura). This name would appear to be formed by a combination of *Rosa* (rose) and *Aura* (breeze), perhaps suggesting the character's beauty as well as her restlessness. *Aura* also recalls the Latin *aurum* (gold), possibly indicating Rossaura's inner worth. Molho 1993 (pp. 238–39) associates the name with the figure of the bear. [Ruh-SORE-uh. The *s*-sound should be pronounced as in *Jessica*.]

Sigismund (Segismundo). Another name that Calderón probably came across in his readings of history, as there were several European monarchs that bore it, including three Polish kings in the sixteenth and seventeenth centuries (see the entries below, adapted from the *Columbia Encyclopedia*). Molho 1993 (pp. 227–29) associates the name with the figure of the wolf. The more familiar, syncopated form of the name is Sigmund. Both versions are Germanic in origin and mean "protector [*mund*] of victories [*sige*]," although it is unlikely that Calderón would have been aware of the etymology. [SIG-iss-mund. The *g*-sound should be pronounced as in *girl*.]

SIGISMUND I. 1467–1548, son of Casimir IV, ruled Poland from 1506–48. Elected to succeed his brother, Alexander I, Sigismund faced the problem of consolidating his domestic power in order successfully to counter external threats to Poland. The enactment during Alexander's rule of the law Nihil Novi (1505), which forbade the kings to enact laws without the consent of the diet, seriously handicapped Sigismund in his struggle with the magnates and nobles. Nevertheless, in 1527 he established a regular army and a fiscal system to finance its maintenance. Intermittent war with Vasily III of Moscow began in 1507; in 1514 Smolensk fell to the Muscovite forces. In 1515 Sigismund entered an alliance with Holy Roman Emperor Maximilian I. Maximilian acknowledged the provisions of the Second Peace of Toru, and Sigismund consented to the marriage of the children of his brother, Wladislaus II of Bohemia and Hungary, to the grandchildren of Maximilian. Through this double marriage contract Bohemia and Hungary passed to the house of Hapsburg upon the death of Sigismund's nephew Louis II in 1526. Sigismund's wars against the Teutonic Knights ended in 1525, when their grand master, Albert of Brandenburg, having converted to Lutheranism, secularized the order and did homage to Sigismund, who invested him with the domains of the order as the first duke of Prussia. Sigismund sought peaceful relations with the khans of Crimea but was still involved in border warfare with them. Sigismund was a humanist; he and his second wife, Bona Sforza, daughter of Gian Galeazzo Sforza of Milan, were patrons of Renaissance culture, which began to flower in Poland during their reign.

SIGISMUND II. 1520–72. Also known as Sigismund Augustus, ruled Poland from 1548–72. Crowned in 1530 to assure his succession, he assumed the royal functions upon the death of his father, Sigismund I. By the Union of Lublin in 1569, he transferred his hereditary grand duchy of Lithuania to the Polish crown, creating the unified Polish-Lithuanian state. His great diplomatic skill enabled him to conciliate the dissident elements both in Poland and among the Lithuanian magnates who opposed the fusion. Upon the dissolution in 1561 of the Livonian Brothers of the Sword, Sigismund gained control over Courland, Latgale, and other parts of Livonia. Opposed in this claim by Holy Roman Emperor Ferdinand I, in 1562 Sigismund granted the elector of Brandenburg hereditary succession in the duchy of

Prussia in exchange for diplomatic support. The widened frontiers brought Sigismund into conflict with Ivan IV of Russia, who took Polotsk in 1563. The Polish Reformation reached its height during Sigismund's reign; in 1570 most of the Protestant sects formed a union to strengthen their cause. An open-minded, tolerant monarch and a loyal Roman Catholic, Sigismund sought peacefully to counteract the Reformation; he abolished the ecclesiastic courts in 1562 but introduced the Society of Jesus in 1565, which successfully preached the Counter Reformation. The Renaissance flowered at this time and Sigismund was an accomplished humanist and theologian. The last of the Jagiello dynasty to rule Poland, Sigismund died childless.

SIGISMUND III. 1566–1632, king of Poland 1587–1632 and of Sweden 1592–99. The son of John III of Sweden and Catherine, sister of Sigismund II of Poland, he united the Vasa and Jagiello dynasties. He was a Roman Catholic, and his marriage to Anne of Hapsburg in 1592 linked him to the Catholic monarchs of Europe. A period of factional strife after the death of King Stephen Báthory in 1586 was ended by the election of Sigismund as king of Poland. In 1592, Sigismund inherited the Swedish throne from his father, but his reluctance to accept Protestantism as the state religion in Sweden involved him in conflict with the Swedes and with his uncle, who was regent. Although finally crowned in 1594, Sigismund was defeated at Stangebro in 1598 and was formally deposed by the Swedish diet in 1599. He retained his claims to Sweden and after 1600 fought intermittently with his uncle and later with his nephew, Gustavus II, to whom he lost most of Livonia in 1629. Sigismund dreamed of conquering all of Russia, and, in 1610, taking advantage of the chaos there after the death of Boris Godunov, he continued his military campaign and took Moscow. In 1612 an improvised Russian army under Prince Pozharski expelled the Poles, who retained Smolensk and other border towns. Peace with Russia came only after Sigismund's death in 1634. Sigismund's pro-Catholic policy helped to effect the union, in 1596, of the Ruthenian Church in Poland-Lithuania with the Church of Rome. Sigismund's rule also saw the start of intermittent war with the Ottoman Empire, lasting until Poland obtained a favourable treaty in 1621. Sigismund's use of Austrian aid to limit the powers of the diet and the dissatisfaction of the Protestants led to a rebellion in 1606-07 under Nicholas Zebrzydowski, the palatine of Krakow. Although the rebels were defeated, their cause triumphed, and no more attempts were made to change the constitution.

Stella (Estrella). Literally *star*, although much more prevalent as a name in Spanish than *Star* is in English. I have chosen the Latin form because its frequency in English is similar to that of *Estrella* in Spanish while still allowing the various puns to which the name gives rise throughout the play.

Vasily (Basilio). A name that seems to arise from an interesting set of coincidences. First, it is derived from the Greek *basileus*, meaning simply "king," suggesting the archetypal nature of Vasily's character. Second, it is one of the proper names in Mendoza's novel, where Basilio is the father (rather than the son) of Eustorgio. Third, it was the name of several early modern Muscovite princes, one of whom, Vasily III, went to war with Sigismund I of Poland (see entry under Sigismund); Ginard de la Rosa 1881 (pp. 296–97) suggests that Calderón could have learned these names through the Polish and Russian ambassadors at the Spanish court. I have adopted the Slavic spelling to reflect the flavour of the play's setting. [Vuh-SIL-ee. The *s*-sound should be pronounced as in *Jessica*.]

Viola (Violante). A name that suggests both *violet* and the *violation* of Clothold's secret wedding vow to this character. [Vie-OH-luh]

6. Wordplay

Wordplay, a defining feature of the language of *Life's a Dream* and of the Spanish baroque in general, bridges many typological divides. Some instances are produced for comic effect; others enhance the gravity of the situation. Some are unintentional on the part of the characters, others quite deliberate. Some arise from a likeness in form, while others are based on similar meanings or concepts. Finally, all characters engage in the phenomenon, from the most humble to the most noble. Consequently, any translation that does not make a serious effort to transmit wordplay cannot but undermine the play's original meaning and flavour. Unfortunately, many previous translators have either suppressed certain instances of wordplay (perhaps because they were unaware of them; perhaps because they considered them inappropriate, insignificant, or impossible to capture in verse) or rendered them so clumsily as to be meaningless. In my translation, I have taken care to render wordplay as closely as possible to the meaning and register of the original. My aim has been to transmit the playfulness of the Spanish in a way that can be apprehended in a performance context (where, it must be noted, a translated pun requiring a footnote to explain it is a resounding failure).

For readers with a working knowledge of Spanish, I include the following commentaries on some of the more significant cases of wordplay. The verse numbers of the original appear in parentheses, followed by my translations. The words in play are underlined.

Apenas llega, cuando llega a penas (v. 20). "<u>Hardly</u> is he come when he comes into <u>hardship</u>." The first and perhaps most famous pun in the play enhances the gravity of Rossaura's desperate circumstances. Based on an ambiguity – whether *a-penas* is interpreted as one word or two – that is lost in performance, the pun shows that readers were perhaps just as important to Calderón as spectators.

[Ros.] Tus pies <u>beso</u> / mil veces. [Bug.] Y yo los <u>viso</u> (vv. 894–95). "I shall <u>adorn</u> your feet a thousand times with my kisses. – I'll just <u>adore</u> them from afar." Given that Spanish *b* and *v* are pronounced identically (as English *b* when they come at the beginning of a word), only the *e-* and *i*-sounds differentiate the two words in play, which of course have very different meanings: one indicating reverence, the other distance. Bugle goes on to invoke the slight phonetic difference to excuse his comical lack of respect.

<u>Despojado</u> y <u>despejado</u> / se asoma a su <u>desvergüenza</u> (vv. 1176–77). "If you're <u>shameless</u> enough, there's more to see in the <u>stands</u> than on the <u>stage</u>." This pun, coming as the culmination of one of the play's more opaque passages, is also among the most difficult to translate not only because of the linguistic play itself but also because the context that would have made it intelligible to spectators of Calderón's time is rather far removed from contemporary theatre audiences. Bugle has just explained how he fought his way into the palace, where he will act as spectator of the drama that has swept up Prince Sigismund. The metaphor is based on the language of public spectacle, where illicit behaviour (*desvergüenza*) in the stands, which involved the removal (*despojado*) of clothing – *i.e.*, prostitution – could prove more entertaining than a clear view (*despejado*) of the stage. Bugle seems to be saying that he intends to enjoy himself in the palace, perhaps more than the prince.

[Sig.] Tú sólo en tan nuevos <u>mundos</u> / me has agradado. [Bug.] Señor, / soy un grande agradador / de todos los <u>Segismundos</u> (vv. 1336–39). "You're the only one in this <u>princely world</u> I find gratifying. – My lord, I'm a great gratifier of all <u>worldly princes</u>." A simple pun based on the similarity of Sigismund's Spanish name (*Segismundo*) to the word for world (*mundo*).

[Serv. 2] Es <u>grande</u>. [Sig.] <u>Mayor</u> soy yo (vv. 1371). "He's <u>titled</u>. – I'm

more <u>entitled</u>!" One of the more significant instances of wordplay in the play. The upper echelons of Spanish nobility, called *grandes* (grandees or peers), were granted the unique privilege of wearing their hats in the king's presence; thus the servant is attempting to defend the duke's behaviour to the prince. Unschooled in courtly etiquette, Sigismund misunderstands the servant's comment and interprets *grande* in the more common sense of "great"; his response means, literally, "I'm greater." Most translators emphasize this second meaning of the word – the one on which Sigismund focuses – but in doing so they elide the first meaning (*i.e.*, a rank of nobility) and thus neutralize the double-entendre on which the wordplay is based.

Aunque el <u>parabién</u> es <u>bien</u> / darme del <u>bien</u> que conquisto, / de sólo haberos hoy visto / os admito el <u>parabién</u>;/ y así, del llegarme a ver / con el <u>bien</u> que no merezco, / el <u>parabién</u> agradezco (vv. 1392–98). "Although it were <u>well</u> to wish me <u>well</u> on the <u>wealth</u> that I inherit, I deserve more <u>well-wishing</u> just for having seen you today; and thus, I appreciate your <u>well-wishing</u> for finding myself before such unmerited <u>wealth</u>." A veritable orgy of internal and end rhyme, this instance of wordplay is meant to imitate (and perhaps to parody) the flowery language characteristic of courtly interaction. The play stems, on the one hand, from the lexical similarity between *parabién* (congratulations) and *bien* and, on the other, from the double grammatical function of the latter as an adverb meaning "well" and a noun meaning "good," "goodness," or "wealth."

Nada me parece <u>justo</u> / en siendo contra mi <u>gusto</u> (vv. 1417–18). "Nothing is <u>right</u> that contradicts my <u>delight</u>." Although the play on *justo* (just, right) and *gusto* (pleasure) is technically a simple rhyme, I have decided, contrary to my normal procedure, to translate it as a rhyme because of the prominence it is accorded in Spanish literature of Calderón's time. Its popularity can be explained by the fact that it neatly encapsulates the tension that gave rise to so many dramatic plots, pitting the desire of the individual against the collective will of society.

Mi <u>primo</u> Astolfo – bastara / que mi <u>primo</u> te dijese (vv. 1794–95). "My <u>first cousin</u> Aistulf – <u>first</u> in more ways than one, if you know what I mean." A pun that plays on the various meanings of *primo* – cousin, peer of the king, spouse (in noble marriages), and first – it also alludes to the Hapsburg practice of endogamy.

[Bug.] ¿A qué fin / me encierran? [Clo.] Eres <u>Clarín</u>. / [Bug.] Pues ya digo que seré / <u>corneta</u>, y que callaré, / que es instrumento ruin (vv. 2044–47). "What's your purpose in locking me up? – You're <u>Bugle</u>. – Well,

I'll call myself <u>Horn</u> from now on, and I'll keep quiet, as befits those with horns." One of the many examples of wordplay involving Bugle's name in Spanish (Clarín), which is lost if the name goes untranslated. In this case, the literal meaning derives from a comparison between the virile bugle, an instrument associated with war, and the more refined cornet; the figurative meaning plays on the association between the Spanish *corneta* and the figure of the *cornudo* (cuckold), who was frequently described as wearing horns and who was obliged to remain silent about his wife's infidelity.

En el filósofo leo / <u>Nicomedes</u>, y las noches / en el concilio <u>Niceno</u> (vv. 2217–19). "This prison's favourite philosopher is <u>Empty-Plato</u> and its only creed is the <u>Frail-Mary</u>." Rivalling the *despojado/despejado* opposition in obscurity, this pun comes in a scene in which Bugle is explaining the treatment he has received since being imprisoned at the end of act 2. High on his list of complaints is the lack of food, which gives rise to the wordplay. Bugle explains that, having nothing else to do, he reads the "philosopher" Nicomedes by day and the teachings of the Nicene Council by night. Because both proper names are historically based, it is plausible that they would have interested readers of Calderón's day, and that minimal degree of plausibility is all that is necessary to facilitate the pun. In truth, none of the individuals named Nicomedes left any known writings, while the canons of the two Nicene Councils would probably have struck Calderón's contemporaries as rather remote.[97] Furthermore, given Bugle's humble station in life, it is doubtful that he would have been able to read at all. This is a case, in fact, where the words are simply shells with no independent meaning or relationship to each other (apart from the curious coincidence that Nicaea, the seat of the Nicene council, was in Bithynia, home to the Nicomedes dynasty). The real import of these proper names lies in their phonetic value, which enables the double-entendre. As with *apenas/a penas*, *Nicomedes* can be read as two words: *ni-comedes*, which means "you get no lunch." Similarly, *Niceno* breaks down into *ni-ceno* or "I get no supper."

[Soldiers.] Danos tus <u>plantas</u>. [Bug.] No puedo / porque las he menester

---

[97] Nicomedes was not a philosopher at all but rather the name assumed by a line of kings of ancient Bithynia from the third to the first century BC; the name also belonged to a little-known Greek mathematician of the second century BC, but it seems unlikely, given his obscurity, that Calderón's allusion would have been made with him in mind. The first Nicene Council convened in AD 325 to deal with the heresy of Arianism (the denial of Christ's divinity); the second met in 787 to address the problem of iconoclasm (the movement, prominent in the Eastern Church, against the worship of images). Both issues had been long defused by Calderón's time.

/ para mí, y fuera defeto / ser príncipe <u>desplantado</u> (vv. 2249–52). "Give us the <u>soles</u> of your feet. – I can't because I need them for myself, and I wouldn't do you much good as a <u>desolated</u> prince." One of Bugle's many humorous puns, this one is based on the similarity between *plantas* (soles of the feet), which the soldiers wish to kiss and *desplantado*, which means, literally, "de-soled" and, figuratively, "uprooted." As is the case with many of the play's puns, most translations capture only one sense of the double-entendre.

Heredera de <u>fortunas</u> / corrí con ella <u>una propia</u> (vv. 2776–77). "My <u>stormy fate</u> drove me to <u>shipwreck</u>." This pun is based on a play between *fortuna*, meaning "luck" or "fortune," and the expression *correr fortuna*, frequent in nautical terminology, which means "to run into stormy weather."

¿Quién creerá, que habiendo sido / una <u>estrella</u> quien conforma / dos amantes, sea una <u>Estrella</u> / la que los divida agora (vv. 2794–97). "Who would guess that lovers brought together by <u>stellar design</u> would now be separated by <u>Stella's design</u>?" One of the many examples of wordplay involving Stella's name in Spanish (Estrella). The pun is lost if the name goes untranslated.

7. Textual Variants and Obscurities

All surviving texts of the late medieval and early modern periods are products of a printing process in its infancy. Technology was primitive at best, and orthographic conventions varied widely. Furthermore, the more popular a book was, the more printings were made of it, and the more subject it became to the fallibility of the process. The works we read today frequently do not represent any single original copy but rather are the fruit of a long, laborious procedure that involves collating and comparing the different versions available in an attempt to come up with an edition that most faithfully represents the author's intentions. Such is the task of textual criticism, and readers must be aware that, just as in literary criticism, the final product always represents an *interpretation*. This is especially the case with dramatic works, whose path from author to printer was especially sinuous and involved long detours through acting companies, where passages were often added, removed, or emended at will.[98]

The text that we are able to reconstruct of *Life's a Dream* comes from two main branches, both of which date back to editions published in 1636, one in Madrid (M) and the other in Zaragoza (Z). According to Ruano de

---

[98] See Varey 1985a (Bibliography, section 8) for more detail on the printing process.

la Haza, the Z-branch, which consists of eight texts, predates the M-branch (four texts) by several years, placing its origin in the late 1620s.[99] Overall, the two branches diverge on about forty percent of the total number of verses,[100] forcing editors to make a significant decision regarding the product that they ultimately present to readers. Because the basic difference seems to be that M represents a more polished, literary version whereas Z is more spontaneous and appropriate for the theatre (it contains more stage directions, for example),[101] choosing one over the other is a particularly difficult decision. One point that tips the balance toward M in my mind is that every major critical edition of the play in Spanish is based on M rather than Z; thus, what people in the Spanish-speaking world know as *La vida es sueño* is, in ninety-nine percent of the cases, a knowledge of M. To publish for the English-speaking world a translation of the play based on Z would create an unreasonable imbalance in popular knowledge of the play and lead to not a few misunderstandings. For instance, Z contains very little of the prince's beautiful and much-admired soliloquy on dreams that appears in M at the end of act 2; because this is one of the passages that have made the play most famous both inside and outside Spain, I find its absence in Z a strong argument in favour of M. Furthermore, and perhaps more importantly, it is clear from Calderón's personal involvement in the Madrid edition of 1636 that M is the text he intended to bequeath to posterity.[102]

After consulting many Spanish-language editions of the play, I have used as the basis of my translation that of J. M. Ruano de la Haza (Castalia 2000). Ruano's phenomenal command of both the play's textual history and its dramatic dimensions, his scrupulous attention to detail, and his always constructive dialogue with his predecessors have resulted in a highly reliable text that renders most previous editions obsolete (along with, I would venture to add, translations based on them). Like many editors, Ruano takes M as his base, but his exceptional knowledge of Z allows him to correct many problematic passages where his predecessors have failed. It is thus an edition that represents the best possible compromise between the literary value of M and the dramatic appeal of Z.

Apart from those passages disputed by textual critics, there are a number of simply enigmatic or obscure passages in which the meaning is not always

---

[99] Ruano de la Haza 2000, pp. 7–9 (Bibliography, section 2).

[100] Ibid., p. 15.

[101] Ibid., pp. 15–18.

[102] Ibid., p. 18.

readily apparent. In many such cases, Ruano's remarkable intuitions, clearly explained in his excellent footnotes, have proved invaluable to me. In some instances, a simple stage direction can clarify an elliptical passage, and I have supplemented the text in this way, always indicating my interpolations in square brackets.[103] A different punctuation, too, can sometimes resolve an otherwise enigmatic passage.[104] Discounting stage directions and punctuation, I have diverged from Ruano's text in only one major instance.[105]

I have been careful, furthermore, not to resolve ambiguities that may have been part of Calderón's design. One passage deserves particular mention in this regard. In act 1 of the play, when Aistulf recounts the royal genealogy to Stella, he explains that her mother was named Clorilyn. Only 120 verses later, Vasily refers to his wife as Clorilyn. Is this an oversight on Calderón's part, or did he have something else in mind? Many previous translators (over half, in fact) evidently see it as an error that must be corrected, and they have either eliminated or altered one of the two references to Clorilyn.[106]

---

[103] Notably scarce in playwrights of Calderón's time (including Shakespeare), stage directions were particularly susceptible to reduction or elimination by penny-pinching printers, and their scarcity is one of the most disorienting elements for modern readers. I have used Ruano de la Haza 1992 and 2000 (Bibliography, section 2) to incorporate stage directions from Z that were, for whatever reason, suppressed in M.

[104] Ruano clarifies some of the play's more perplexing passages through a simple change in punctuation. One instance in which he could have applied this principle but does not involves the punctuation of verses 237–42: "Fuera, más que muerte fiera, / ira, rabia y dolor fuerte; / fuera muerte – desta suerte / su rigor he ponderado – , / pues dar vida a un desdichado / es dar a un dichoso muerte." After a personal correspondence with Ruano, I have decided to read the verses as follows: "Fuera más que muerte; fiera / ira, rabia y dolor fuerte / fuera muerte desta suerte – / su rigor he ponderado – / pues dar vida a un desdichado / es dar a un dichoso muerte." I am grateful to Ruano for his helpful suggestions regarding the punctuation of these lines as well as their translation.

[105] I read *estorbe* in v. 2864 as *estorbé* ("thwarted"); otherwise, the unaccented, subjunctive form makes the thwarting appear to come at the behest of Clothold, which clearly cannot be the case given Clothold's loyalty to the king, as vv. 2870–75 confirm: "...Clothold, convinced that Aistulf should marry the lovely Stella and rule jointly with her, advised me, in an affront to my honour, to end my crusade." I also diverge from Ruano in the accentuation of *aun/aún* on several occasions (see vv. 226, 396, 1981, 2098, 2758, and 3004), in each case following Rull 1980.

[106] Birch and Trend 1925, pp. 11/13; Stirling 1942, pp. 47/55; Colford 1958, pp. 16/20; Campbell 1959, pp. 232/235; Raine and Nadal 1968, pp. 16/20; Honig 1993, pp. 304/306; Clifford 1998, pp. 18/20; FitzGerald 2000, pp. 390/392 (Bibliography, sections 1a, 1b). Editors of the Spanish text, for their part, either ignore the coincidence, as does Morón Arroyo 2000, or take care to point out that the two names refer to different people, as does Ruano de la Haza 2000 (Bibliography, section 2).

I believe, in fact, that this passage may provide an important key to the play's interpretation (see Introduction, section 4) and that, at the very least, it should be left to the readers or spectators to decide. As a general rule, I prefer to let stand a possible error than to neutralize a potentially meaningful ambiguity.

***

In conclusion, I hope to acquaint a new generation of students and theatre-goers with a translation of Calderón that is accurate, accessible, and, most of all, playable, for I firmly agree with the contention that drama translators must "see written text and performance as *indissolubly linked*."[107] The major problem with previous translations of *Life's a Dream* stems from a failure to recognize that indissoluble link, resulting in a formal stiffness of language that is little conducive to oral reception. All of the decisions I have made, in one way or another, are aimed at avoiding such stiffness. As a final example, the reader will note that I have made liberal use of contractions, as evidenced in my translation of the play's title. A few previous translators have done so as well, but most have not. (In the past thirty years, only Mitchell and Barton's adaptation has used a contraction in the title.) Although we are admonished against their use in standard written English, contractions more accurately represent the norms of the spoken language and are thus more appropriate to the oral context of theatre.

There is no doubt that *Life's a Dream* stands up to the highest of literary standards; I hope to have preserved its literary qualities while at the same time creating a genuine *script* for the performance of this extraordinary play.

---

[107] Bassnett-McGuire 1991, p. 121 (Bibliography, section 4).

SUGGESTIONS FOR DIRECTORS

(Before reading this section, the reader may wish to review the description of Comedia staging techniques offered in section 2 of the Introduction. Similarly, the analysis and interpretation in section 4 of the Introduction offers a fuller discussion of the thematic issues mentioned below.)

Like many classical plays, *Life's a Dream* can be productively staged with true minimalist principles. Only three settings are implied throughout the play: Sigismund's tower and surroundings (1.1, 2.2, 3.1) the royal palace (1.2, 2.1, 3.2), and a wilderness area somewhere between the two (3.3). As Ruano de la Haza has pointed out, there is no mention at all, in either the dialogue or the stage directions, of stage decor in the palace scenes, which, consequently, were probably meant to be played on a bare stage in front of a neutral curtain.[108] The tower and wilderness scenes imply some background elements – mountains, shrubs, *etc.* – but Ruano's observations are again instructive: "The function of these sets was iconic rather than realistic in the sense that they served to establish a conventional, analogical relationship with the place they were meant to represent."[109] A ramp leading from one of the balconies (with its detachable railing removed to permit access), perhaps decorated with rocks and branches or boulders cut from cardboard, would have been sufficient to indicate the nature of the setting to the audience. Rossaura and Bugle's descent from the mountain would have coincided with their initial dialogue, so that by the time they reach stage level they are in a position to see Sigismund's tower.

The tower is undoubtedly the most important element of the outdoor scenes. In Calderón's day, it would have been represented in the discovery space or "inner stage" on the first level of the *vestuario*, although in 3.1 there is a spatial inversion through which the interior of the tower comes to be represented on the main stage while the soldiers who break down the door enter from the discovery space.[110] In the first scene, the dialogue and the sound of chains would have been all that was necessary to transform the discovery space into a tower, while the dim lantern that serves Sigismund – visible against the darker ambient light of the inner stage – and the animal skins in which he is dressed would have indicated the poverty of

---

[108] Ruano de la Haza 1987, p. 57 (Bibliography, section 8)
[109] Ibid., pp. 51–52.
[110] Ibid., p. 58.

his surroundings. In 3.1, Bugle immediately mentions that he is in prison, thus clarifying the spatial inversion that has taken place.

By the seventeenth century, the sparseness of stage decor had come to stand in inverse relation to the richness and diversity of costume. It has even been suggested that the lavish costumes represented a certain draw to spectators, who were bound by strict sumptuary laws that did not apply to actors on the stage.[111] In any case, it would certainly appear that Calderón intends the wardrobe of *Life's a Dream* to be taken seriously because he devotes a large portion of the minimal stage directions to its description. In addition to indicating setting (at least as much as stage scenery does), the play's wardrobe also identifies certain symbolic aspects of the characters. Rossaura appears in three different outfits (a male traveller in 1.1, a lady-in-waiting in 2.1, and a half-man, half-woman soldier in 3.3) and Sigismund in two (animal skins in 1.1, 2.2, 3.1, 3.3 and a prince in 2.1), indicating the inner conflicts that bring them together and link them to the image of the hippogriff. Vasily appears both as the elderly king and, significantly, cloaked in disguise in 2.2, an act viewed as beneath the dignity of a monarch (hence Clothold's surprised reaction). Other important wardrobe items are the pistol carried by Clothold and the masks worn by the soldiers in 1.1, and the hat worn by the duke that so offends Sigismund in 2.1. Besides these details, there are no indications that Clothold and Aistulf would have worn anything contrary to what would be expected of a duke and a king's minister. The same goes for Stella, who would have worn the outfit of a princess; for Bugle, who would have dressed in a simple, perhaps ragged outfit reflecting his lowly social standing; and for the various guards, servants, musicians, and soldiers that appear throughout the play. Two important props are the sword with which Rossaura makes her entrance in 1.1 and the locket that Aistulf wears in 1.2 and 2.1. The sword links Rossaura to Clothold while the locket links her to the duke, and neither can be eliminated without seriously marring the visual complement they offer to the play's dialogue.

These, then, are the minimal conditions necessary for performing the play today and those in which it most likely would have been performed in Calderón's time. Contemporary directors, of course, should feel free to modify and elaborate as much their tastes dictate and their budgets permit. If there is any indicator of a play's greatness, it is its ability to constantly refashion itself in the eyes of posterity. Elegant sets, advanced lighting techniques, and a rich musical score would all add to the performance of

---

[111] Ruano de la Haza and Allen 1994, p. 298 (Bibliography, section 8).

Life's a Dream. My only suggestion in this regard would be to maintain the basic visual oppositions that complement the play's verbal imagery. Calderón was a great lover of vivid contrasts, and he builds them into the stage directions: between the neutral palace and the wild mountainside; between Rossaura's initial entry atop the mountain and her resting point at stage level; between Sigismund's dark tower and the light he carries; between the diverse costumes worn by the same character, *etc*. The specific elements that form the contrasts may by freely changed to represent different or more modern settings, but the contrasts themselves can be profitably maintained in any performance. Whether Rossaura descends from a mountaintop or from the rooftop of an apartment building matters little as long as the essential vertical opposition is maintained. Likewise, if Sigismund's role as prince is to be transformed into that of a modern businessman, then an appropriate substitute for the animal skins he wears in the tower should be used to contrast with his business suit.

Happily for directors and actors, the minimal number of stage directions (even in my translation, which adds significantly to those of the original) gives ample freedom in moulding not just the superficial characteristics of the performance but the way in which the play will be interpreted. The character Bugle, for example, given how little is known about him (How old is he? Why is he in the service of Rossaura at the beginning of the play? How does he come to intuit the relationship between Rossaura and Clothold? *etc*.), represents a virtual blank slate in which the actor's creative talents can truly shine.[112] The way he pronounces a certain line or combines it with a gesture can make a drastic difference in reception. Regarding such issues, it may prove useful to read the very thoughtful article by Colin Thompson, which mentions a number of passages where speech modulation, intonation, and gestures are likely to have a great impact.[113] What follows is an elaboration and expansion of Thompson's list.

The deep oedipal rivalry between the king and the prince, so crucial to the play's plot and symbolism, is a gold mine for psychologically oriented actors. In the prince's first encounter with his father in 2.1, the king's language and gestures might easily be played as a provocation designed to assure the prince's failure, a failure that would both justify the king's original decision to jail Sigismund and assuage his conscience upon returning him to the tower (and thus assure that Vasily will remain in power). Conversely, the

---

[112] Ruano de la Haza 2000, pp. 64–65 (Bibliography, section 2).

[113] Thompson 1994 (Bibliography, section 8).

actor who plays Sigismund might wish to reflect on the fact that the prince's confrontational nature in this exchange and, in general, his barbaric conduct throughout the court scene of 2.1, may be partially due to the drug cocktail that he is made to drink at the beginning of the act.[114] Another father-son scene ripe for interpretation comes in the much-disputed moment at the end of the play in which Sigismund apparently repents: "And I – inferior to him in years, valour, and knowledge – shall succeed where he failed. Rise, my lord, and give me your hand; now that the stars have shown you the error in your attempts to overcome them, my neck humbly awaits your vengeance. I am at your mercy." The precise way in which the actor interprets these lines and what he does in the all-important pauses between the sentences (Does he anguish over the decision? Does he avoid eye contact with his father? Does he give him a paternalistic pat on the shoulder? Does he kneel upon saying "I am at your mercy"? *etc.*) will have a major impact on the audience's interpretation of this crucial scene.

Similar pivotal scenes take place between Rossaura and Clothold in 1.1 and 3.2, where the many double entendres seem to suggest that Rossaura has intuited her relationship to Clothold and may be attempting to force a confession from him; between Aistulf and Sigismund in 2.1, where the duke's loaded language seems intent on provoking the prince's ire and thus dooming his chances at becoming king; and in the encounter between Aistulf and Stella in 1.2, also charged with double entendres and sarcasm.

One final note regarding reception. Depending on the venue, some of the allusions in the text may not be familiar to all audience members, and directors may wish to consider substituting them with the suggestions found in brackets at the end of the glossary entries. If the original terms are maintained, care should be taken to coach the actress who plays Rossaura so that, when she pronounces the all-important *hippogriff* in scene 1, it does not come out sounding like *hypocrite*. Suggestions for the correct pronunciation of proper names are found in brackets at the end of the entries explaining the character names in the Translator's Notes.

---

[114] Ruano de la Haza 2000, pp. 39–42 (Bibliography, section 2); see also the entry under "henbane" in the glossary.

SELECTED BIBLIOGRAPHY

1. *Previous English Versions of* La vida es sueño
1a. *Translations*

Appelbaum, S. 2002. *Life Is a Dream*. Mineola, NY: Dover.

Birch, F., and J. B. Trend. 1925. *Life's a Dream*. Cambridge: W. Heffer and Sons.

Campbell, R. 1985 [original publication 1959]. *Life Is a Dream*. In *Life Is a Dream and Other Spanish Classics*. Ed. E. Bentley. New York: Applause Theatre Book Publishers. 219–92.

Clifford, J. 1998. *Life Is a Dream*. London: Nick Hern Books.

Colford, W. E. 1958. *Life Is a Dream*. Woodbury, NY: Barron's Educational Series.

Edwards, G. 1991. *Life Is a Dream*. In *Calderón. Plays: One*. London: Methuen. 101–200.

Honig, E. 1993 [original publication 1970]. *Life Is a Dream*. In *Calderón de la Barca: Six Plays*. New York: Iasta Press, 1993. 287–364. [Reprinted 1985 in *Our Dramatic Heritage*. Ed. P. G. Hill. Vol. 2 (*The Golden Age*). Rutherford, NJ: Fairleigh Dickinson University Press. 453–90.]

Huberman, E., and E. Huberman. 1962. *Life Is a Dream*. In *Spanish Drama*. Ed. Á. Flores. New York: Bantam. 191–242. [Reprinted 1963 in *The Golden Age*. Ed. N. Houghton. Laurel Masterpieces of Continental Drama 1. New York: Dell. 83–147; and 1991 in *Great Spanish Plays in English Translation*. Ed. A. Flores. New York: Dover. 191–242.]

Mac-Carthy, D. F. 1873. *Life Is a Dream*. In *Calderón's Dramas*. London: Henry S. King and Company. 1–116. [Revised and reprinted in *Calderón de la Barca: Six Plays* . Ed. H. W. Wells. New York: Las Américas Publishing Company, 1961. 13–95.]

Oxenford, J. 1842. *Life Is a Dream*. In *The Monthly Magazine* 549: 255–70, 550: 389–410, 551: 470–89.

Trench, R. C. 1856. *Life's a Dream*. In *Calderon: His Life and Genius with Specimens of His Plays*. New York: Redfield. 117–69. [An incomplete translation, reprinted with slight modifications (but still incomplete) in *An Essay on the Life and Genius of Calderon*. New York: Haskell House, 1970. 152–94.]

Raine, K., and R. M. Nadal. 1968. *Life's a Dream: A Play in Three Acts*. London: Hamish Hamilton.

Stirling, W. F. 1942. *Life Is a Dream: A Play in Three Acts*. Ediciones "1616." Havana, Cuba: La Verónica.

1b. *Loose Translations and Adaptations*

FitzGerald, E. 2000 [original publication 1865]. *Such Stuff as Dreams Are Made Of.* In *Eight Dramas of Calderón.* Urbana: University of Illinois Press. 375–440.

Mandel, O. 1988. *Sigismund, Prince of Poland: A baroque Entertainment.* Lanham, MD: University Press of America.

Mitchell, A., and J. Barton. 1990. *Life's a Dream.* Woodstock, IL: Dramatic Publishing Company.

Williamson, L. 1998. *Life Is a Dream: A New Adaptation.* Ashland, OR: Oregon Shakespeare Festival [2001].

2. *Major Spanish Critical Editions of* La vida es sueño *and other works by* Calderón

Buchanan, M. A. 1909. Toronto: University of Toronto Library.

Cilveti, A. L. 1970. Salamanca: Anaya.

Hartzenbusch, J. E. 1918 [original publication 1848]. In *Comedias de Don Pedro Calderón de la Barca.* Vol. 1. Biblioteca de Autores Españoles 7. Madrid: Rivadeneyra. 1–19.

Krenkel, M. 1881. In *Klassische Bühnendichtungen der Spanier.* Vol. 1. Leipzig: Johann Ambrosius Barth. 37–154. (Volume includes *El príncipe constante.*)

Morón Arroyo, C. 2000 [original publication 1976]. 27th ed. Madrid: Cátedra.

Riquer, M. de. 1945. Barcelona: Juventud.

Rodríguez Cuadros, E. 1987. Madrid: Espasa-Calpe.

Ruano de la Haza, J. M. 1992. *La primera versión de* La vida es sueño, *de Calderón.* Hispanic Studies TRAC 5. Liverpool: Liverpool University Press.

Ruano de la Haza, J. M. 2000 [original publication 1994]. 2nd ed. Clásicos Castalia 208. Madrid: Castalia.

Rull, E. 1980. Madrid: Alhambra. (Volume includes the *loa* and *auto sacramental* of the same title.)

Sloman, A. E. 1961. Manchester: Manchester University Press.

Valbuena Briones, Á. 1952–62. *Obras completas.* 3 vols. Madrid: Aguilar. (*La vida es sueño* is found in Volume 1, pp. 357–98.)

Valverde, J. M. 1981. Barcelona: Planeta. (Volume includes the *auto sacramental* of the same title.)

Vega García-Luengos, G., D. W. Cruickshank, and J. M. Ruano de la Haza. 2000. *La segunda versión de* La vida es sueño, *de Calderón.* Hispanic Studies TRAC 19. Liverpool: Liverpool University Press.

3. Poetry and Poetics

Alonso, D. 1993. *Poesía española: ensayo de métodos y límites estilísticos.* 5th ed. Madrid: Gredos.

Aristotle. 1961. *Poetics.* Trans. Francis Fergusson. New York: Hill and Wang.

Baehr, R. 1970. *Manual de versificación española.* Trans. K. Wagner and F. López Estrada. Madrid: Gredos.

Greenblatt, S., general editor. 1997. *The Norton Shakespeare, Based on the Oxford Edition.* Ed. W. Cohen, J. E. Howard, and K. Eisaman Maus. New York: W. W. Norton and Company.

Kayser, W. 1954. *Interpretación y análisis de la obra literaria.* Trans. M. D. Mouton and V. García Yebra. Biblioteca Románica Hispánica. Madrid: Gredos.

Kinzie, M. 1999. *A Poet's Guide to Poetry.* Chicago: University of Chicago Press.

Mallarmé, S. 1965. "À Léo d'Orfer." In *Correspondance.* Ed. H. Mondor and L. James Austin. Vol. 2. Paris: Gallimard. 266.

Navarro Tomás, T. 1991. *Métrica española.* Barcelona: Labor.

Rivers, El. L. 1988. *Renaissance and baroque Poetry of Spain with English Prose Translations.* Prospect Heights, IL: Waveland Press.

Shaw, R. B. 2007. *Blank Verse: A Guide to Its History and Use.* Athens: Ohio University Press.

Vega Carpio, L. F. de. 1989. *Arte nuevo de hacer comedias en este tiempo, dirigido a la Academia de Madrid.* In *Antología del teatro del Siglo de Oro.* Ed. E. Suárez-Galbán Guerra. Madrid: Orígenes. 779–89.

Williamsen, V. G. 1984. "Rhyme as a Form of Audible 'Sign' in Two Calderonian Plays." *Neophilologus* 68: 546-56.

4. Linguistics and Translation Theory

Bassnett-McGuire, S. 1991. "Translating Dramatic Texts." In *Translation Studies.* Rev. ed. London: Routledge. 120–35.

Dixon, V. 1989. "Arte nuevo de traducir comedias en este tiempo: hacia una versión inglesa de *Fuenteovejuna.*" 11–25.

Dixon, V. 2008. "Translating the Polymetric *Comedia* for Performance (with Special Reference to Lope de Vega's Sonnets)." In Paun de García and Larson. 54–65.

Edwards, G. "La traducción de textos clásicos dramáticos españoles al inglés." *Cuadernos de Teatro Clásico* 4 (1989): 27–43.

Frota, S., and M. Vigário. 2001. "On the Correlates of Rhythmic Distinctions: The European / Brazilian Portuguese Case." *Probus* 13: 247–275.

Gitlitz, D. "Confesiones de un traductor." *Cuadernos de Teatro Clásico* 4 (1989): 45–52.

Grabe, E., and E. Ling Low. 2002. "Durational Variability in Speech and the Rhythm Class Hypothesis." *Laboratory Phonology 7.* Ed. C. Gussenhoven and N. Warner. Berlin: Mouton de Gruyter. 515–546.

Lesser, W. 2002. "The Mysteries of Translation." *Chronicle of Higher Education* 49.5: B5.

MacKenzie, A. L. "*La cisma de Inglaterra*: dos versiones inglesas del monólogo de Carlos sobre Ana Bolena." *Cuadernos de Teatro Clásico* 4 (1989): 53–77.

McGaha, M. "Hacia la traducción representable." *Cuadernos de Teatro Clásico* 4 (1989): 79–86.

Muir, K. "Algunos problemas en torno a la traducción del teatro del Siglo de Oro." *Cuadernos de Teatro Clásico* 4 (1989): 87–93.

Paterson, A. K. G. "Reflexiones sobre una traducción inglesa de *El pintor de su deshonra*." *Cuadernos de Teatro Clásico* 4 (1989): 113–32.

Paun de García, S., and D. R. Larson, eds. 2008. *The* Comedia *in English: Translation and Performance.* London: Tamesis.

Whitley, M. Stanley. 1986. *Spanish/English Contrasts: A Course in Spanish Linguistics.* Washington, DC: Georgetown University Press.

5. Dictionaries, Encyclopedias, and Handbooks

Ara Sánchez, J. A. 1996. *Bibliografía crítica comentada de* La vida es sueño *(1682–1994).* New York: Peter Lang.

The Catholic Encyclopedia. 1917. Available on line at http://www.newadvent.org/cathen/.

The Columbia Encyclopedia (Sixth Edition). 2002. Available on line at http://www.bartleby.com/65/.

Hartnoll, P., and P. Found, eds. 1993. *The Concise Oxford Companion to the Theatre.* Oxford: Oxford University Press.

Real Academia Española. 1726-39. *Diccionario de Autoridades.* Available on line at http://buscon.rae.es/ntlle/SrvltGUILoginNtlle.

Rose, H. J. 1991. *Handbook of Classical Mythology.* New York: Penguin.

6. Calderón's Life

Alonso Cortés, N. 1915. "Algunos datos relativos a D. Pedro Calderón." *Revista de Filología Española* 2: 41–51.

Alonso Cortés, N. 1951. "Genealogía de Calderón." *Boletín de la Real Academia Española* 31: 299–309.

Cotarelo y Mori, E. 1924. *Ensayo sobre la vida y obras de D. Pedro Calderón de la Barca*. Madrid: Revista de Archivos, Bibliotecas y Museos.

Marcos Rodríguez, F. 1959. "Un pleito de D. Pedro Calderón de la Barca, estudiante en Salamanca." *RABM* 47: 717–31.

Pérez Pastor, C. 1905. *Documentos para la biografía de D. Pedro Calderón de la Barca*. Madrid: Fortanet.

Valbuena Briones, A. J. 2001. "Don Pedro Calderón de la Barca: biografía, formación y cultura." *Calderón desde el 2000: simposio internacional complutense*. N. pl.: Ollero y Ramos. 17–35.

7. Spain and Early Modern Europe: History, Religion, Culture

Bataillon, M. 1966. *Erasmo y España*. Trans. Antonio Alatorre. 2nd ed. Mexico City: Fondo de Cultura Económica.

Beardsley, T. S. Jr. 1970. *Hispano-Classical Translations Printed between 1482 and 1699*. Pittsburgh: Duquesne University Press.

Biskupski, M. B. 2000. *The History of Poland*. Westport, CT: Greenwood Press.

Caro Baroja, J. 1965. "Honour and Shame: A Historical Account of Several Conflicts." *Honour and Shame: The Values of Mediterranean Society*. Ed. J. G. Peristiany. London: Weindenfeld and Nicolson. 79–137.

Castro, A. 1916. "Algunas observaciones acerca del concepto del honour en los siglos XVI y XVII." *Revista de Filología Española* 3: 1–50, 357–85.

Castro, A. 1954. *The Structure of Spanish History*. Trans. E. L. King. Princeton: Princeton University Press.

Castro, A. 1972. *De la edad conflictiva: crisis de la cultura española en el siglo XVII*. 3rd ed. Madrid: Taurus.

Curtius, E. R. 1983. *European Literature and the Latin Middle Ages*. Trans. W. R. Trask. Bollingen Ser. 36. Princeton: Princeton University Press.

Díaz-Regañón López, J. M. 1955–56. *Los trágicos griegos en España*. Anales de la Universidad de Valencia 29: 1–374.

Dios, Salustiano de. 1999. "Representación doctrinal de la propiedad en los juristas de la Corona de Castilla (1480–1640)." In *Historia de la propiedad en España, siglos XV–XX*. Ed. Salustiano de Dios et al. Madrid: J. San José.

Domínguez Ortiz, A. 1973. *El antiguo régimen: los Reyes Católicos y los Austrias*. Madrid: Alianza.

Elliott, J. H. 1963. *Imperial Spain: 1469–1716*. New York: Mentor-New American Library.

Gerber, J. S. 1992. *The Jews of Spain: A History of the Sephardic Experience*. New York: Free Press.

Gingerich, O. 1993. *The Eye of Heaven: Ptolemy, Copernicus, Kepler*. New York: American Institute of Physics.

Green, O. H. 1963–66. *Spain and the Western Tradition: The Castilian Mind in Literature from El Cid to Calderón*. 4 vols. Madison: University of Wisconsin Press.

Greenblat, S. J. 1980. *Renaissance Self-Fashioning: From More to Shakespeare*. Chicago : University of Chicago Press.

Huizinga, J. 1995. *The Autumn of the Middle Ages*. Trans. R. J. Payton and Ulrich Mammitzsch. Chicago: University of Chicago Press.

Kamen, H. 1991. *Spain, 1469–1714: A Society of Conflict*. 2nd ed. New York: Longman.

Kamen, H. 1985. *Inquisition and Society in Spain in the Sixteenth and Seventeeth Centuries*. Bloomington: Indiana University Press.

Kristeller, P. O. 1979. *Renaissance Thought and Its Sources*. New York: Columbia University Press.

López Piñero, J. M. 1979. *Ciencia y técnica en la sociedad española de los siglos XVI y XVII*. Barcelona: Labor.

McCluskey, S. C. 1988. *Astronomers and Cultures in Early Medieval Europe*. Cambridge: Cambridge University Press.

Murillo, L. A. 1990. *A Critical Introduction to* Don Quixote. New York: Peter Lang.

O'Callaghan, J. F. 1975. *A History of Medieval Spain*. Ithaca: Cornell University Press.

Ozment, S. E. 1980. *The Age of Reform (1250–1550): An Intellectual and Religious History of Late Medieval and Reformation Europe*. New Haven: Yale University Press.

Pennington, D. H. 1989. *Europe in the Seventeenth Century*. 2nd ed. London: Longman.

Rabil, A., ed. 1988. *Renaissance humanism: Foundations, Forms, and Legacy*. Philadelphia: University of Pennsylvania Press.

Seznec, J. 1953. *The Survival of the Pagan Gods: The Mythological Tradition and Its Place in Renaissance humanism and Art*. Trans. Barbara F. Sessions. Bollingen Ser. 38. Princeton: Princeton University Press.

Teresa of Ávila. 1990. *Libro de la vida*. Ed. Dámaso Chicharro. 8th ed. Madrid: Cátedra.

Spitzer, L. 1980. "El barroco español." *Estilo y estructura en la literatura española*. Barcelona: Crítica. 310–25.

Vernet Ginés, J. 1974. *Astrología y astronomía en el Renacimiento*. Barcelona: Ariel.

Zayas, María de. 1993. *Desengaños amorosos*. Ed. Alicia Yllera. 2nd ed. Madrid: Cátedra.

8. *The Spanish Comedia and* **Life's a Dream***: Context, Performance, Editing, and Interpretation*

Abel, L. 1963. "Metatheatre: Shakespeare and Calderón." In *Metatheatre: A New View of Dramatic Form*. New York: Hill and Wang. 59–72.

Alcalá-Zamora, J. 1978. "Despotismo, libertad política y rebelión popular en el pensamiento calderoniano de *La vida es sueño*." *Cuadernos de Investigación Histórica* 2: 39–113.

Allen, J. J. 1983. *The Reconstruction of a Spanish Golden Age Playhouse: El Corral del Príncipe, 1583–1744*. Gainesville: University Presses of Florida.

Allen, J. J. 1993. "Staging." In De Armas 1993: 27–38.

Allen, J. J. 1996. "La división de la comedia en cuadros." In *En torno al teatro del Siglo de Oro: actas de las Jornadas XII–XIII celebradas en Almería*. Ed. J. Berbel *et al.* Almería: Instituto de Estudios Almerienses. 85–94.

Allen, J. J. 2001. "Staging Calderón with the TESO Data Base." *Bulletin of the Comediantes* 53.1: 15–39.

Bandera, C. 1967. "El itinerario de Segismundo en *La vida es sueño*." *Hispanic Review* 35: 69–84.

Bandera, C. 1971. "Significación de Clarín en *La vida es sueño*." *Atlántida* 9: 638–46.

Baczynska, B. 1991. "La recepción de *La vida es sueño* en Polonia." *Castilla* 16: 19–38.

Balachov, N. I. 1969. "Les thèmes slaves chez Calderón et la question renaissance-baroque dans la littérature espagnole." In *Actes du Ve congrès de l'Association international de littérature comparée, Belgrade 1967*. Ed. N. Banasevic. Amsterdam: Swets and Zeitlinger. 119–24.

Blanco Asenjo, R. 1870. "Hamlet y Segismundo." *Boletín-Revista de la Universidad de Madrid* 3: 219–30.

Bradburn-Ruster, M. 1997. "Awakening from the Dream: Calderón and the Perennial Philosophy." *Bulletin of the Comediantes* 49.1: 35–54.

Brody, E. C. 1969. "Poland in Calderón's *Life Is a Dream*: Poetic Illusion or Historical Reality?" *The Polish Review* 14.2: 21–62.

Bueno, L. 1999. "Rosaura o la búsqueda de la propia identidad en *La vida es sueño*." *Bulletin of Hispanic Studies* (Glasgow) 76: 365–82.

Callois, R. 1966. "Logical and Philosophical Problems of the Dream." In *The Dream and Human Societies*. Ed. G. E. von Grunebaum and R. Callois. Berkeley: University of California Press. 23–52.

Carrera Artau, T. 1927. "La filosofía de la libertad en *La vida es sueño*, de Calderón."

In *Estudios eruditos in memoriam de Adolfo Bonilla y San Martín*. Vol. 1. Madrid: Facultad de Filosofía y Letras de la Universidad Central. 151–79.

Cascardi, A. J. 1984. "*La vida es sueño*: Calderón's Idea of a Theatre." In *The Limits of Illusion: A Critical Study of Calderón*. Cambridge: Cambridge University Press. 11–23.

Cilveti, A. L. 1973. "La función de la metáfora en *La vida es sueño*." *Nueva Revista de Filología Hispánica* 22: 17–38.

Connolly, E. M. 1972. "Further Testimony in the Rebel Soldier Case." *Bulletin of the Comediantes* 24: 11–15.

Correa, G. 1958. "El doble aspecto de la honra en el teatro del siglo XVII." *Hispanic Review* 26: 99–107.

Cotarelo y Mori, E. 1914. "Don Diego Jiménez de Enciso y su teatro." *Boletín de la Real Academia Española* 1: 209–48, 385–415, 510–50.

Cruickshank, D. W., and J. E. Varey. 1973. *Comedias: A Facsimile Edition with Textual and Critical Studies*. Farnborough, England: Gregg International. 19 vols.

De Armas, F. A. 1986. *The Return of Astraea: An Astral-Imperial Myth in Calderón*. Lexington, KY: University Press of Kentucky.

De Armas, F. A. 1987. "Icons of Saturn: Astrologer-Kings in Calderón's *comedias*." *Forum for Modern Language Studies* 23: 117–30.

De Armas, F. A.1990. "The Hyppogryph as Vehicle: Layers of Myth in *La vida es sueño*." In *Estudios en Homenaje a Enrique Ruiz-Fornells*. Ed. J. Fernández Jiménez *et al*. Erie, PA: ALDEEU. 18–26.

De Armas, F. A. 2001. Segismundo/Philip IV: The Politics of Astrology in *La vida es sueño*. *Bulletin of the Comediantes* 53.1: 83–100.

De Armas, F. A., ed. 1993. *The Prince in the Tower: Perceptions of* La vida es sueño. Lewisburg, PA: Bucknell University Press.

Durán, M., and R. González Echevarría, eds. 1976. *Calderón y la crítica: historia y antología*. Madrid: Gredos. 2 vols.

Egginton, W. 2000. "Psychoanalysis and the Comedia: Skepticism and the Paternal Function in *La vida es sueño*." *Bulletin of the Comediantes* 52.1: 97–122.

Farinelli, A. 1916. *La vita è un sogno*. 2 vols. Turin: Fratelli Bocca.

Feal, G., and C. Feal-Deibe. 1974. "Calderón's *Life Is a Dream*: From Psychology to Myth." *Hartford Studies in Literature* 6: 1–28.

Febrer, M. 1934. "Los problemas filosóficos en *La vida es sueño*." *Contemporánea* 5: 86-101, 262–78.

Ferdinandy, M. de. 1961. "El príncipe preso: una perspectiva mítica en la historia de España." *En torno al pensar mítico*. Berlin: Colloquium. 220–37.

Fischer, S. L. 2001. "Del texto 'original' al espectáculo actual: la fuerza de la intertextualidad en *La vida es sueño*." *Hispanic Review* 69: 209–37.

Flasche, H., ed. *Calderón de la Barca*. 1971. Darmstadt: Wissenschatliche Buchgesellschaft.

Fox, D. 1986. *Kings in Calderón: A Study in Characterization and Political Theory*. London: Tamesis.

Fox, D. 1989. "In Defence of Segismundo." *Bulletin of the Comediantes* 41.1: 141–54.

Frenzel, E. 1970. *Stoff der Weltliteratur*. Stuttgart: Alfred Kröner.

Galmés de Fuentes, Á. 1986. "Una leyenda oriental y *La vida es sueño* de Calderón de la Barca." *Studia in honourem profesor Martín de Riquer*. Vol. 1. Barcelona: Quaderns Crema. 299–309.

García Bacca, J. D. 1964. "Sentido 'dramático' de la filosofía española: *La vida es sueño*, en tres jornadas filosóficas." In *Introducción literaria a la filosofía*. Caracas: Universidad Central de Venezuela. 227–68.

García Barroso, M. 1974. "*La vie est un songe*: Un essai psychanalytique." *Revue Française de Psychanalyse* 38, 5–6: 1155–70.

García Lorenzo, L., ed. 1983. *Calderon: Actas del Congreso Internacional sobre Calderón y el teatro español del Siglo de Oro. (Madrid, 8–13 de junio de 1981)*. 3 vols. Madrid: CSIC.

Gennaro, G. de, ed. 1983. *Colloquium Calderonianum Internationale. L'Aquila 16-19 settembre 1981*. L'Aquila: Università dell'Aquila, 1983.

Ginard de la Rosa, R. 1881. "*La vida es sueño*: consideraciones críticas." In *Homenaje a Calderón*. Ed. N. González. Madrid: Nicolás González. 287–339.

Ginard de la Rosa, R.1895. "*La vida es sueño*, comedia de don Pedro Calderón de la Barca. Estudio crítico." In *Hombres y obras*. Madrid: Fernando Fe. 5–150.

Halkhoree, P. 1972. "A Note on the Ending of Calderón's *La vida es sueño*." *Bulletin of the Comediantes* 24: 8–11.

Hall, H. B. 1968. "Segismundo and the Rebel Soldier." *Bulletin of Hispanic Studies* 45: 189–200.

Hall, H. B. 1969. "Poetic Justice in *La vida es sueño*: A Further Comment." *Bulletin of Hispanic Studies* 46: 128–31.

Hall, J. B. 1982. "The Problem of Pride and the Interpretation of Evidence in *La vida es sueño*." *Modern Language Review* 77: 339–47.

Hartzenbusch, J. E. 1924. "Prólogo del colector." In *Comedias escogidas de Fray Gabriel Téllez (El maestro Tirso de Molina)*. Biblioteca de Autores Españoles 5. Ed. Hartzenbusch. 7th ed. Madrid: Sucesores de Hernando. v–x.

Heiple, D. L. 1973. "The Tradition Behind the Punishment of the Rebel Soldier in *La vida es sueño*." *Bulletin of Hispanic Studies* 50: 1–17.

Hesse, E. W. 1966. "Some Observations on Imagery in *La vida es sueño*." *Hispania* 49: 421–29.

Hesse, E. W. 1977. "El doble criterio de valores en la comedia." In *Interpretando la comedia*. Madrid: José Porrúa Turranzas. 131–52.

Hesse, E. W. 1982. "*La vida es sueño* and the Divided Self." In *Theology, Sex and the Comedia and Other Essays*. Madrid: José Porrúa Turanzas. 112–26.

Hilborn, H. W. 1938. *A Chronology of the Plays of D. Pedro Calderón de la Barca*. Toronto: University of Toronto Press.

Homstad, A. 1989. "Segismundo: The Perfect Machiavellian Prince." *Bulletin of the Comediantes* 41.1: 127–39.

Howe, E. T. 1977. "Fate and Providence in Calderón de la Barca." *Bulletin of the Comediantes* 29: 103–17.

Hurtado Torres, A. 1983. "La astrología en el teatro de Calderón de la Barca." In García Lorenzo 2: 925–37.

Jones, C. A. 1958. "Honour in Spanish Golden-Age Drama: Its Relation to Real Life and to Morals." *Bulletin of Hispanic Studies* 35: 199–210.

Lapesa, R. 1983. "Lenguaje y estilo de Calderón." García Lorenzo 1983: 169–225.

Lavroff, E. C. 1976. "Who Is Rosaura? Another Look at *La vida es sueño*." *Revue des Langues Vivantes* 42: 482–96.

León, P. R. 1983. "El caballo desbocado, símbolo de la pasión desordenada en la obra de Calderón." *Romanische Forschungen* 95: 23–35.

Levi, E. 1920. *Il Principe Don Carlos nella leggenda e nella poesia*. Rome: Fratelli Treves.

Lieder, F. W. C. 1930. "The Don Carlos Theme." *Harvard Studies and Notes in Philology and Literature* 12: 1–73.

Lorenz, E. 1961. "Calderón und die Astrologie." *Romanistisches Jahrbuch* 12: 265–77.

McGaha, M. D., ed. 1982. *Approaches to the Theatre of Calderón*. Lanham, MD: University Press of America.

McGrady, D. 1985. "Calderón's Rebel Soldier and Poetic Justice Reconsidered." *Bulletin of Hispanic Studies* 62: 181–84.

McKendrick, M. 1989. *Theatre in Spain, 1490–1700*. Cambridge: Cambridge University Press.

Maravall, J. A. 1990. *Teatro y literatura en la sociedad barroca*. 2nd ed. Barcelona: Crítica.

Maurin, M. S. 1967. "The Monster, the Sepulchre, and the Dark: Related Patterns of Imagery in *La vida es sueño*." *Hispanic Review* 35: 161–78.

May, T. E. 1970. "Segismundo y el soldado rebelde." In *Hacia Calderón: Coloquio anglogermano, Exeter 1969.* Ed. Hans Flasche. Berlin: Walter de Gruyter. 71–75.

May, T. E. 1972. "Brutes and Stars in *La vida es sueño.*" In *Hispanic Studies in Honour of Joseph Manson.* Ed. D. M. Atkinson and A. H. Clarke. Oxford: Dolphin. 167–84.

Millé y Giménez, J. 1925. "Una nota a *La vida es sueño.*" *Revue Hispanique* 65: 144–45.

Molho, M. 1993. *Mitologías: Don Juan, Segismundo.* Mexico City: Siglo XXI.

Morales San Martín, B. 1918. "El teatro griego y el teatro español: Esquilo y Calderón, Prometeo y Segismundo." *Revista Quincenal* 6: 260–75, 343–59.

Morón Arroyo, C. 1990. "Semiótica del texto y semiótica de la representación." In *Teatro del Siglo de Oro: homenaje a Alberto Navarro González.* Ed. V. García de la Concha *et al.* Kassel: Reichenberger. 437–54.

Navarro González, A. 1977. "Segismundo y Prometeo encadenados." *La Estafeta Literaria* 607: 29–30.

Olmedo, F. G. 1928. *Las fuentes de* La vida es sueño. Madrid: Voluntad.

Parker, A. A. 1957. *The Spanish Drama of the Golden Age: A Method of Analysis and Interpretation.* London: Hispanic and Luso-Brazilian Councils. Reprinted in *The Great Playwrights: Twenty-Five Plays with Commentaries by Critics and Scholars.* Ed. E. Russell Bentley. Vol. 1. Garden City, NY: Doubleday, 1970. 679–707. 2 vols.

Parker, A. A. 1966. "The Father-Son Conflict in the Drama of Calderón." *Forum for Modern Language Studies* 2: 99–113.

Parker, A. A. 1969. "Calderón's Rebel Soldier and Poetic Justice." *Bulletin of Hispanic Studies* 46: 120–27.

Parker, A. A. 1982. "Segismundo's Tower: A Calderonian Myth." *Bulletin of Hispanic Studies* 59: 247–56.

Praag, J. A. van. 1936. "*Eustorgio y Clorilene, historia moscovica* (1629), de Enrique Suárez de Mendoza y Figueroa." *Boletín de la Real Academia Española* 23: 282–314. Republished in *Bulletin Hispanique* 41 (1939): 236–65.

Rank, O. 1992. *The Incest Theme in Literature and Legend: Fundamentals of a Psychology of Literary Creation.* Trans. Gregory C. Richter. Baltimore: Johns Hopkins University Press.

Reichenberger, A. G. 1959, 1970. "The Uniqueness of the Comedia." *Hispanic Review* 27: 303–16; 38: 163–73.

Rennert, H. A. 1963. *The Spanish Stage in the Time of Lope de Vega.* New York: Dover Publications.

Resina, J. R. 1983. "Honour y razón en *La vida es sueño*." *Cuadernos de Investigación Filológica* 9: 129–49.

Richthofen, E., Freiherr von. 1970. "Espíritu hispánico en una forma galorromana, I." *Nuevos estudios épicos medievales*. Madrid: Gredos. 147–215.

Riquer, M. de, and J. M. Valverde. 1958. *Historia de la literatura universal, II: del renacimiento al romanticismo*. Barcelona: Noguer.

Rodríguez López-Vázquez, A. 1978. "La significación política del incesto en el teatro de Calderón." In *Les mentalités dans la péninsule Ibérique et en Amérique Latine aux XVIe et XVIIe siècles: histoire et problematique*. Tours: Université de Tours. 107–112.

Rozik, E. 1989. "The Generation of *Life Is a Dream* from *Oedipus the King*." In *The Play Out of Context: Transferring Plays from Culture to Culture*. Ed. H. Skolnikov and P. Holland. Cambridge: Cambridge University Press. 121–34.

Ruano de la Haza, J. M. 1987. "The Staging of Calderón's *La vida es sueño* and *La dama duende*." *Bulletin of Hispanic Studies* 64: 51–63.

Ruano de la Haza, J. M., and J. J. Allen. 1994. *Los teatros comerciales del siglo XVII y la escenificación de la comedia*. Nueva Biblioteca de Erudición y Crítica 8. Madrid: Castalia.

Ruiz Ramón, F. 1990. "El 'mito de Uranus' en *La vida es sueño*." In *Teatro del Siglo de Oro: homenaje a Alberto Navarro González*. Eds. V. García de la Concha *et al.* Kassel: Reichenberger. 547–62.

Rull, E. 1975. "La literalidad del 'soldado rebelde' en *La vida es sueño*." *Segismundo* 21–22 (1975): 117–25.

Rupp, S. 1990. "Reason of State and Repetition in *The Tempest* and *La vida es sueño*." *Comparative Literature* 42: 289–318.

Rupp, S. 1996. *Allegories of Kingship: Calderón and the Anti-Machiavellian Tradition*. University Park, PA: Penn State University Press.

Schevill, R. 1903. "The *comedias* of Diego Ximénez de Enciso." *PMLA* 18: 194–210.

Shergold, N. D. 1967. *A History of the Spanish Stage: From Medieval Times until the End of the Seventeenth Century*. Oxford: Clarendon.

Sloman, A. E. 1958. *The Dramatic Craftsmanship of Calderon: His Use of Earlier Plays*. Oxford: Dolphin.

Soufas, C. C. Jr. 1985. "Thinking in *La vida es sueño*." *PMLA* 100: 287–98.

Soufas, T. S. 1993. "*La vida es sueño* as Forerunner of Calderón's Mythological Dramas." *Bulletin of Hispanic Studies* 70: 293–303.

Strzalko, M. 1959. "La Pologne et les polonais dans le théâtre espagnol du XVIIe et XVIIIe siècles." In *Comparative Literature: Proceedings of the Second Congress at the University of North Carolina, September 8–12, 1958*. Ed. W. P. Friederich.

Vol. 2. Chapel Hill: University of North Carolina. 635–49.

Sullivan, H. W. 1979. "'Tam clara et evidens': 'Clear and Distinct Ideas' in Calderón, Descartes and Francisco Suárez S. J." In *Perspectivas de la comedia*. Ed. A. V. Ebersole. Vol. 2. Valencia: Albatros/Hispanófila. 127–36.

Sullivan, He. W. 1993. "The Oedipus Myth: Lacan and Dream Interpretation." In De Armas 1993: 111–17.

Thomas, L.-P. 1910. "La genêse de la philosophie et le symbolisme dan *La vie est un songe* de Calderón." *Mélanges de philologie romane et d'histoire littéraire offerts à M. Maurice Wilmotte*. Vol. 2. Paris: Honouré Champion. 751–83.

Thompson, C. 1994. "Calderon's *La vida es sueño*: A More Theatrical Approach." In *The Discerning Eye: Studies Presented to Robert Pring-Mill on His Seventieth Birthday*. Ed. N. Griffin *et al*. Llangrannog, Wales: Dolphin Book Co. 77–94.

Valbuena Briones, Á. 1961. "El concepto del hado en el teatro de Calderón." *Bulletin Hispanique* 63: 48–53.

Valbuena Briones, Á. 1962. "El simbolismo en el teatro de Calderón: la caída del caballo." *Romanische Forschungen* 74: 60–76.

Valbuena Prat, Á. 1956. "El drama de la problemática de la vida." In *Historia del teatro español*. Barcelona: Noguer. 347–64.

Varey, J. E. 1982. "Cavemen in Calderón (and Some Cavewomen)." In McGaha 1982: 231–44.

Valbuena Briones, Á. 1985a. "Stages and Stage Directions." In *Editing the Comedia*. Ed. M. McGaha and F. P. Casa. Michigan Romance Studies 5. Ann Arbor: University of Michigan. 146–61.

Valbuena Briones, Á. 1985b. "The Use of Costume in Some Plays of Calderón." In *Calderón and the baroque Tradition*. Ed. K. Levy, J. Ara, and G. Hughes. Waterloo, Ontario: Wilfrid Laurier University Press. 109–18.

Valbuena Briones, Á. 1986. "Valores visuales en la comedia española en la época de Calderón." In *Edad de Oro*. Ed. P. Jauralde Pou. Vol. 5. Madrid: Ediciones de la Universidad Autónoma. 271–97.

Valbuena Briones, Á. 1988. "'Sale en lo alto de un monte': un problema escenográfico." In *Hacia Calderón: Octavo Coloquio Anglogermano, Bochum 1987*. Ed. H. Flasche. Stuttgart: Franz Steiner. 162–72.

Vida Nájera, F. 1944. "Las fuentes de *La vida es sueño*." *Revista de la Universidad de Oviedo* 5: 93–147.

Wardropper, B. W. 1960. "Apenas llega cuando llega a penas." *Modern Philology* 57: 240–44.

Wardropper, B. W., ed. 1965. *Critical Essays on the Theatre of Calderón*. New York: New York University Press.

Warnke, F. J. 1969. "The World as Theatre: baroque Variations on a Traditional Topos." In *Festschrift für Edgar Mertner*. Ed. B. Fabian and U. Seurbaum. Munich: Wilhelm Fink. 185–200.

Whitby, W. 1960. "Rosaura's Role in the Structure of *La vida es sueño*." *Hispanic Review* 28: 16–27.

Wilson, E. M., and D. Moir. 1971. *The Golden Age: Drama, 1492–1700*. London: Benn.

Zaidi, A. S. 1996. "Hidden Treasure: The Marvelous Present and Magical Reality in *The Tempest* and *La vida es sueño*." *Bulletin of the Comediantes* 48.2: 213–14, 295–313.

Ziomek, H. 1975. "Historic Implications and Dramatic Influences in Calderón's Life Is a Dream." *The Polish Review* 20.1: 111–28.

Ziomek, H. 1983. "Polonia en la obra de Calderón de la Barca." In G. Lorenzo 1983: 987–95.

LIFE'S A DREAM

LA VIDA ES SUEÑO

LA VIDA ES SUEÑO

Comedia famosa de
Don Pedro Calderón de la Barca

Personas que hablan en ella:

ROSAURA, dama
SEGISMUNDO, príncipe
CLOTALDO, viejo
ESTRELLA, infanta
SOLDADOS

CLARÍN, gracioso
BASILIO, Rey
ASTOLFO, príncipe
GUARDAS
MÚSICOS

ACTO 1

Escena 1

(Sale en lo alto de un monte ROSAURA en hábito de hombre, de camino, y en representando los primeros versos va bajando.)

ROSAURA.	Hipogrifo violento,	
	que corriste parejas con el viento,	
	¿dónde, rayo sin llama,	
	pájaro sin matiz, pez sin escama,	
	y bruto sin instinto	5
	natural, al confuso laberinto	
	de esas desnudas peñas,	
	te desbocas, te arrastras y despeñas?	
	¡Quédate en este monte,	
	donde tengan los brutos su Faetonte,	10
	que yo, sin más camino	
	que el que me dan las leyes del destino,	
	ciega y desesperada,	
	bajaré la cabeza enmarañada	
	deste monte eminente,	15

LIFE'S A DREAM

by
Pedro Calderón de la Barca
(Translated by Michael Kidd)

Characters:

ROSSAURA, a lady   BUGLE, a foolish lackey
SIGISMUND, a prince   VASILY, the king
CLOTHOLD, an old man   AISTULF, a prince [and duke]
STELLA, a princess   GUARDS
SOLDIERS   MUSICIANS
[SERVANTS and COURT ATTENDANTS]

Note: Bracketed items are editorial interpolations.

ACT 1

Scene 1

([Deserted mountainside at twilight, near the entrance to a tower.] Enter ROSSAURA at the top of a mountain, disguised as a man dressed for the road. She makes her way down the mountain as she begins to speak, [addressing the horse from which she has been thrown].)

ROSSAURA.   Hippogriff, monstrous hippogriff, peer of the wind! You're a lightning bolt with no flame, a bird with no colour, a fish with no scales, a brute with no base instinct. Where do you speed off to: bucking, lurching, and bolting before the obscure labyrinth of those barren crags? Stay, then, on this mountaintop, a Phaethon to the brutes; while I, a woman with no direction but that offered by the laws of fate, will descend in blindness and desperation the twisted face of this

que arruga el sol el ceño de la frente!
Mal, Polonia, recibes
a un extranjero, pues con sangre escribes
su entrada en tus arenas,
y apenas llega cuando llega a penas.   20
Bien mi suerte lo dice,
mas ¿dónde halló piedad un infelice?

(Sale CLARÍN, gracioso.)

CLARÍN.   Di dos, y no me dejes
en la posada a mí cuando te quejes;
que si dos hemos sido   25
los que de nuestra patria hemos salido
a probar aventuras,
dos los que entre desdichas y locuras
aquí habemos llegado,
y dos los que del monte hemos rodado,   30
¿no es razón que yo sienta
meterme en el pesar y no en la cuenta?

ROSAURA.   No quise darte parte
en mis quejas, Clarín, por no quitarte,
llorando tu desvelo,   35
el derecho que tienes al consuelo;
que tanto gusto había
en quejarse, un filósofo decía,
que, a trueco de quejarse,
habían las desdichas de buscarse.   40

CLARÍN.   El filósofo era
un borracho barbón. ¡Oh, quién le diera
más de mil bofetadas!
Quejárase después de muy bien dadas.
Mas ¿qué haremos, señora,   45
a pie, solos, perdidos y a esta hora,
en un desierto monte,
cuando se parte el sol a otro horizonte?

ROSAURA.   ¡Quién ha visto sucesos tan estraños!
Mas, si la vista no padece engaños   50
que hace la fantasía,
a la medrosa luz que aún tiene el día,
me parece que veo
un edificio.

lofty cliff, whose scowling brow withers in the sun. Poorly, Poland, do you greet the foreigner, for you write his entrance to your sands in blood, and hardly is he come when he comes into hardship. I'm at the mercy of my luck, but where did an unlucky wretch ever turn for mercy?

(Enter BUGLE, a foolish lackey.)

BUGLE. Make that two unlucky wretches, and don't forget me back at camp when you start lodging complaints. For if it was two of us who left our fatherland to seek adventures, and two of us who, amid misfortune and madness, arrived at this spot, and two of us who came rolling down the mountain, can't I rightly complain if you make me party to the sorrow and leave me out of the settlement?

ROSSAURA. I didn't want to involve you in my complaints, Bugle, and take away your right to consolation through the expression of your own distress; for there is such pleasure to be gained from complaining, a philosopher once said, that one should go in search of misfortunes just to be able to complain about them.

BUGLE. That philosopher was a scruffy drunk who deserves a thousand slaps in the face! I'd like to see how he enjoys lamenting then. But really, my lady, what are we to do now: on foot, alone, and lost at such an hour on a deserted mountainside, with the sun heading fast for the horizon?

ROSSAURA. Who ever heard of such strange happenings? Yet unless my vision suffers from the deceptions of fantasy, I think I see some kind of building in the flickering twilight.

CLARÍN.	O miente mi deseo,	
	o termino las señas.	55
ROSAURA.	Rústico yace, entre desnudas peñas,	
	un palacio tan breve	
	que el sol apenas a mirar se atreve.	
	Con tan rudo artificio	
	la arquitectura está de su edificio,	60
	que parece, a las plantas	
	de tantas rocas y de peñas tantas	
	que al sol tocan la lumbre,	
	peñasco que ha rodado de la cumbre.	
CLARÍN.	Vámonos acercando,	65
	que este es mucho mirar, señora, cuando	
	es mejor que la gente	
	que habita en ella generosamente	
	nos admita.	
ROSAURA.	La puerta	
	– mejor diré funesta boca – abierta	70
	está, y desde su centro	
	nace la noche, pues la engendra dentro.	

(Suena ruido de cadenas.)

CLARÍN.	¡Qué es lo que escucho, cielo!	
ROSAURA.	Inmóvil bulto soy de fuego y hielo.	
CLARÍN.	Cadenita hay que suena,	75
	¡mátenme si no es galeote en pena!	
	Bien mi temor lo dice.	

(Dentro SEGISMUNDO.)

SEGISMUNDO.	¡Ay, mísero de mí! ¡Y ay, infelice!	
ROSAURA.	¡Qué triste voz escucho!	
	Con nuevas penas y tormentos lucho.	80
CLARÍN.	Yo, con nuevos temores.	
ROSAURA.	Clarín.	
CLARÍN.	Señora.	
ROSAURA.	Huyamos los rigores	
	desta encantada torre.	
CLARÍN.	Yo aun no tengo	
	ánimo de hüir, cuando a eso vengo.	
ROSAURA.	¿No es breve luz aquella	85
	caduca exhalación, pálida estrella,	

BUGLE.	Either my desire is deceiving me, or I see the same thing.
ROSSAURA.	Lying crudely among the barren crags, it's a palace so minute that even the sunlight barely reaches it. Its crude architecture is such that it could pass for a boulder that rolled off the mountaintop and settled at the foot of all these rocks and crags that strive toward the sun's warmth.
BUGLE.	Let's draw closer and not lose time in speculation, my lady, for it's preferable to be received with generosity by whoever lives inside.
ROSSAURA.	The door – or better yet, the gloomy mouth – is open, and from its depths the night, conceived inside, issues forth.

(They hear the sound of chains [from inside the tower].)

BUGLE.	What's that sound, heavens!
ROSSAURA.	I'm paralyzed, a mass of frozen fire.
BUGLE.	I hear the sound of chains; I'll be damned if it's not the ghost of a galley slave. My fear says it all.

(SIGISMUND's voice is heard from inside the tower.)

SIGISMUND.	Oh, what a miserable, unlucky wretch am I!
ROSSAURA.	What's that sad voice I hear! I'm struggling with new sufferings and torments!
BUGLE.	And I with new fears.
ROSSAURA.	Bugle!
BUGLE.	My lady!
ROSSAURA.	We must flee the severities of this haunted tower!
BUGLE.	I don't even have the stomach to flee, should I be forced to.
ROSSAURA.	Is there not a faint light in that decrepit glow, that pale star,

que en trémulos desmayos,
pulsando ardores y latiendo rayos,
hace más tenebrosa
la obscura habitación con luz dudosa?   90
Sí, pues a sus reflejos
puedo determinar – aunque de lejos –
una prisión obscura,
que es de un vivo cadáver sepultura.
Y, porque más me asombre,   95
en el traje de fiera yace un hombre,
de prisiones cargado
y sólo de la luz acompañado.
Pues hüir no podemos,
desde aquí sus desdichas escuchemos.   100
Sepamos lo que dice.

(Descúbrese SEGISMUNDO con una cadena y a la luz, vestido de pieles.)

SEGISMUNDO.   ¡Ay, mísero de mí! ¡Y ay, infelice!
Apurar, cielos, pretendo,
ya que me tratáis así,
qué delito cometí   105
contra vosotros naciendo.
Aunque si nací, ya entiendo
qué delito he cometido.
Bastante causa ha tenido
vuestra justicia y rigor,   110
pues el delito mayor
del hombre es haber nacido.
Sólo quisiera saber,
para apurar mis desvelos,
dejando a una parte, cielos,   115
el delito de nacer,
¿qué más os pude ofender,
para castigarme más?
¿No nacieron los demás?
Pues si los demás nacieron,   120
¿qué privilegios tuvieron
que yo no gocé jamás?
Nace el ave y, con las galas
que le dan belleza suma,
apenas es flor de pluma   125

which, in faltering swoons, flickering warmth, and trembling radiance, makes the dark room more shadowy with its feeble glow? Yes, for in its flicker I can make out, though from afar, a dark prison that serves as grave to a living corpse. And to my even greater astonishment, clothed in the skins of a beast lies a man bound in chains and accompanied only by the light. Since we can't flee, let's listen to his misfortunes from here and see what he says.

(A curtain is drawn back to reveal SIGISMUND with a candle, bound in chains and dressed in animal skins.)

SIGISMUND.   Oh, what a miserable, unlucky wretch am I! I seek to understand, heavens, given the way you treat me, what crime I committed against you with my birth; although if I was born, I already understand my crime. Your sentence and its harshness have due cause, for birth itself is man's greatest offence. But I would just like to know, to ease my distress – leaving aside, heavens, the offence of birth – what else I did to merit further punishment. Weren't others born? And if so, what privileges were they granted that I've never enjoyed? Birds are born, and with the regalia that decorates them in finest beauty, hardly do they attain the stature of a feathered

o ramillete con alas
cuando las etéreas salas
corta con velocidad,
negándose a la piedad
del nido que deja en calma,   130
¿y teniendo yo más alma,
tengo menos libertad?
Nace el bruto y, con la piel
que dibujan manchas bellas,
apenas signo es de estrellas,   135
gracias al docto pincel,
cuando, atrevido y crüel,
la humana necesidad
le enseña a tener crueldad,
monstruo de su laberinto,   140
¿y yo, con mejor instinto,
tengo menos libertad?
Nace el pez, que no respira,
aborto de ovas y lamas,
y apenas bajel de escamas   145
sobre las ondas se mira
cuando a todas partes gira,
midiendo la inmensidad
de tanta capacidad
como le da el centro frío,   150
¿y yo, con más albedrío,
tengo menos libertad?
Nace el arroyo, culebra
que entre flores se desata,
y apenas, sierpe de plata,   155
entre las flores se quiebra
cuando músico celebra
de los cielos la piedad,
que le dan con majestad
el campo abierto a su huida,   160
¿y teniendo yo más vida
tengo menos libertad?
En llegando a esta pasión,
un volcán, un Etna hecho,
quisiera sacar del pecho   165
pedazos del corazón.

flower or a winged bouquet when they cut swiftly through the ethereal chambers, overcoming devotion to the nest that they leave behind in tranquillity. Yet I, with more soul, have less liberty? Brutes are born, with their coats of dappled beauty, and hardly do they reflect the constellations above, thanks to divine artistry, when they become reckless and cruel, and human necessity, teaching them cruelty, makes them monsters in its labyrinth. Yet I, with gentler instinct, have less liberty? Fish are born, unbreathing miscarriages of algae and slime, and hardly do these scaly ships see themselves upon the waves when they begin to lurch in all directions, measuring the ocean's vastness with the full capacity of their frigid core. Yet I, with greater will, have less liberty? Streams are born, snakes winding through the flowers, and hardly do these silvery serpents begin to twist among the flowers when they celebrate with music the mercy of the heavens that grant them majestic flight through the open field. Yet I, with more life, have less liberty? Suffering like this turns me into a volcano, an Etna, and I should like to rip pieces of my heart from my breast. What law, what sentence, what cause is

¿Qué ley, justicia, o razón
negar a los hombres sabe
privilegio tan süave,
excepción tan principal,   170
que Dios le ha dado a un cristal,
a un pez, a un bruto y a un ave?

ROSAURA.   Temor y piedad en mí
sus razones han causado.

SEGISMUNDO.   ¿Quién mis voces ha escuchado?   175
¿Es Clotaldo?

CLARÍN.   (*Aparte. Di que sí.*)

ROSAURA.   No es sino un triste, ¡ay de mí!,
que en estas bóvedas frías
oyó tus melancolías.

(*Ásela.*)

SEGISMUNDO.   Pues la muerte te daré,   180
porque no sepas que sé,
que sabes flaquezas mías.
Sólo porque me has oído,
entre mis membrudos brazos,
te tengo de hacer pedazos.   185

CLARÍN.   Yo soy sordo, y no he podido
escucharte.

ROSAURA.   Si has nacido
humano, baste el postrarme
a tus pies para librarme.

SEGISMUNDO.   Tu voz pudo enternecerme,   190
tu presencia suspenderme,
y tu respeto turbarme.
¿Quién eres? Que aunque yo aquí
tan poco del mundo sé,
que cuna y sepulcro fue   195
esta torre para mí;
y aunque desde que nací,
si esto es nacer, sólo advierto
este rústico desierto
donde miserable vivo,   200
siendo un esqueleto vivo,
siendo un animado muerto;
y aunque nunca vi ni hablé

capable of denying men the sweet privilege, the fundamental charter that God grants to crystalline waters, to fish, to brutes, and to birds?

ROSSAURA. His words have filled me with fear and pity.

SIGISMUND. Who's been listening to me? Is it Clothold?

BUGLE. *(Aside.)* Say yes.

ROSSAURA. It's only a poor wretch – Oh, miserable me! – who in these frigid caverns has overheard your melancholy words.

(SIGISMUND grabs her.)

SIGISMUND. Then you shall die by my hand, so you won't know that I know that you know my frailties. Simply because you've overheard me, I'm going to rip you to shreds in my mighty arms.

BUGLE. I'm deaf and haven't heard a word you've said.

ROSSAURA. If you're human by birth, my kneeling at your feet will be sufficient cause for you to spare me.

SIGISMUND. Your voice has filled me with sympathy; your appearance, with awe; and your deference, with confusion. Who are you? For although I know so little of the world here, for this tower is both my cradle and my grave; and although since birth, if mine can be called a birth, I know only this crude wasteland where I live miserably like a living skeleton or a breathing cadaver; and although I've never seen or spoken to

sino a un hombre solamente
que aquí mis desdichas siente,   205
por quien las noticias sé
de cielo y tierra; y aunque
aquí, porque más te asombres
y monstruo humano me nombres,
entre asombros y quimeras,   210
soy un hombre de las fieras,
y una fiera de los hombres;
y aunque, en desdichas tan graves,
la política he estudiado,
de los brutos enseñado,   215
advertido de las aves,
y de los astros süaves
los círculos he medido,
tú sólo, tú, has suspendido
la pasión a mis enojos,   220
la suspensión a mis ojos,
la admiración al oído.
Con cada vez que te veo,
nueva admiración me das;
y cuando te miro más,   225
aun más mirarte deseo.
Ojos hidrópicos creo
que mis ojos deben ser,
pues, cuando es muerte el beber,
beben más, y, desta suerte,   230
viendo que el ver me da muerte,
estoy muriendo por ver.
Pero véate yo y muera;
que no sé, rendido ya,
si el verte muerte me da,   235
el no verte qué me diera.
Fuera más que muerte; fiera
ira, rabia y dolor fuerte
fuera muerte desta suerte –
su rigor he ponderado –   240
pues dar vida a un desdichado
es dar a un dichoso muerte.

ROSAURA.   Con asombro de mirarte,
              con admiración de oírte,

anyone but the man who frequents this place and understands my misfortunes, from whom I know something of Heaven and earth; and although here – to give you more cause for astonishment, that you may call me a human monster – amid bewilderment and chimeras, I am a man among beasts and a beast among men; and although, amid such grim misfortunes, I have studied the art of government through the example of brutes and the counsel of birds, and have measured the orbits of the gentle heavenly bodies; you alone – you – have eased the agony of my anger, the bewilderment of my eyes, the amazement of my ears. Each glimpse of you increases my amazement, and the more I look at you the more I desire to look. My eyes must suffer from the dropsy, since when drinking means death, they drink more, and thus, seeing that sight kills me, I'm dying to see. But let me see you and die, for now that I've succumbed I can't imagine, if seeing you brings me death, what not seeing you would bring. It would be beyond death; death of that sort – I've pondered its severity – would be savage ire, rage, and intense grief, for to give life to an unfortunate wretch is tantamount to giving death to a happy soul.

ROSSAURA.   I'm so astonished by looking at you and so amazed by

ni sé qué pueda decirte,   245
ni qué pueda preguntarte.
Sólo diré que a esta parte
hoy el cielo me ha guïado
para haberme consolado;
si consuelo puede ser,   250
del que es desdichado, ver
a otro que es más desdichado.
Cuentan de un sabio que, un día,
tan pobre y mísero estaba
que sólo se sustentaba   255
de unas yerbas que comía.
¿Habrá otro, entre sí decía,
más pobre y triste que yo?
Y, cuando el rostro volvió,
halló la respuesta, viendo   260
que iba otro sabio cogiendo
las hojas que él arrojó.
Quejoso de la fortuna,
yo en este mundo vivía,
y cuando entre mí decía: 265
«¿habrá otra persona alguna
de suerte más importuna?»,
piadoso me has respondido,
pues volviendo en mi sentido,
hallo que las penas mías,   270
para hacerlas tú alegrías,
las hubieras recogido.
Y por si acaso mis penas
pueden aliviarte en parte,
óyelas atento y toma   275
las que dellas me sobraren.
Yo soy...

CLOTALDO.   *(Dentro.)* ¡Guardas desta torre,
que, dormidas o cobardes,
disteis paso a dos personas
que han quebrantado la cárcel!   280

ROSAURA.   *(Aparte.* Nueva confusión padezco.)
SEGISMUNDO.   Éste es Clotaldo, mi alcaide.
Aún no acaban mis desdichas.

CLOTALDO.   *(Dentro.)* Acudid y, vigilantes,

listening to you that I don't know what to say to you or what to ask you. I will say only that Heaven has led me here today in order to console me, if he who is unfortunate can gain consolation from seeing another even more so. The story is told of a wise man who one day reached such a point of poverty and misery that his only nourishment came from eating the grasses he picked. Can there be anyone else, he would say to himself, poorer and sadder than I? And when he turned his head he found the answer, for there was another wise man gathering the blades that he'd discarded. I lived in this world resentful of fortune, and just when I was asking myself, Can there be anyone else with more miserable luck? you responded mercifully, for in applying the moral of my story, I find that you would have taken up my sufferings and treated them as joys. And if by chance my sufferings might give you some relief, listen to them carefully, and feel free to take any that are left over. I am...

CLOTHOLD   *(Offstage.)* Tower guards! Through sleep or cowardice, you've given passage to two people who've broken through the prison perimeter.

ROSSAURA.   *(Aside.)* What new confusion is this!

SIGISMUND.   That's Clothold, my jailer; my misfortunes haven't ended yet.

CLOTHOLD.   *(Offstage.)* Come quickly and, with vigilance, seize them or

	sin que puedan defenderse,	285
	o prendeldes o mataldes.	
TODOS.	*(Dentro.)* ¡Traición!	
CLARÍN.	Guardas desta torre,	
	que entrar aquí nos dejasteis,	
	pues que nos dais a escoger,	
	el prendernos es más fácil.	290

(Sale CLOTALDO con escopeta, y SOLDADOS, todos con los rostros cubiertos.)

CLOTALDO.	Todos os cubrid los rostros;	
	que es diligencia importante,	
	mientras estamos aquí,	
	que no nos conozca nadie.	
CLARÍN.	¿Enmascaraditos hay?	295
CLOTALDO.	¡Oh vosotros que, ignorantes	
	de aqueste vedado sitio,	
	coto y término, pasasteis	
	contra el decreto del Rey,	
	que manda que no ose nadie	300
	examinar el prodigio	
	que entre estos peñascos yace,	
	rendid las armas y vidas,	
	o aquesta pistola, áspid	
	de metal, escupirá	305
	el veneno penetrante	
	de dos balas, cuyo fuego	
	será escándalo del aire!	
SEGISMUNDO.	Primero, tirano dueño,	
	que los ofendas y agravies,	310
	será mi vida despojo	
	destos lazos miserables;	
	pues en ellos, ¡vive Dios!,	
	tengo de despedazarme	
	con las manos, con los dientes,	315
	entre aquestas peñas, antes	
	que su desdicha consienta	
	y que llore sus ultrajes.	
CLOTALDO.	Si sabes que tus desdichas,	
	Segismundo, son tan grandes	320
	que antes de nacer moriste	
	por ley del cielo; si sabes	
	que aquestas prisiones son,	

| | kill them before they can defend themselves! (*In unison with the GUARDS, offstage.*) Treason! |
| BUGLE. | Tower guards who let us in here: since we have a choice, I think seizing us would be easier. |

(Enter CLOTHOLD with a gun, accompanied by SOLDIERS, all with their faces covered.)

CLOTHOLD.	Keep your faces covered, all of you; it's an important precaution that will keep anyone from recognizing us while we're here.
BUGLE.	What's this, a damn costume party?
CLOTHOLD.	O you, whose ignorance of this forbidden site has led you past its enclosed perimeter against the decree of the king, who has prohibited anyone from daring to behold the monstrosity that lies amidst these boulders; surrender your arms and your lives, or this pistol, a metallic viper, will spit forth a piercing venom of two bullets, deafening the air with its shots.
SIGISMUND.	Before, O tyrannical master, you can offend or injure them, my life will become the spoils of these miserable fetters. For despite their restraint, by God, I will tear myself to shreds with own my hands and teeth, here among these very crags, before I consent to the misfortune of these strangers and bewail their abuse.
CLOTHOLD.	If you know that your misfortunes, Sigismund, are so great that even before your birth you were condemned to die by the dictates of the stars; if you know that these prison walls were

	de tus furias arrogantes,	
	un freno que las detenga	325
	y una rienda que las pare,	
	¿por qué blasonas? La puerta	
	cerrad desa estrecha cárcel.	
	Escondelde en ella.	

(Ciérranle la puerta, y dice dentro.)

SEGISMUNDO.	¡Ah, cielos,	
	qué bien hacéis en quitarme	330
	la libertad, porque fuera	
	contra vosotros gigante	
	que, para quebrar al sol	
	esos vidrios y cristales,	
	sobre cimientos de piedra,	335
	pusiera montes de jaspe!	
CLOTALDO.	Quizá, por que no los pongas,	
	hoy padeces tantos males.	
ROSAURA.	Ya que vi que la soberbia	
	te ofendió tanto, ignorante	340
	fuera en no pedirte, humilde,	
	vida que a tus plantas yace.	
	Muévate en mí la piedad,	
	que será rigor notable	
	que no hallen favor en ti	345
	ni soberbias ni humildades.	
CLARÍN.	Y si humildad y soberbia	
	no te obligan, personajes	
	que han movido y removido	
	mil autos sacramentales,	350
	yo, ni humilde ni soberbio,	
	sino entre las dos mitades	
	entreverado, te pido	
	que nos remedies y ampares.	
CLOTALDO.	¡Hola!	
SOLDADOS.	Señor.	
CLOTALDO.	A los dos	355
	quitad las armas, y ataldes	
	los ojos, por que no vean	
	cómo ni de dónde salen.	
ROSAURA.	Mi espada es ésta, que a ti	

built to serve as brake and rein to your arrogant fury, what are you boasting about? Guards, close the door to that narrow cell and lock him away inside.

(They lock him in the tower, and he speaks from within.)

SIGISMUND.   Oh, heavens, how rightly you act in stripping me of my liberty, for otherwise I would fight you like a giant who, to shatter the crystal sphere of the sun, piles mountains of jasper atop foundations of stone.

CLOTHOLD.   Perhaps, precisely so that you won't do so, you suffer so many hardships today.

ROSSAURA.   I see how his pride so offended you, and I would be a fool if I didn't beg you humbly for my life, which lies in your power. Let yourself be moved by my submission, for it would be unduly severe if neither pride nor humility found favour with you.

BUGLE.   And if you're unmoved by Humility and Pride, two characters that have moved and stirred a thousand allegorical plays, I shall, neither humbly nor proudly but somewhere in between, ask you for your help and shelter.

CLOTHOLD.   *[To the SOLDIERS.]* Attention!

SOLDIERS.   Sir!

CLOTHOLD.   Strip them both of their arms and blindfold them, so they won't see how or from where they're leaving.

ROSSAURA.   *[Touching her sword, still in its sheath.]* Here's my sword,

	solamente ha de entregarse;	360
	porque, al fin, de todos eres	
	el principal, y no sabe	
	rendirse a menos valor.	
CLARÍN.	La mía es tal que puede darse	
	al más ruin. Tomalda vos.	365
ROSAURA.	Y si he de morir, dejarte	
	quiero, en la fe desta piedad,	
	prenda que pudo estimarse	
	por el dueño que algún día	
	se la ciñó; que la guardes	370
	te encargo, porque, aunque yo	
	no sé qué secreto alcance,	
	sé que esta dorada espada	
	encierra misterios grandes,	
	pues sólo fiado en ella	375
	vengo a Polonia a vengarme	
	de un agravio.	
CLOTALDO.	(*Aparte.* ¡Santos cielos!	
	¿Qué es esto? Ya son más graves	
	mis penas y confusiones,	
	mis ansias y mis pesares.)	380
	¿Quién te la dio?	
ROSAURA.	Una mujer.	
CLOTALDO.	¿Cómo se llama?	
ROSAURA.	Que calle	
	su nombre es fuerza.	
CLOTALDO.	¿De qué	
	infieres agora o sabes	
	que hay secreto en esta espada?	385
ROSAURA.	Quien me la dio, dijo: «Parte	
	a Polonia, y solicita,	
	con ingenio, estudio o arte,	
	que te vean esa espada	
	los nobles y principales,	390
	que yo sé que alguno dellos	
	te favorezca y ampare»;	
	que por si acaso era muerto,	
	no quiso entonces nombrarle.	
CLOTALDO.	(*Aparte.* ¡Válgame el cielo! ¿Qué escucho?	395
	Aun no sé determinarme	

which can be surrendered only to you because, after all, you're the commander, and it is incapable of surrendering to anyone of lesser rank.

BUGLE. Mine is such that it can be given to the lowest of the low. *[To one of the SOLDIERS.]* Here, you take it.

ROSSAURA. And if I am to die, I wish to leave you, as proof of my loyalty, an item whose value was determined by he who once wore it. I ask you to keep it safe because, although I don't know what secret it holds, I do know that this golden sword conceals great mysteries, for I have come to Poland to avenge a dishonour with nothing else to vouch for me. *[She unsheathes the sword and hands it to CLOTHOLD, who cannot contain his astonishment.]*

CLOTHOLD. *(Aside.)* Good heavens! What's the meaning of this? My sufferings and confusions, my anxieties and sorrows, are now compounded.

[To ROSSAURA.] Who gave it to you?

ROSSAURA. A woman.

CLOTHOLD. What was her name?

ROSSAURA. I'm obliged not to reveal that.

CLOTHOLD. How do you suspect or know that it holds some secret?

ROSSAURA. She who gave it to me said: "Leave for Poland and, through ingenuity, deliberation, or artifice, let the noble and powerful see you with this sword, for I know that one of them will offer you favour and shelter." She wouldn't say whom she meant in case he might be dead.

CLOTHOLD. *(Aside.)* Heaven help me! What am I hearing! Is this an

si tales sucesos son
ilusiones o verdades.
Esta espada es la que yo
dejé a la hermosa Violante,   400
por señas que, el que ceñida
la trujera, había de hallarme
amoroso como hijo,
y piadoso como padre.
Pues ¿qué he de hacer, ¡ay de mí!,   405
en confusión semejante,
si quien la trae por favor
para su muerte la trae,
pues que sentenciado a muerte
llega a mis pies? ¡Qué notable   410
confusión! ¡Qué triste hado!
¡Qué suerte tan inconstante!
Éste es mi hijo, y las señas
dicen bien con las señales
del corazón, que por verle   415
llama el pecho, y en él bate
las alas, y no pudiendo
romper los candados, hace
lo que aquél que está encerrado
y, oyendo ruido en la calle,   420
se asoma por la ventana.
Y él así, como no sabe
lo que pasa y oye el ruido,
va a los ojos a asomarse,
que son ventanas del pecho,   425
por donde en lágrimas sale.
¿Qué he de hacer? ¡Válgame el cielo!
¿Qué he de hacer? Porque llevarle
al Rey es llevarle, ¡ay, triste!,
a morir. Pues ocultarle   430
al Rey no puedo, conforme
a la ley del homenaje.
De una parte, el amor propio,
y la lealtad, de otra parte,
me rinden. Pero ¿qué dudo?   435
¿La lealtad al Rey no es antes
que la vida y que el honor?

illusion or reality? This is the sword I left with the lovely Viola, signalling that anyone who came back wearing it would find me as loving as a son and as faithful as a father. So what am I to do now – Oh, miserable me! – amid such confusion, when he who brings the sword seeking favour can find only death, insofar as he comes before me doomed by the king's edict? What terrible confusion! What sad fate! What inconstant luck! This is my son; his appearance confirms what I know in my heart, which, longing to see him, calls to my breast, beats its wings within, and, unable to break the lock, does as he who, confined indoors, leans out of the window upon hearing a noise in the street. And thus, not knowing what's happening, my heart hears the noise and rushes to look out through my eyes – the windows to my soul – through which it escapes in the form of tears. What am I to do? Heaven help me! What am I to do? To take him to the king is to take him – Oh, what tragedy! – to his death, and I can't hide him from the king without violating the laws of fealty. On the one hand I am swayed by self-interest, on the other by loyalty to the king. But how can there really be any doubt? Doesn't loyalty to the king come before all else?

Pues ella viva y él falte.
Fuera de que, si ahora atiendo
a que dijo que a vengarse   440
viene de un agravio, hombre
que está agraviado es infame:
no es mi hijo, no es mi hijo,
ni tiene mi noble sangre.
Pero si ya ha sucedido   445
un peligro, de quien nadie
se libró, porque el honor
es de materia tan fácil
que con una acción se quiebra
o se mancha con un aire,   450
¿qué más puede hacer, qué más
el que es noble, de su parte,
que, a costa de tantos riesgos,
haber venido a buscarle?
Mi hijo es; mi sangre tiene,   455
pues tiene valor tan grande.
Y así, entre una y otra duda,
el medio más importante
es irme al Rey y decirle
que es mi hijo y que le mate.   460
Quizá la misma lealtad
de mi honor podrá obligarle.
Y si le merezco vivo,
yo le ayudaré a vengarse
de su agravio; mas si el Rey,   465
en sus rigores constante,
le da muerte, morirá
sin saber que soy su padre.)
Venid conmigo, extranjeros.
No temáis, no, de que os falte   470
compañía en las desdichas;
pues en duda semejante
de vivir o de morir,
no sé cuáles son más grandes.

(Vanse.)

So loyalty it shall be, and away with self-interest. Besides, I recall now that he said he's come to Poland to avenge a dishonour, and everyone knows that a dishonoured man is contemptible, so he can't be my son. He's not my son and doesn't share my noble blood. But then again, if the affront was inescapable – for honour is of such fragile substance that it can be shattered with a single deed or blemished with a whisper – what more could a nobleman do in his defence, what more than to go looking for his remedy at all cost? He *is* my son, he *does* share my blood, for his courage is great! And thus, in the face of so much doubt, my best option is go to the king, inform him that he's my son, and acknowledge that he must die. Perhaps the very depth of my loyalty will move his heart; and if I manage to preserve my son's life, then I'll help him avenge his dishonour; but if the king remains steadfast in his severity and sentences him to death, then he shall die without knowing that I'm his father.

[To ROSSAURA and BUGLE.] Come with me, foreigners. Fear not, no, that you lack company in your misfortunes; for amid such doubt, where life hangs in the balance, I don't know whose misfortunes are greater. *[Exit all.]*

Escena 2

(Sale por una parte ASTOLFO, con acompañamiento de soldados, y por otra ESTRELLA con damas. Suena música.)

ASTOLFO.	Bien, al ver los excelentes	475
	rayos que fueron cometas,	
	mezclan salvas diferentes	
	las cajas y las trompetas,	
	los pájaros y las fuentes,	
	siendo, con música igual	480
	y con maravilla suma,	
	a tu vista celestial,	
	unos, clarines de pluma,	
	y otras, aves de metal.	
	Y así os saludan, señora,	485
	como a su reina las balas,	
	los pájaros como a Aurora,	
	las trompetas como a Palas,	
	y las flores como a Flora;	
	porque sois, burlando el día,	490
	que ya la noche destierra,	
	Aurora en el alegría,	
	Flora en paz, Palas en guerra	
	y reina en el alma mía.	
ESTRELLA.	Si la voz se ha de medir	495
	con las acciones humanas,	
	mal habéis hecho en decir	
	finezas tan cortesanas	
	donde os pueda desmentir	
	todo ese marcial trofeo,	500
	con quien ya atrevida lucho;	
	pues no dicen, según creo,	
	las lisonjas que os escucho	
	con los rigores que veo.	
	Y advertid que es baja acción,	505
	que sólo a una fiera toca,	
	madre de engaño y traición,	
	el halagar con la boca	
	y matar con la intención.	
ASTOLFO.	Muy mal informada estáis,	510
	Estrella, pues que la fe	

Scene 2

([Palace of King VASILY of Poland.] Enter, on one side, AISTULF in the company of SOLDIERS, and on the other, STELLA with her LADIES-IN-WAITING. Music plays in the background.)

AISTULF.   Upon seeing the brilliant flashes that were comets, the drums and the trumpets along with the birds and the streams do well in mixing their diverse greetings; for, with equal music and awesome wonder before your celestial image, the birds are feathered bugles and the instruments, metallic birds. And thus you are greeted, my lady, as Queen by the salvos, as Aurora by the birds, as Pallas by the trumpets, and as Flora by the flowers. Because, in mocking the day that the night now banishes, you are Aurora in happiness, Flora in peace, Pallas in war, and Queen in my soul.

STELLA.   If words are to be judged by actions, you do not fare well in pronouncing courtly compliments that are so easily contradicted by all that clamorous brass *[pointing to the SOLDIERS]*, which has already met my bold resistance; for the flattery I'm hearing from you, as I see it, does not agree with the severe show of force that I'm observing. And take note that it's a base action, worthy only of the deception and treachery of beasts, to flatter with the mouth and kill with the mind.

AISTULF.   You're very poorly informed, Stella, in questioning the

de mis finezas dudáis;
y os suplico que me oigáis
la causa, a ver si la sé.
Falleció Eustorgio tercero,   515
rey de Polonia, y quedó
Basilio por heredero,
y dos hijas, de quien yo
y vos nacimos. No quiero
cansar con lo que no tiene   520
lugar aquí. Clorilene,
vuestra madre y mi señora,
que en mejor imperio agora
dosel de luceros tiene,
fue la mayor, de quien vos   525
sois hija. Fue la segunda,
madre y tía de los dos,
la gallarda Recisunda,
que guarde mil años Dios.
Casó en Moscovia, de quien   530
nací yo. Volver agora
al otro principio es bien.
Basilio, que ya, señora,
se rinde al común desdén
del tiempo, más inclinado   535
a los estudios que dado
a mujeres, enviudó
sin hijos; y vos y yo
aspiramos a este Estado.
Vos alegáis que habéis sido   540
hija de hermana mayor;
yo, que varón he nacido
y, aunque de hermana menor,
os debo ser preferido.
Vuestra intención y la mía   545
a nuestro tío contamos;
él respondió que quería
componernos y aplazamos
este puesto y este día.
Con esta intención salí   550
de Moscovia y de su tierra;
con ésta llegué hasta aquí,
en vez de haceros yo guerra,
a que me la hagáis a mí.

sincerity of my compliments, so I beseech you: hear my cause before you judge my intentions. When Eustorgius the Third, King of Poland, passed away, he left Vasily as his heir, along with two daughters, from whom you and I were born. I won't tire you with details that have no place here. Clorilyn, your mother and my superior, who now rests under a canopy of stars in a sweeter realm, was the eldest, and you're her daughter. Next came my mother and your aunt, the gallant Grethissunda, may God keep her a thousand years. She married the Duke of Muscovy and gave birth to me. Now here's the issue, my lady: Vasily, who's already succumbing to the inevitable contempt of time, and who was always more inclined to academic pursuits than to women, is widowed and childless, and you and I both aspire to this country's throne. You contend that you're the daughter of the elder sister; I, that I was born a man and that, even though my mother was the younger sister, I should receive preference. We have both informed our uncle of our intentions; he responded that he wished to resolve our dispute, and we settled on this place and this day. With this intention I left my land in Muscovy; with the same intention I have arrived here, unprepared to go to war, only to find you waging it against me. Oh, would

	¡Oh, quiera Amor, sabio dios,	555
	que el vulgo, astrólogo cierto,	
	hoy lo sea con los dos,	
	y que pare este concierto	
	en que seáis reina vos,	
	pero reina en mi albedrío,	560
	dándoos, para más honor,	
	su corona nuestro tío,	
	sus triunfos vuestro valor,	
	y su imperio el amor mío!	
ESTRELLA.	A tan cortés bizarría	565
	menos mi pecho no muestra;	
	pues, la imperial monarquía,	
	para sólo hacerla vuestra,	
	me holgara que fuese mía.	
	Aunque no está satisfecho	570
	mi amor de que sois ingrato,	
	si en cuanto decís sospecho	
	que os desmiente ese retrato	
	que está pendiente del pecho.	
ASTOLFO.	Satisfaceros intento	575
	con él, mas lugar no da	
	tanto sonoro instrumento,	
	que avisa que sale ya	
	el Rey con su parlamento.	

(Tocan, y sale el Rey BASILIO, viejo, y acompañamiento.)

ESTRELLA.	Sabio Tales,	
ASTOLFO.	Docto Euclides,	580
ESTRELLA.	…que entre signos,	
ASTOLFO.	…que entre estrellas,	
ESTRELLA.	…hoy gobiernas,	
ASTOLFO.	…hoy resides,	
ESTRELLA.	…y sus caminos	
ASTOLFO.	…sus huellas	
ESTRELLA.	…describes,	
ASTOLFO.	…tasas y mides,	
ESTRELLA.	…deja que en humildes lazos	585
ASTOLFO.	…deja que en tiernos abrazos	
ESTRELLA.	…yedra dese tronco sea.	
ASTOLFO.	…rendido a tus pies me vea.	
BASILIO.	Sobrinos, dadme los brazos,	

that Love, a wise god, move the people, always a sound astrologer, to grant us a sound judgment today and end this meeting by making you Queen – Queen of my will. Thus you would be, to your greater honour, crowned by our uncle, rewarded by your valour, and recognized as sovereign by my love.

STELLA. To such courtly generosity my heart responds no less in turn, for I, simply to make this imperial monarchy yours, would be happy to claim it as mine; yet, though my love is not convinced that you are insincere, in all you say I fear you are contradicted by that locket hanging about your breast.

AISTULF. I'll resolve your doubts about that... but not now, for all those clamorous instruments indicate that the king and his court are approaching.

(Flourish. Enter King VASILY – an old man – and his ATTENDANTS.)

STELLA.	Wise Thales,
AISTULF.	Learned Euclid,
STELLA.	who governs today
AISTULF.	who lives today
STELLA.	by the constellations
AISTULF.	by the stars
STELLA.	and charts
AISTULF.	and glosses and measures
STELLA.	their courses,
AISTULF.	their tracks,
STELLA.	allow me, with humble bonds,
AISTULF.	allow me, with tender embraces,
STELLA.	to be the ivy upon your trunk.
AISTULF.	to surrender myself at your feet.
VASILY.	Dear niece and nephew, let me embrace you. And insofar

y creed, pues que leales   590
a mi precepto amoroso
venís con afectos tales,
que a nadie deje quejoso,
y los dos quedéis iguales.
Y así, cuando me confieso   595
rendido al prolijo peso,
sólo os pido en la ocasión
silencio, que admiración
ha de pedirla el suceso.
Ya sabéis, estadme atentos,   600
amados sobrinos míos,
corte ilustre de Polonia,
vasallos, deudos, y amigos;
ya sabéis que yo, en el mundo,
por mi ciencia he merecido   605
el sobrenombre de docto,
pues, contra el tiempo y olvido,
los pinceles de Timantes,
los mármoles de Lisipo,
en el ámbito del orbe,   610
me aclaman el gran Basilio.
Ya sabéis que son las ciencias
que más curso y más estimo
matemáticas sutiles,
por quien al tiempo le quito,   615
por quien a la fama rompo
la jurisdición y oficio
de enseñar más cada día;
pues, cuando en mis tablas miro
presentes las novedades   620
de los venideros siglos,
le gano al tiempo las gracias
de contar lo que yo he dicho.
Esos círculos de nieve,
esos doseles de vidrio,   625
que el sol ilumina a rayos,
que parte la luna a giros;
esos orbes de diamantes,
esos globos cristalinos,
que las estrellas adornan   630
y que campean los signos,
son el estudio mayor

as you both come here, true to my loving ways, with your own show of affection, trust that I will leave neither of your with cause for complaint, and you shall both be treated fairly. And now, confessing weariness from the heavy burden of my years, I solicit only your silence, for the subject matter itself will solicit your amazement. You know well – and please listen carefully, my beloved niece and nephew, illustrious court of Poland, vassals, relatives, and friends – you know well that my knowledge has earned me the nickname of Learned in world opinion; thus, in defiance of time and oblivion, paintings worthy of Timanthes and sculptures worthy of Lysippus proclaim me the great Vasily around the globe. You know also that the knowledge I most cultivate and admire lies in subtle mathematics, in whose name I rob time and exempt fame of the jurisdiction and task of making new revelations with the passing of each day. For when in my charts I witness happenings of the coming centuries, I earn the thanks owed to time for revealing what I have told. Those snowy spheres, those glass canopies illuminated by the sun's rays and encircled by the moon's beams, those diamond orbs, those crystalline globes adorned by the stars and crisscrossed by the Zodiac, have received the greatest

de mis años; son los libros
donde, en papel de diamante,
en cuadernos de zafiros,   635
escribe con líneas de oro,
en caracteres distintos,
el cielo nuestros sucesos,
ya adversos o ya benignos.
Éstos leo tan veloz,   640
que con mi espíritu sigo
sus rápidos movimientos
por rumbos y por caminos.
¡Pluguiera al cielo, primero
que mi ingenio hubiera sido   645
de sus márgenes comento
y de sus hojas registro,
hubiera sido mi vida
el primero desperdicio
de sus iras, y que en ellas   650
mi tragedia hubiera visto!
Porque de los infelices,
aun el mérito es cuchillo;
que a quien le daña el saber,
homicida es de sí mismo.   655
Dígalo yo, aunque mejor
lo dirán sucesos míos,
para cuya admiración
otra vez silencio os pido.
En Clorilene, mi esposa,   660
tuve un infelice hijo,
en cuyo parto los cielos
se agotaron de prodigios
antes que a la luz hermosa
le diese el sepulcro vivo   665
de un vientre, porque el nacer
y el morir son parecidos.
Su madre, infinitas veces,
entre ideas y delirios
del sueño, vio que rompía   670
sus entrañas atrevido
un monstruo en forma de hombre;
y, entre su sangre teñido,

attention of my years; they are the books in which, on diamond-studded paper bound in sapphire, with diverse characters etched in gold lines, Heaven records our deeds, whether adverse or auspicious. These books I read with such swiftness that I follow in spirit their rapid movements across the sky's corridors and pathways. If only Heaven had taken my life as the first casualty of its ire, if only I had foreseen my tragedy in its writings before my ingenuity began to gloss the margins and index the pages. Even success is a double-edged sword for the unlucky, and he who is pricked by knowledge ends up destroying himself. I say this to you myself, although my actions will speak more eloquently, and once again I ask that silence accompany your amazement. By Clorilyn, my wife, I had an unlucky son, upon whose birth the heavens ran out of omens before he had been freed into the beautiful light from the living grave of the womb, for thus are birth and death akin. Time and again his mother, seized by the images and hallucinations of dreams, watched as a monster in human form brazenly broke through her entrails

le daba muerte, naciendo
víbora humana del siglo.   675
Llegó de su parto el día,
y, los presagios cumplidos,
porque tarde o nunca son
mentirosos los impíos,
nació en horóscopo tal,   680
que el sol, en su sangre tinto,
entraba sañudamente
con la luna en desafío;
y, siendo valla la tierra,
los dos faroles divinos   685
a luz entera luchaban,
ya que no a brazo partido.
El mayor, el más horrendo
eclipse que ha padecido
el sol, después que con sangre   690
lloró la muerte de Cristo,
éste fue, porque, anegado
el orbe entre incendios vivos,
presumió que padecía
el último parasismo: 695
los cielos se escurecieron,
temblaron los edificios,
llovieron piedras las nubes,
corrieron sangre los ríos.
En este mísero, en este   700
mortal planeta o signo
nació Segismundo, dando
de su condición indicios,
pues dio la muerte a su madre,
con cuya fiereza dijo: 705
«Hombre soy, pues que ya empiezo
a pagar mal beneficios».
Yo, acudiendo a mis estudios,
en ellos y en todo miro
que Segismundo sería   710
el hombre más atrevido,
el príncipe más crüel
y el monarca más impío;
por quien su reino vendría

and, drenched in her blood, killed her, a once-in-a-century
human viper. The day of the birth arrived, and, in fulfilment
of the omens – for the irreverent are often proved true – he
was born under such a horoscope that the sun, reddened by
its blood, was viciously entering into a duel with the moon;
and with Earth as spectator, the two divine torches fought not
in hand to hand combat but with the volleys of their brilliant
rays. It was the greatest, most horrendous eclipse the sun
has ever suffered since it shed tears of blood over Christ's
death; and the globe, bathed in raging fires, presumed itself
to be in the grips of the apocalypse. The heavens darkened,
buildings trembled, the clouds rained stones, and the rivers
ran with blood. Under this miserable, under this fatal planet
or sign Sigismund was born, indicating his nature with the
death of his mother, a savage act of which he said: "I am
man, for already I've begun poorly to repay my benefactors."
Resorting to my studies, I saw in them and in everything
that Sigismund would be the wildest of men, the cruellest
of princes, and the most perverse of monarchs, bringing

a ser parcial y diviso,   715
escuela de las traiciones
y academia de los vicios;
y él, de su furor llevado,
entre asombros y delitos,
había de poner en mí   720
las plantas, y yo, rendido
a sus pies me había de ver
(¡con qué congoja lo digo!),
siendo alfombra de sus plantas
las canas del rostro mío.   725
¿Quién no da crédito al daño,
y más al daño que ha visto
en su estudio, donde hace
el amor propio su oficio?
Pues dando crédito yo   730
a los hados que, adivinos,
me pronosticaban daños
en fatales vaticinios,
determiné de encerrar
la fiera que había nacido,   735
por ver si el sabio tenía
en las estrellas dominio.
Publicóse que el Infante
nació muerto y, prevenido,
hice labrar una torre   740
entre las peñas y riscos
desos montes, donde apenas
la luz ha hallado camino,
por defenderle la entrada
sus rústicos obeliscos.   745
Las graves penas y leyes
que, con públicos editos,
declararon que ninguno
entrase a un vedado sitio
del monte se ocasionaron   750
de las causas que os he dicho.
Allí Segismundo vive,
mísero, pobre y cautivo,
adonde solo Clotaldo
le ha hablado, tratado y visto.   755

polarization and division to the kingdom, like a school of treachery or an academy of vice; and that, driven by his fury and wavering between bewilderment and transgression, he would trample me beneath his heels, and I, vanquished and prostrate before his feet, would – what anxiety it causes me to say the words! – offer the grey hair of my beard as a doormat to his boots. Who doesn't take peril seriously, especially when it is revealed through the research on which his self-interest depends? Thus, lending credence to the soothsaying fates that had foretold the peril in their fatal prophecies, I determined to lock up the beast that had been born, to see if a wise man might master the stars. It was announced that the prince was stillborn, and I, ever cautious, had a tower built among the crags and bluffs of those mountains, where the light of day scarcely makes its way, so heavily do the crude obelisks guard the entrance. The severe penalties and laws that, by public proclamation, prohibited anyone from entering the mountain's forbidden zone were made necessary by the reasons I have told you. There lives Sigismund, in misery, destitution, and confinement, where only Clothold has spoken to him, dealt with him, and seen him. The only

Éste le ha enseñado ciencias;
éste en la ley le ha instruido
católica, siendo solo
de sus miserias testigo.
Aquí hay tres cosas: la una,   760
que yo, Polonia, os estimo
tanto que os quiero librar
de la opresión y servicio
de un rey tirano, porque
no fuera señor benigno   765
el que a su patria y su imperio
pusiera en tanto peligro;
la otra es considerar
que, si a mi sangre le quito
el derecho que le dieron   770
humano fuero y divino,
no es cristiana caridad,
pues ninguna ley ha dicho
que, por reservar yo a otro
de tirano y de atrevido,   775
pueda yo serlo, supuesto
que si es tirano mi hijo,
porque él delitos no haga,
vengo yo a hacer los delitos;
es la última y tercera   780
el ver cuánto yerro ha sido
dar crédito fácilmente
a los sucesos previstos,
pues, aunque su inclinación
le dicte sus precipicios,   785
quizá no le vencerán,
porque el hado más esquivo,
la inclinación más violenta,
el planeta más impío
sólo el albedrío inclinan,   790
no fuerzan el albedrío.
Y así, entre una y otra causa
vacilante y discursivo,
previne un remedio tal
que os suspenda los sentidos.   795
Yo he de ponerle mañana,
sin que él sepa que es mi hijo
y rey vuestro, a Segismundo,

witness to his miseries, Clothold has taught him natural law and instructed him in the Catholic faith. Three conclusions may be drawn from all this. First, that I hold you in such esteem, Poland, that I wish to spare you the oppression and rule of a tyrannical king, because any ruler who put his fatherland and empire in such danger couldn't be considered benevolent. Second is the consideration that to deprive my heir of the right he was given by human and divine sanction is not an act of Christian charity, for no law allows me, in trying to keep someone else from becoming tyrannical and barbaric, to become so myself; yet if my son is a tyrant, in order to prevent him from committing crimes, I must commit them myself. Third and last, I realize how erroneous it was to place easy credence in predictions of the future; for although the prince's inclination may place ruinous obstacles in his path, he might very well avoid them, because even the most contemptuous fate, the most monstrous inclination, or the most perverse planet can only influence the will, not force it. And so, after hesitating and reflecting over my options, I've come up with a solution that is sure to leave you dumbstruck. Tomorrow I shall place Sigismund – for this is his name – without his knowing that he is my son and your king, under

que aqueste su nombre ha sido,
en mi dosel, en mi silla   800
y, en fin, en el lugar mío,
donde os gobierne y os mande,
y donde todos, rendidos,
la obediencia le juréis;
pues con aquesto consigo   805
tres cosas, con que respondo
a las otras tres que he dicho.
Es la primera, que siendo
prudente, cuerdo y benigno,
desmintiendo en todo al hado,   810
que de él tantas cosas dijo,
gozaréis el natural
príncipe vuestro, que ha sido
cortesano de unos montes
y de sus fieras vecino.   815
Es la segunda que, si él,
soberbio, osado, atrevido
y crüel, con rienda suelta
corre el campo de sus vicios,
habré yo, piadoso entonces,   820
con mi obligación cumplido,
y luego, en desposeerle,
haré como rey invicto,
siendo el volverle a la cárcel
no crueldad, sino castigo.   825
Es la tercera que, siendo
el príncipe como os digo,
por lo que os amo, vasallos,
os daré reyes más dignos
de la corona y el cetro,   830
pues serán mis dos sobrinos,
juntando en uno el derecho
de los dos, y, convenidos
con la fe del matrimonio,
tendrán lo que han merecido.   835
Esto como rey os mando,
esto como padre os pido,
esto como sabio os ruego,
esto como anciano os digo,
y, si el Séneca español,   840

my canopy, upon my throne, and in place of me, where he will govern and command you and where you will all swear docile obedience to him. In this way I shall accomplish three things, with which I can now respond to the three conclusions I pointed out earlier. First, that if he turns out to be prudent, rational, and kind, in complete contradiction of the fate that predicted so many things of him, you will all enjoy the reign of your rightful prince, who has grown up a courtier to the mountain and a neighbour to its beasts. Second, that if he turns out to be defiant, brazen, barbaric, and cruel and runs with free rein through the field of his vices, I shall have loyally fulfilled my obligation; and then, in ousting him, I shall behave as a successful king, for returning him to prison would not be cruelty but rather punishment. Third, that if he turns out to be the prince I just described, out of my love for you, my subjects, I shall give you a king and queen more worthy of my crown and sceptre: for my niece and nephew, uniting their two claims to the throne and reconciled to each other through the sanctity of marriage, will have what they have earned. This I command of you as a king; this I ask of you as a father; this I beg of you as a sage; this I say to you as an elder; and if kings are the humble slaves of their republics

que era humilde esclavo, dijo,
de su república un rey,
como esclavo os lo suplico.

ASTOLFO.   Si a mí el responder me toca,
como el que, en efeto, ha sido   845
aquí el más interesado,
en nombre de todos digo
que Segismundo parezca,
pues le basta ser tu hijo.

TODOS.   ¡Danos al príncipe nuestro,   850
que ya por rey le pedimos!

BASILIO.   Vasallos, esa fineza
os agradezco y estimo.
Acompañad a sus cuartos
a los dos atlantes míos,   855
que mañana le veréis.

TODOS.   ¡Viva el grande Rey Basilio!

(Éntranse todos. Antes que se entre el REY salen CLOTALDO, ROSAURA y CLARÍN, y CLOTALDO detiene al REY.)

CLOTALDO.   ¿Podréte hablar?

BASILIO.   ¡Oh, Clotaldo,
tú seas muy bien venido!

CLOTALDO.   Aunque viniendo a tus plantas   860
es fuerza el haberlo sido,
esta vez rompe, señor,
el hado triste y esquivo
el privilegio a la ley
y a la costumbre el estilo.   865

BASILIO.   ¿Qué tienes?

CLOTALDO.   Una desdicha,
señor, que me ha sucedido,
cuando pudiera tenerla
por el mayor regocijo.

BASILIO.   Prosigue.

CLOTALDO.   Este bello joven,   870
osado o inadvertido,
entró en la torre, señor,
adonde al príncipe ha visto,
y es...

BASILIO.   No te aflijas, Clotaldo.
Si otro día hubiera sido,   875

	as Seneca the Spaniard said, this I beseech of you as a slave.
AISTULF.	If it's up to me to respond, as he who presumably has the greatest interest here in the matter, I'll speak for everyone in saying let Sigismund come forward, for his being your son is reason enough.
ALL.	Give us our prince, for we want him as our king!
VASILY.	Vassals, I appreciate and value your goodwill. Accompany my niece and nephew, Atlases of my old age, to their quarters, and tomorrow you will see him.
ALL.	Long live the great King Vasily!

(Exit all. Before the king can leave, CLOTHOLD enters with ROSSAURA and BUGLE and detains him.)

CLOTHOLD.	May I speak with you?
VASILY.	Oh, Clothold! You are most welcome.
CLOTHOLD.	Although bowing before your presence is always welcoming, this time, my lord, a gloomy and contemptuous fate has forced a break in the norms of protocol and custom.
VASILY.	What's the matter?
CLOTHOLD.	A grave misfortune, my lord, has befallen me, when it could have been a source of greatest joy.
VASILY.	Explain.
CLOTHOLD.	*[Pointing to ROSSAURA.]* This handsome young man, either daring or unknowing, entered the tower, my lord, where he saw the prince. And he's...
VASILY.	Don't fret, Clothold. If this had happened another day,

confieso que lo sintiera;
pero ya el secreto he dicho,
y no importa que él lo sepa,
supuesto que yo lo digo.
Vedme después, porque tengo   880
muchas cosas que advertiros,
y muchas que hagáis por mí;
que habéis de ser, os aviso,
instrumento del mayor
suceso que el mundo ha visto.   885
Y a esos presos, porque al fin
no presumáis que castigo
descuidos vuestros, perdono.

(Vase.)

CLOTALDO.   ¡Vivas, gran señor, mil siglos!
                 (*Aparte.* Mejoró el cielo la suerte;   890
                 ya no diré que es mi hijo,
                 pues que lo puedo excusar.)
                 Extranjeros peregrinos,
                 libres estáis.
ROSAURA.   Tus pies beso
                 mil veces.
CLARÍN.   Y yo los viso,   895
                 que una letra más o menos
                 no reparan dos amigos.
ROSAURA.   La vida, señor, me has dado;
                 y, pues a tu cuenta vivo,
                 eternamente seré   900
                 esclavo tuyo.
CLOTALDO.   No ha sido
                 vida la que yo te he dado;
                 porque un hombre bien nacido,
                 si está agraviado, no vive.
                 Y supuesto que has venido   905
                 a vengarte de un agravio,
                 según tú propio me has dicho,
                 no te he dado vida yo,
                 porque tú no la has traído;
                 que vida infame no es vida.   910
                 (*Aparte.* Bien con aquesto le animo.)

I confess I would have been alarmed. But I just spoke the tower's secret, so it doesn't matter that he knows it because I've revealed it. Come and see me later, because I have many things to report to you and much to ask of you; for you are to be, take note, the instrument of the greatest event the world has ever seen. And to those prisoners, so that you won't conclude I'm punishing your oversight, I grant pardon.

(Exit.)

CLOTHOLD.   May you live a thousand centuries, great lord!
(Aside.) Heaven has improved my luck. I won't tell anyone that he's my son now, since I can get by without doing so.
[To ROSSAURA and BUGLE.] Errant strangers, you are free to go.

ROSSAURA.   I shall *adorn* your feet a thousand times with my kisses.

BUGLE.   I'll just *adore* them from afar, for what's a letter or two between friends?

ROSSAURA.   You have given me, sire, my life; and since I live in your debt, I shall be your eternal slave.

CLOTHOLD.   What I've given you isn't life, for a well-born man has no life as long as he's dishonoured; and given that you've come here to avenge a dishonour, as you yourself have told me, I can't have given you life because you bring none with you; for a life lived in disrepute is no life.
(Aside.) In this way I'll spur him on.

ROSAURA.	Confieso que no la tengo,
	aunque de ti la recibo;
	pero yo, con la venganza,
	dejaré mi honor tan limpio 915
	que pueda mi vida luego,
	atropellando peligros,
	parecer dádiva tuya.
CLOTALDO.	Toma el acero bruñido
	que trujiste, que yo sé 920
	que él baste, en sangre teñido
	de tu enemigo, a vengarte;
	porque acero que fue mío
	– digo este instante, este rato
	que en mi poder le he tenido – 925
	sabrá vengarte.
ROSAURA.	En tu nombre
	segunda vez me le ciño,
	y en él juro mi venganza,
	aunque fuese mi enemigo
	más poderoso.
CLOTALDO.	¿Eslo mucho? 930
ROSAURA.	Tanto, que no te lo digo;
	no porque de tu prudencia
	mayores cosas no fío,
	sino porque no se vuelva
	contra mí el favor que admiro 935
	en tu piedad.
CLOTALDO.	Antes fuera
	ganarme a mí con decirlo,
	pues fuera cerrarme el paso
	de ayudar a tu enemigo.
	(*Aparte.* ¡Oh, si supiera quién es!) 940
ROSAURA.	Porque no pienses que estimo
	tan poco esa confianza,
	sabe que el contrario ha sido
	no menos que Astolfo, duque
	de Moscovia.
CLOTALDO.	(*Aparte.* Mal resisto 945
	el dolor, porque es más grave
	que fue imaginado, visto.)
	Apuremos más el caso.
	Si moscovita has nacido,

ROSSAURA.	I confess that I remain without life despite receiving it from you; but through vengeance I shall leave my honour so unblemished that my life, in overcoming danger, may be recognized as your gift.
CLOTHOLD.	Take back this burnished blade you brought with you, for I know that, when dyed in the blood of your enemy, it will be sufficient to avenge your dishonour; because any blade that was once mine – I mean "mine" in this instant, this brief period that I've held it in my power – is capable of avenging you.
ROSSAURA.	In your name I arm myself with it a second time, and upon it I swear myself to revenge, even if my enemy were more powerful.
CLOTHOLD.	Is he? By a lot?
ROSSAURA.	So much so that I shall not tell you: not because I wouldn't entrust greater matters to your prudence but rather so that the advantage I behold in your devotion won't backfire on me.
CLOTHOLD.	On the contrary, in telling me you would keep me on your side, for you would keep me from aiding your enemy. *(Aside.)* Oh, if only I could know who it is!
ROSSAURA.	So that you won't think I underestimate your trust, know that my enemy is none other than Aistulf, Duke of Muscovy.
CLOTHOLD.	*(Aside.)* This is more than I can bear, much worse than I'd imagined! *[To ROSSAURA.]* Let's clarify matters. If you were born a

	el que es natural señor	950
	mal agraviarte ha podido.	
	Vuélvete a tu patria, pues,	
	y deja el ardiente brío	
	que te despeña.	
ROSAURA.	Yo sé	
	que, aunque mi príncipe ha sido,	955
	pudo agraviarme.	
CLOTALDO.	No pudo,	
	aunque pusiera, atrevido,	
	la mano en tu rostro.	
	(*Aparte.* ¡Ay cielos!)	
ROSAURA.	Mayor fue el agravio mío.	
CLOTALDO.	Dilo ya, pues que no puedes	960
	decir más que yo imagino.	
ROSAURA.	Sí dijera, mas no sé	
	con qué respeto te miro,	
	con qué afecto te venero,	
	con qué estimación te asisto,	965
	que no me atrevo a decirte	
	que es este exterior vestido	
	enigma, pues no es de quien	
	parece. Juzga advertido,	
	si no soy lo que parezco	970
	y Astolfo a casarse vino	
	con Estrella, si podrá	
	agraviarme. Harto te he dicho.	

(*Vanse ROSAURA y CLARÍN.*)

CLOTALDO.	¡Escucha, aguarda, detente!	
	¿Qué confuso laberinto	975
	es éste, donde no puede	
	hallar la razón el hilo?	
	Mi honor es el agraviado;	
	poderoso el enemigo;	
	yo vasallo; ella mujer.	980
	Descubra el cielo camino;	
	aunque no sé si podrá	
	cuando, en tan confuso abismo,	
	es todo el cielo un presagio	
	y es todo el mundo un prodigio.	985

	Muscovite, your natural lord cannot have dishonoured you; return to your fatherland, then, and cast aside the burning impetuousness that propels you.
ROSSAURA.	I'm certain that, even though he's my prince, he has dishonoured me.
CLOTHOLD.	Impossible, even if he had dared to slap you in the face. *(Aside.)* Heavens!
ROSSAURA.	My dishonour was greater.
CLOTHOLD.	State it then, for you can't say anything more than I can imagine.
ROSSAURA.	I would do so, but such is the respect with which I look upon you, the affection with which I worship you, the esteem in which I hold you, that I dare not tell you that my external trappings are a riddle, for their owner is not what appearances suggest. You decide: if I am not what I appear to be, and Aistulf has come here to marry Stella, can he not dishonour me? I have said enough.

(Exit ROSSAURA and BUGLE.)

| CLOTHOLD. | Listen! Wait! Stop! What confusing labyrinth is this, where reason has lost its thread? My honour is besmirched, the enemy is powerful, I'm his vassal, and she's a woman: show me the way out, heavens! Although I'm not sure there is a way out when, in such a confusing abyss, Heaven is full of omens and earth is full of aberrations. |

ACTO 2

Escena 1
(Salen el REY BASILIO y CLOTALDO.)

CLOTALDO.	Todo, como lo mandaste,
	queda efetuado.
BASILIO.	Cuenta,
	Clotaldo, cómo pasó.
CLOTALDO.	Fue, señor, desta manera.

Con la apacible bebida 990
que, de confecciones llena,
hacer mandaste mezclando
la virtud de algunas hierbas,
cuyo tirano poder
y cuya secreta fuerza 995
así el humano discurso
priva, roba y enajena
que deja vivo cadáver
a un hombre, y cuya violencia,
adormecido, le quita 1000
los sentidos y potencias...
No tenemos que argüir
que aquesto posible sea,
pues tantas veces, señor,
nos ha dicho la experiencia, 1005
y es cierto, que de secretos
naturales está llena
la medicina; y no hay
animal, planta ni piedra
que no tenga calidad 1010
determinada; y, si llega
a examinar mil venenos
la humana malicia nuestra
que den la muerte, ¿qué mucho
que, templada su violencia, 1015
pues hay venenos que maten,
haya venenos que aduerman?
Dejando aparte el dudar
si es posible que suceda,

ACT 2

Scene 1

([The palace.] Enter VASILY and CLOTHOLD.)

CLOTHOLD.	Everything has been carried out as you ordered.
VASILY.	Tell me, Clothold, how it happened.
CLOTHOLD.	In this way, my lord. With the soothing concoction you had compounded from a mixture of medicinal herbs, whose tyrannical properties and secret powers so dissipate, rob, and disorient human reasoning that they can turn a man into a living corpse, and whose potent qualities divest anyone under their influence of his senses and faculties... There's no need to prove that this is possible, for so many times, my lord, experience shows us, and it's true, that medicine is full of natural secrets, and there's no animal, plant, or stone that doesn't have a determined property; and if our human malice has experimented with a thousand poisons in search of their lethal qualities, is it surprising that, with a little less potency, a poison that kills could be made to induce sleep? Leaving aside doubts about whether this is possible, for it's been

pues que ya queda probado   1020
con razones y evidencias,
con la bebida, en efeto,
que el opio, la adormidera
y el beleño compusieron,
bajé a la cárcel estrecha   1025
de Segismundo. Con él
hablé un rato de las letras
humanas que le ha enseñado
la muda naturaleza
de los montes y los cielos,   1030
y en cuya divina escuela
la retórica aprendió
de las aves y las fieras.
Para levantarle más
el espíritu a la empresa   1035
que solicitas, tomé
por asunto la presteza
de un águila caudalosa
que, despreciando la esfera
del viento, pasaba a ser,   1040
en las regiones supremas
del fuego, rayo de pluma
o desasido cometa.
Encarecí el vuelo altivo
diciendo: «Al fin eres reina   1045
de las aves, y así a todas
es justo que te prefieras».
Él no hubo menester más,
que, en tocando esta materia
de la majestad, discurre   1050
con ambición y soberbia
– porque, en efecto, la sangre
le incita, mueve y alienta
a cosas grandes – y dijo:
«¡Que en la república inquieta   1055
de las aves también haya
quien les jure la obediencia!
En llegando a este discurso,
mis desdichas me consuelan;
pues, por lo menos, si estoy   1060

demonstrated through argument and evidence, I'll continue my story: with the concoction compounded of opium, belladonna, and henbane, I descended to Sigismund's narrow prison. I talked with him a bit about the moral lessons he has been taught by the silence of the mountains and heavens, under whose divine instruction he has learned rhetoric from the birds and the beasts. To better elevate his spirit to the task you have in store for him, I proposed for discussion the swiftness of a majestic eagle that, as it scorned the sphere of the wind, was transformed, in the lofty regions of fire, into a feathery flare or a runaway comet. I praised its imperious flight, saying: "You are, after all, sovereign among birds, and thus it is natural that you consider yourself superior to all the rest." He needed no further prompting, for whenever the topic of sovereign power is discussed, he reasons with ambition and pride because his blood, of course, incites, moves, and animates him to great things, and he said: "To think that in the restive realm of birds there is one who commands obedience from all! In this matter my misfortunes console me, since, if I'm subservient to another, it's only by

sujeto, lo estoy por fuerza;
porque, voluntariamente,
a otro hombre no me rindiera».
Viéndole ya enfurecido
con esto, que ha sido el tema   1065
de su dolor, le brindé
con la pócima, y apenas
pasó desde el vaso al pecho
el licor cuando las fuerzas
rindió al sueño, discurriendo   1070
por los miembros y las venas
un sudor frío, de modo
que, a no saber yo que era
muerte fingida, dudara
de su vida. En esto llegan   1075
las gentes de quien tú fías
el valor desta experiencia,
y, poniéndole en un coche
hasta tu cuarto le llevan,
donde prevenida estaba   1080
la majestad y grandeza
que es digna de su persona.
Allí en tu cama le acuestan,
donde, al tiempo que el letargo
haya perdido la fuerza,   1085
como a ti mismo, señor,
le sirvan, que así lo ordenas.
Y si haberte obedecido
te obliga a que yo merezca
galardón, sólo te pido   1090
– perdona mi inadvertencia –
que me digas qué es tu intento,
trayendo desta manera
a Segismundo a palacio.
BASILIO.   Clotaldo, muy justa es esa   1095
duda que tenéis, y quiero
sólo a vos satisfacerla.
A Segismundo, mi hijo,
el influjo de su estrella
– vos lo sabéis – amenaza   1100
mil desdichas y tragedias.

force, because I would never submit of my own free will to another man." Seeing him enraged by this idea, which tells the story of his grief, I invited him to drink from the potion, and hardly had the elixir passed from the glass to his breast when he surrendered his powers to sleep and a chill ran through his veins and organs such that, if I hadn't known it was a simulated death, I would have feared for his life. At this moment the people to whom you have entrusted the success of this endeavour are arriving and, placing him in a coach, are taking him to your quarters, which have been prepared with the majesty and grandeur worthy of his person. They will lay him upon your bed where, when the stupor wears off, they will attend to him as they do to you, my lord, for you have ordered it thus. And if having obeyed you has earned me any favour, I ask only – and forgive me my impropriety – that you tell me your intention in bringing Sigismund to the palace in this way.

VASILY. Clothold, your doubt is well founded, and I wish to satisfy it for you alone. The influence of my son Sigismund's star, as you know, threatens a thousand misfortunes and tragedies. I

Quiero examinar si el cielo
– que no es posible que mienta
y más habiéndonos dado
de su rigor tantas muestras   1105
en su crüel condición –
o se mitiga o se templa
por lo menos, y, vencido
con valor y con prudencia,
se desdice, porque el hombre   1110
predomina en las estrellas.
Esto quiero examinar
trayéndole donde sepa
que es mi hijo y donde haga
de su talento la prueba.   1115
Si magnánimo se vence,
reinará; pero si muestra
el ser crüel y tirano,
le volveré a su cadena.
Agora preguntarás   1120
que, para aquesta experiencia,
¿qué importó haberle traído
dormido desta manera?
Y quiero satisfacerte,
dándote a todo respuesta.   1125
Si él supiera que es mi hijo
hoy, y mañana se viera
segunda vez reducido
a su prisión y miseria,
cierto es de su condición   1130
que desesperara en ella;
porque, sabiendo quién es,
¿qué consuelo habrá que tenga?
Y así he querido dejar
abierta al daño esta puerta   1135
del decir que fue soñado
cuanto vio. Con esto llegan
a examinarse dos cosas:
su condición, la primera,
pues él, despierto, procede   1140
en cuanto imagina y piensa;
y el consuelo, la segunda,

wish to study whether the stars – which are incapable of lying, especially when they've already given us, in the prince's cruel character, so many examples of their correctness – at least soften or temper their judgment and, won over through courage and prudence, retract their prediction; for man has mastery over the stars. I wish to study this matter by bringing the prince to a place where he'll discover he's my son and have his talent put to the test. If he overcomes his inclinations through magnanimity, he shall become king; but if he shows his cruel and tyrannical nature, I will return him to his chains. Now you'll ask why, for the purposes of the experiment, it was necessary to bring him asleep in this way. And I wish to answer all your doubts. If he were to discover today that he's my son and tomorrow found himself reduced again to his chains and misery, given his character he would no doubt fall into the sin of despair, because with the knowledge of who he is, what consolation would he have? And thus I have tried to leave myself an escape from that jeopardy by telling him that everything he saw was a dream. In this way two things may be examined. First: his character, for when he awakens, his actions will show us what he imagines and thinks. Second:

	pues, aunque agora se vea	
	obedecido y después	
	a sus prisiones se vuelva,	1145
	podrá entender que soñó;	
	y hará bien cuando lo entienda,	
	porque en el mundo, Clotaldo,	
	todos los que viven sueñan.	
CLOTALDO.	Razones no me faltaran	1150
	para probar que no aciertas,	
	mas ya no tiene remedio;	
	y, según dicen las señas,	
	parece que ha despertado	
	y hacia nosotros se acerca.	1155
BASILIO.	Yo me quiero retirar;	
	tú, como ayo suyo, llega	
	y, de tantas confusiones	
	como su discurso cercan,	
	le saca con la verdad.	1160
CLOTALDO.	En fin, ¿que me das licencia	
	para que lo diga?	
BASILIO.	Sí,	
	que podrá ser, con saberla,	
	que, conocido el peligro,	
	más fácilmente se venza.	1165

(Vase BASILIO, y sale CLARÍN.)

CLARÍN.	(*Aparte.* A costa de cuatro palos	
	que el llegar aquí me cuesta	
	de un alabardero rubio	
	que barbó de su librea,	
	tengo que ver cuanto pasa;	1170
	que no hay ventana más cierta	
	que aquella que, sin rogar	
	a un ministro de boletas,	
	un hombre se trae consigo;	
	pues para todas las fiestas,	1175
	despojado y despejado,	
	se asoma a su desvergüenza.)	
CLOTALDO.	(*Aparte.* Éste es Clarín, el criado	
	de aquella, ¡ay cielos!, de aquella	
	que, tratante de desdichas,	1180
	pasó a Polonia mi afrenta.)	
	Clarín, ¿qué hay de nuevo?	

	a way to console him if he finds himself obeyed now and later reawakens in his cell, for he will conclude that he was dreaming, and he will be correct in that assumption because in this world, Clothold, everyone who lives dreams.
CLOTHOLD.	I wouldn't be lacking in reasons to prove your error, but it's too late now for, from the look of things, the prince has awoken and is drawing near.
VASILY.	I'm going to step out. You're his mentor; go to him and, with the truth, confront the many confusions that must be assailing his thoughts.
CLOTHOLD.	So you give me permission to tell him the truth?
VASILY.	Yes, for it may be that when he finds out, the danger will be more easily overcome because it's been understood.

(Exit VASILY; enter BUGLE.)

BUGLE.	*(Aside.)* At the expense of a good beating from a blond, halberd-brandishing sentry whose beard matched the colour of his livery, I've pushed my way in to see all that's happening; because the best way to get an eyeful without bribing the usher is to focus elsewhere, for if you're shameless enough, there's more to see in the stands than on the stage.
CLOTHOLD.	*(Aside.)* That's Bugle, servant to she who – Good heavens! – she who, dealing in misfortune, has relayed my offence to Poland. *[To BUGLE.]* Bugle, what's the news?

CLARÍN.	Hay,
	señor, que tu gran clemencia,
	dispuesta a vengar agravios
	de Rosaura, la aconseja 1185
	que tome su propio traje.
CLOTALDO.	Y es bien, por que no parezca
	liviandad.
CLARÍN.	Hay que, mudando
	su nombre y tomando, cuerda,
	nombre de sobrina tuya, 1190
	hoy tanto honor se acrecienta
	que dama en palacio ya
	de la singular Estrella
	vive.
CLOTALDO.	Es bien que, de una vez,
	tome su honor por mi cuenta. 1195
CLARÍN.	Hay que ella se está esperando
	que ocasión y tiempo venga
	en que vuelvas por su honor.
CLOTALDO.	Prevención segura es ésa,
	que al fin el tiempo ha de ser 1200
	quien haga esas diligencias.
CLARÍN.	Hay que ella está regalada,
	servida como una reina
	en fe de sobrina tuya,
	y hay que, viviendo con ella, 1205
	estoy yo muriendo de hambre;
	y naide de mí se acuerda,
	sin mirar que soy Clarín,
	y que, si el tal Clarín suena,
	podrá decir cuanto pasa 1210
	al Rey, a Astolfo y a Estrella;
	porque Clarín y crïado
	son dos cosas que se llevan
	con el secreto muy mal;
	y podrá ser, si me deja 1215
	el silencio de su mano,
	se cante por mí esta letra:
	«Clarín que rompe el albor
	no suena mejor».
CLOTALDO.	Tu queja está bien fundada; 1220
	yo satisfaré tu queja,
	y, en tanto, sírveme a mí.

BUGLE.	The news, my lord, is that the great generosity you show in your willingness to help Rossaura avenge her dishonour has encouraged her to resume dressing in her own clothing.
CLOTHOLD.	A good decision, so that she not be judged indecent.
BUGLE.	The news is that, changing her name and wisely calling herself your niece, she has enhanced her stature to such a degree that the remarkable Princess Stella has employed her as her lady-in-waiting.
CLOTHOLD.	It is fitting that my name be used to defend her honour once and for all.
BUGLE.	The news is that she's eagerly awaiting the moment in which you will act on behalf of her honour.
CLOTHOLD.	That's a safe bet, for good things come to those who wait.
BUGLE.	The news is that she is being pampered and attended to like a queen, thanks to calling herself your niece. And the news is that I, living beside her, am dying of hunger, for no one thinks about me, forgetting that my name is Bugle, and that if such a Bugle sounds off, it can inform the king, Aistulf, and Stella of everything that's happening; because bugles and servants are two things that don't get on very well with secrecy. And if silence ever abandons me, I may become the subject of that familiar tune, *A bugle that heralds the sun / Plays second to none.*
CLOTHOLD.	Your complaint is well founded, and I shall attend to it; in the meantime, you may work for me.

CLARÍN.   Pues ya Segismundo llega.

(Salen músicos cantando, y criados, dando de vestir a SEGISMUNDO, que sale como asombrado.)

SEGISMUNDO.   ¡Válgame el cielo, qué veo!
¡Válgame el cielo, qué miro!   1225
¡Con poco espanto lo admiro!
¡Con mucha duda lo creo!
¿Yo en palacios suntuosos?
¿Yo entre telas y brocados?
¿Yo cercado de crïados   1230
tan lucidos y briosos?
¿Yo despertar de dormir
en lecho tan excelente?
¿Yo en medio de tanta gente
que me sirva de vestir?   1235
Decir que sueño es engaño;
bien sé que despierto estoy.
¿Yo Segismundo no soy?
Dadme, cielos, desengaño.
Decidme: ¿qué pudo ser   1240
esto que a mi fantasía
sucedió mientras dormía,
que aquí me he llegado a ver?
Pero sea lo que fuere,
¿quién me mete en discurrir?   1245
Dejarme quiero servir,
y venga lo que viniere.

CRIADO 2.   ¡Qué melancólico está!

CRIADO 1.   Pues ¿a quién le sucediera
esto que no lo estuviera?   1250

CLARÍN.   A mí.

CRIADO 2.   Llega a hablarle ya.

CRIADO 1.   ¿Volverán a cantar?

SEGISMUNDO.   No,
no quiero que canten más.

CRIADO 2.   Como tan suspenso estás,
quise divertirte.

SEGISMUNDO.   Yo   1255
no tengo de divertir
con sus voces mis pesares;
las músicas militares
sólo he gustado de oír.

BUGLE.   Well here comes Sigismund.

*(Enter MUSICIANS in song and SERVANTS who are busily dressing SIGISMUND.
The prince enters in astonishment.)*

SIGISMUND.   Heaven help me, what am I seeing! Heaven help me, what am
                   I watching! My doubt surpasses my dread. I, in a sumptuous
                   palace? I, dressed in fine fabrics and brocades? I, surrounded
                   by such elegant and refined servants? I, waking from sleep
                   in such an exquisite bed? I, amid so many people intent on
                   dressing me? To say I'm dreaming is deception; I know
                   quite well that I'm awake. Am I not Sigismund? Heavens,
                   reveal the truth to me. Tell me: what could have befallen my
                   imagination as I slept, that I should find myself here? But
                   whatever it was, why waste time wondering about it? Better
                   to enjoy being served and let come what may.
SERVANT 2.   He's so melancholy!
SERVANT 1.   Well who wouldn't be, after going through this?
BUGLE.   Me.
SERVANT 2.   Go speak to him now.
SERVANT 1.   *[To SIGISMUND.]* Shall I have them sing again?
SIGISMUND.   No, I don't want any more singing.
SERVANT 2.   You seem so shocked, I thought you might enjoy some
                   entertainment.
SIGISMUND.   I can't comfort my sorrows with their voices; military
                   marches are the only music I enjoy listening to.

CLOTALDO.	Vuestra Alteza, gran señor,	1260
	me dé su mano a besar;	
	que el primero le ha de dar	
	esta obediencia mi honor.	
SEGISMUNDO.	(*Aparte.* Clotaldo es; pues ¿cómo así,	
	quien en prisión me maltrata,	1265
	con tal respeto me trata?	
	¿Qué es lo que pasa por mí?)	
CLOTALDO.	Con la grande confusión	
	que el nuevo estado te da,	
	mil dudas padecerá	1270
	el discurso y la razón.	
	Pero ya librarte quiero	
	de todas — si puede ser — ,	
	porque has, señor, de saber	
	que eres príncipe heredero	1275
	de Polonia. Si has estado	
	retirado y escondido,	
	por obedecer ha sido	
	a la inclemencia del hado,	
	que mil tragedias consiente	1280
	a este imperio cuando en él	
	el soberano laurel	
	corone tu augusta frente.	
	Mas fiando a tu atención	
	que vencerás las estrellas,	1285
	porque es posible vencellas	
	a un magnánimo varón,	
	a palacio te han traído	
	de la torre en que vivías,	
	mientras al sueño tenías	1290
	el espíritu rendido.	
	Tu padre, el Rey mi señor,	
	vendrá a verte, y dél sabrás,	
	Segismundo, lo demás.	
SEGISMUNDO.	Pues vil, infame y traidor,	1295
	¿qué tengo más que saber,	
	después de saber quién soy,	
	para mostrar desde hoy	
	mi soberbia y mi poder?	
	¿Cómo a tu patria le has hecho	1300

CLOTHOLD.   Your Highness, my lord, allow me to kiss your hand; for my
                   honour will be the first to offer you obedience.

SIGISMUND.   *(Aside.)* This is Clothold, so how is it that he who mistreats me
                   in prison now treats me with such respect? What's happening
                   to me?

CLOTHOLD.   In the immense confusion of your new surroundings, your
                   thought and reason must be plagued by thousands of doubts.
                   But I want to free you from all of them if – if that's possible
                   – because you need to know, my lord, that you are the Crown
                   Prince of Poland. If you have lived secluded and hidden from
                   sight, it was due to the inclemency of fate, which sanctions a
                   thousand tragedies for this realm once the kingly laurel leaf
                   adorns your noble brow. Yet in the hope that, with caution,
                   you might overcome the stars, for a virtuous man can do so,
                   you've been brought to the palace from the tower in which
                   you lived while your spirit was in the power of sleep. Your
                   father, the king my lord, will come to see you shortly, and
                   from him, Sigismund, you'll learn the rest.

SIGISMUND.   Why you vile, contemptible traitor! What more need I learn,
                   now that I know my true identity, in order to proclaim my
                   pride and power from this point forward? How could you

	tal traición que me ocultaste	
	a mí, pues que me negaste,	
	contra razón y derecho,	
	este estado?	
CLOTALDO.	¡Ay de mí triste!	
SEGISMUNDO.	Traidor fuiste con la ley,	1305
	lisonjero con el Rey,	
	y crüel conmigo fuiste;	
	y así el Rey, la ley y yo,	
	entre desdichas tan fieras,	
	te condenan a que mueras	1310
	a mis manos.	
CRIADO 2.	¡Señor!	
SEGISMUNDO.	No	
	me estorbe nadie, que es vana	
	diligencia; y, ¡vive Dios!,	
	si os ponéis delante vos,	
	que os eche por la ventana.	1315
CRIADO 1.	¡Huye, Clotaldo!	
CLOTALDO.	(*Aparte.* ¡Ay de ti,	
	que soberbia vas mostrando	
	sin saber que estás soñando!)	

(Vase.)

CRIADO 2.	Advierte...	
SEGISMUNDO.	Apartad de aquí.	
CRIADO 2.	... que a su Rey obedeció.	1320
SEGISMUNDO.	En lo que no es justa ley,	
	no ha de obedecer al Rey;	
	y su príncipe era yo.	
CRIADO 2.	Él no debió examinar	
	si era bien hecho o mal hecho.	1325
SEGISMUNDO.	Que estáis mal con vos, sospecho,	
	pues me dais que replicar.	
CLARÍN.	Dice el príncipe muy bien,	
	y vos hicistes muy mal.	
CRIADO 1.	¿Quién os dio licencia igual?	1330
CLARÍN.	Yo me la he tomado.	
SEGISMUNDO.	¿Quién	
	eres tú? Di.	

betray your fatherland by hiding me away, for you have denied me, against reason and law, my entitlement?

CLOTHOLD. Oh, miserable me!

SIGISMUND. You were a traitor to the law, a sycophant to the king, and a cruel jailor to me; and thus the king, the law, and I, amid such monstrous misfortune, condemn you to die by my hands.

SERVANT 2. My lord...

SIGISMUND. Let no one try to stop me, for it would be a useless endeavour and, by God, if you get in my way, I'll throw you out that window.

SERVANT 1. Flee, Clothold.

CLOTHOLD. *(Aside.)* Poor Sigismund, what excessive pride you demonstrate, unaware that it's all a dream! *(He flees.)*

SERVANT 2. Beware that...

SIGISMUND. Out of my way.

SERVANT 2. ...he was obeying his king.

SIGISMUND. When the law isn't just, the king needn't be obeyed; and at any rate, I was his prince.

SERVANT 2. It wasn't for him to decide whether it was just or not.

SIGISMUND. You're asking for it, it would seem, with all that yapping.

BUGLE. What the prince says is very right, and what you did was very wrong.

SERVANT 1. Who gave you permission to speak?

BUGLE. I took it upon myself.

SIGISMUND. Who are you, pray tell?

CLARÍN.   Entremetido,
                    y deste oficio soy jefe,
                    porque soy el mequetrefe
                    mayor que se ha conocido.   1335

SEGISMUNDO.   Tú solo, en tan nuevos mundos,
                    me has agradado.

CLARÍN.   Señor,
                    soy un grande agradador
                    de todos los Segismundos.

(Sale ASTOLFO.)

ASTOLFO.   ¡Feliz mil veces el día,   1340
                    oh príncipe, que os mostráis
                    sol de Polonia, y llenáis
                    de resplandor y alegría
                    todos estos horizontes
                    con tan divino arrebol,   1345
                    pues que salís como el sol
                    de debajo de los montes!
                    Salid, pues, y aunque tan tarde
                    se corona vuestra frente
                    del laurel resplandeciente,   1350
                    tarde muera.
SEGISMUNDO.   Dios os guarde.
ASTOLFO.   El no haberme conocido
                    sólo por disculpa os doy
                    de no honrarme más; yo soy
                    Astolfo, duque he nacido   1355
                    de Moscovia, y primo vuestro.
                    Haya igualdad en los dos.
SEGISMUNDO.   Si digo que os guarde Dios,
                    ¿bastante agrado no os muestro?
                    Pero ya que, haciendo alarde   1360
                    de quien sois, desto os quejáis,
                    otra vez que me veáis
                    le diré a Dios que no os guarde.
CRIADO 2.   *(A ASTOLFO.)* Vuestra Alteza considere
                    que, como en montes nacido,   1365
                    con todos ha procedido.
                    (A SEGISMUNDO.) Astolfo, señor, prefiere…

BUGLE.	A busybody, a job in which I reign supreme, because I'm the nosiest person on the face of the earth.
SIGISMUND.	You're the only one in this princely world I find gratifying.
BUGLE.	My lord, I'm a great gratifier of all worldly princes.

(Enter AISTULF [hat in hand].)

AISTULF.	Infinitely lucky is this day, O prince, in which you proclaim yourself Poland's sun and fill its horizons with the brightness and bliss of your divine radiance, for you appear like the sun from beneath the mountains! Rise, then, and may the shining laurel leaf, so slow in crowning your brow, be as slow in withering. *[He dons his hat.]*
SIGISMUND.	God keep you.
AISTULF.	I'll forgive your meagre greeting only because you don't recognize me. I am Aistulf, Duke of Muscovy, and your cousin; we must treat each other as equals.
SIGISMUND.	I said "God keep you." What more do you want? But since you don't find my greetings suitable to your high birth, next time I'll say "God damn you!"
SERVANT 2.	*(To AISTULF.)* Consider, your highness, that he was raised in the mountains and treats everyone accordingly. *(To SIGISMUND.)* Aistulf, my lord, prefers to be addressed as…

SEGISMUNDO.	Cansóme cómo llegó
	grave a hablarme, y lo primero
	que hizo, se puso el sombrero. 1370
CRIADO 2.	Es grande.
SEGISMUNDO.	Mayor soy yo.
CRIADO 2.	Con todo eso, entre los dos,
	que haya más respeto es bien
	que entre los demás.
SEGISMUNDO.	¿Y quién
	os mete conmigo a vos? 1375

(Sale ESTRELLA.)

ESTRELLA.	Vuestra Alteza, señor, sea
	muchas veces bien venido
	al dosel, que agradecido
	le recibe y le desea;
	adonde, a pesar de engaños, 1380
	viva augusto y eminente;
	donde su vida se cuente
	por siglos y no por años.
SEGISMUNDO.	Dime tú agora, ¿quién es
	esta beldad soberana? 1385
	¿Quién es esta diosa humana
	a cuyos divinos pies
	postra el cielo su arrebol?
	¿Quién es esta mujer bella?
CLARÍN.	Es, señor, tu prima Estrella. 1390
SEGISMUNDO.	Mejor dijeras el sol.
	Aunque el parabién es bien
	darme del bien que conquisto,
	de sólo haberos hoy visto
	os admito el parabién; 1395
	y así, del llegarme a ver
	con el bien que no merezco,
	el parabién agradezco.
	Estrella, que amanecer
	podéis y dar alegría 1400
	al más luciente farol,
	¿qué dejáis que hacer al sol
	si os levantáis con el día?
	Dadme a besar vuestra mano,
	en cuya copa de nieve 1405
	el aura candores bebe.

SIGISMUND.	I found it irritating the way he spoke to me so gravely, and the first thing he did was don his hat.
SERVANT 2.	He's titled.
SIGISMUND.	I'm more entitled!
SERVANT 2.	All the same, it's fitting that there be greater decorum between the two of you than with others.
SIGISMUND.	Who asked for your opinion anyway?

(Enter STELLA.)

STELLA.	Your highness, my lord, I welcome you warmly to the royal family, which gratefully receives you and desires your presence, and where, despite past deceptions, we wish you an august and celebrated reign and a life measured in centuries rather than years.
SIGISMUND.	Tell me now, who is this imperial beauty? Who is this human goddess at whose divine feet Heaven surrenders its radiance? Who is this beautiful woman?
BUGLE.	She is, my lord, your cousin Stella.
SIGISMUND.	Stella...Stellar? More like Solar! *[To STELLA.]* Although it were well to wish me well on the wealth that I inherit, I deserve more well-wishing just for having seen you today; and thus, I appreciate your well-wishing for finding myself before such unmerited wealth. Stella – whose waking is enough to please the brightest star – what is left for the sun to do if you rise with the day? Allow me to kiss your hand, from whose snowy chalice the gentle breeze drinks in radiance.

ESTRELLA.	Sed más galán cortesano.
ASTOLFO.	(*Aparte.* Si él toma la mano, yo soy perdido.)
CRIADO 2.	*(Aparte.* El pesar sé
	de Astolfo, y le estorbaré.) 1410
	Advierte, señor, que no
	es justo atreverte así,
	y estando Astolfo...
SEGISMUNDO.	¿No digo
	que vos no os metáis conmigo?
CRIADO 2.	Digo lo que es justo.
SEGISMUNDO.	A mí 1415
	todo eso me causa enfado.
	Nada me parece justo
	en siendo contra mi gusto.
CRIADO 2.	Pues yo, señor, he escuchado
	de ti que en lo justo es bien 1420
	obedecer y servir.
SEGISMUNDO.	También oíste decir
	que, por un balcón, a quien
	me canse, sabré arrojar.
CRIADO 2.	Con los hombres como yo 1425
	no puede hacerse eso.
SEGISMUNDO.	¿No?
	Por Dios, que lo he de probar.

(Cógele en los brazos y éntrase, y todos tras él, y torna a salir.)

ASTOLFO.	¿Qué es esto que llego a ver?
ESTRELLA.	¡Llegad todos a ayudar!

(Vase.)

SEGISMUNDO.	Cayó del balcón al mar. 1430
	¡Vive Dios, que pudo ser!
ASTOLFO.	Pues medid con más espacio
	vuestras acciones severas,
	que lo que hay de hombres a fieras
	hay desde un monte a palacio. 1435
SEGISMUNDO.	Pues en dando, tan severo,
	en hablar con entereza,
	quizá no hallaréis cabeza
	en que se os tenga el sombrero.

(Vase ASTOLFO y sale el REY.)

STELLA.	Be a little more gentlemanly in the presence of the court.
AISTULF.	*(Aside.)* If he takes her hand, I'm finished!
SERVANT 2.	*(Aside.)* Aistulf's dismay is palpable; I must put a stop to this. *(To SIGISMUND.)* Beware, my lord, that it's not right to be so forward, and Aistulf is…
SIGISMUND.	Didn't I tell you to stay out of my way?
SERVANT 2.	I'm only saying what's right.
SIGISMUND.	Everything you say annoys me. Nothing is right that contradicts my delight.
SERVANT 2.	But my lord, I remember hearing you say that it's well to obey and serve what's right.
SIGISMUND.	You also heard me say that I'd throw anyone who annoyed me off that balcony.
SERVANT 2.	Men of my standing can't be treated that way.
SIGISMUND.	Oh no? So help me God, I'll test that theory!

(He grabs the SERVANT and rushes offstage, followed by the others. He returns shortly [with the others, minus the SERVANT].)

AISTULF.	I can't believe what I've just seen!
STELLA.	Help, everyone! *(Exit.)*
SIGISMUND.	Did you see how he dropped from the balcony to the sea below? By God, the test succeeded!
AISTULF.	You should keep your rash impulses in greater check; for what separates men from beasts also separates a mountainside from a palace.
SIGISMUND.	If you persist in acting so gravely and speaking with such presumption, next time you might not have a head to wear that hat on.

(Exit AISTULF; enter VASILY.)

BASILIO.	¿Qué ha sido esto?
SEGISMUNDO.	Nada ha sido. 1440
	A un hombre que me ha cansado
	de ese balcón he arrojado.
CLARÍN.	Que es el Rey está advertido.
BASILIO.	¿Tan presto una vida cuesta
	tu venida el primer día? 1445
SEGISMUNDO.	Díjome que no podía
	hacerse y gané la apuesta.
BASILIO.	Pésame mucho que cuando,
	príncipe, a verte he venido,
	pensando hallarte advertido, 1450
	de hados y estrellas triunfando,
	con tanto rigor te vea,
	y que la primera acción
	que has hecho en esta ocasión
	un grave homicidio sea. 1455
	¿Con qué amor llegar podré
	a darte agora mis brazos,
	si de sus soberbios lazos,
	que están enseñados sé
	a dar muerte? ¿Quién llegó 1460
	a ver desnudo el puñal
	que dio una herida mortal
	que no temiese? ¿Quién vio,
	sangriento, el lugar adonde
	a otro hombre dieron muerte 1465
	que no sienta? Que el más fuerte
	a su natural responde.
	Yo así, que en tus brazos miro
	desta muerte el instrumento
	y miro el lugar sangriento, 1470
	de tus brazos me retiro;
	y, aunque en amorosos lazos
	ceñir tu cuello pensé,
	sin ellos me volveré,
	que tengo miedo a tus brazos. 1475
SEGISMUNDO.	Sin ellos me podré estar
	como me he estado hasta aquí;
	que un padre que contra mí
	tanto rigor sabe usar

VASILY.   What's going on here?
SIGISMUND.   Nothing. I threw a man who annoyed me off that balcony.
BUGLE.   *[To SIGISMUND.]* Be aware that you're speaking to the king.
VASILY.   Your first day here has already cost a life?
SIGISMUND.   He told me it couldn't be done, and I won the bet.
VASILY.   It's very distressing that, when I come to see you as prince, expecting to find you mindful, triumphing over fate and the stars, I find you acting with such severity that your first deed in power is a grave murder. How can I offer you love with open arms now, when I know your prideful embrace is trained in bringing death? Who ever looked without fear upon a naked dagger fresh from the kill? Who ever looked without emotion upon the bloody spot in which a man was murdered? Even the strongest among us responds to his instinct. And thus, seeing in your arms the instrument of this murder and recognizing the bloody spot where it happened, I withdraw from your arms; and, although I had planned to encircle your neck with loving embraces, I shall turn away empty-handed, for I fear the intent of your arms.
SIGISMUND.   I can survive without your embraces as I have until now, for when a father is capable of using such severity against me

	que, con condición ingrata,	1480
	de su lado me desvía,	
	como a una fiera me cría	
	y como a un monstruo me trata,	
	y mi muerte solicita,	
	de poca importancia fue	1485
	que los brazos no me dé	
	cuando el ser de hombre me quita.	
BASILIO.	Al cielo y a Dios pluguiera	
	que a dártele no llegara;	
	pues ni tu voz escuchara,	1490
	ni tu atrevimiento viera.	
SEGISMUNDO.	Si no me le hubieras dado,	
	no me quejara de ti;	
	pero una vez dado, sí,	
	por habérmele quitado;	1495
	que, aunque el dar el acción es	
	más noble y más singular,	
	es mayor bajeza el dar	
	para quitarlo después.	
BASILIO.	Bien me agradeces el verte,	1500
	de un humilde y pobre preso,	
	príncipe ya.	
SEGISMUNDO.	Pues en eso,	
	¿qué tengo que agradecerte?	
	Tirano de mi albedrío,	
	si, viejo y caduco, estás	1505
	muriéndote, ¿qué me das?	
	¿Dasme más de lo que es mío?	
	Mi padre eres y mi rey;	
	luego toda esta grandeza	
	me da la naturaleza	1510
	por derechos de su ley.	
	Luego, aunque esté en este estado,	
	obligado no te quedo,	
	y pedirte cuentas puedo	
	del tiempo que me has quitado	1515
	libertad, vida y honor;	
	y así, agradéceme a mí	
	que yo no cobre de ti,	
	pues eres tú mi deudor.	
BASILIO.	Bárbaro eres y atrevido.	1520
	Cumplió su palabra el cielo;	

and ungratefully casts me off, raises me like a beast, treats me like a monster, and solicits my death, it matters little that he withhold his embraces, for he has already denied me my humanity.

VASILY.

By God and Heaven above, I wish I had never brought you into existence so as not to hear your voice and see your defiance now.

SIGISMUND.

If you'd never brought me into existence, I'd have no complaint with you; but since you did, I do, because you then took it from me; for though to give is the noblest and most unique of all actions, to give only to take away later is the most despicable.

VASILY.

What thanks I get for turning you from a poor and humble prisoner into the prince of Poland!

SIGISMUND.

Well what's there to thank you for in that? You've been a tyrant to my free will. Old and decrepit, you're already at death's door, so what can you give me? Anything more than what's rightfully mine? You're my father and my king; thus all this splendour is mine by the rights of natural law. Thus, whatever rank I now enjoy I owe you nothing for, and I could even denounce you for the time you've kept me without liberty, life, and honour; so it is you who should thank me for not exacting from you what you owe.

VASILY.

You are barbaric and reckless; the heavens have kept their

	y así, para él mismo apelo.	
	¡Soberbio, desvanecido!	
	Y aunque sepas ya quién eres	
	y desengañado estés,	1525
	y aunque en un lugar te ves	
	donde a todos te prefieres,	
	mira bien lo que te advierto:	
	que seas humilde y blando,	
	porque quizá estás soñando,	1530
	aunque ves que estás despierto.	

(Vase.)

SEGISMUNDO.   ¿Que quizá soñando estoy,
aunque despierto me veo?
No sueño, pues toco y creo
lo que he sido y lo que soy.   1535
Y aunque agora te arrepientas,
poco remedio tendrás:
sé quién soy y no podrás,
aunque suspires y sientas,
quitarme el haber nacido   1540
desta corona heredero.
Y, si me viste primero
a las prisiones rendido,
fue porque ignoré quién era;
pero ya informado estoy   1545
de quién soy y sé que soy
un compuesto de hombre y fiera.

(Sale ROSAURA, dama.)

ROSAURA.   (*Aparte.* Siguiendo a Estrella vengo;
y gran temor de hallar a Astolfo tengo,
que Clotaldo desea   1550
que no sepa quién soy y no me vea,
porque dice que importa al honor mío;
y de Clotaldo fío
su efeto, pues le debo agradecida
aquí el amparo de mi honor y vida.)   1555
CLARÍN.   ¿Qué es lo que te ha agradado
más de cuanto hoy has visto y admirado?
SEGISMUNDO.   Nada me ha suspendido,

word, and thus I appeal to the heavens now. So full of pride and presumption you are! And though you may now know your lineage and understand the deception in which you have lived, and though you find yourself in a place where you consider yourself superior to everyone else, take my advice seriously: act with humility and gentleness, for you might be dreaming even though your think you're awake. *(Exit.)*

SIGISMUND.
Might be dreaming even though I think I'm awake? Impossible, for I feel and perceive the continuity between my past and present. And though you may be having second thoughts, there's no going back now; I know who I am, and you cannot, no matter how much you wail and moan, take away my birthright to this crown. And if you saw me before, weighed down by my chains, that was when I was unaware of my identity. But I know who I am now, and I know that I'm a composite of man and beast.

(Enter ROSSAURA, dressed as a lady-in-waiting.)

ROSSAURA.
(Aside.) Now that I'm in the service of Stella, I'm in constant fear of running into Aistulf, for Clothold doesn't want him to know who I am or to see me because he says it's important for my honour. And I trust Clothold's intentions because I owe him a debt of gratitude for the refuge he has given my life and honour here in the palace.

BUGLE.
What has pleased you most of all the wondrous things you've seen today?

SIGISMUND.
Nothing has shocked me, for I was prepared for everything.

	que todo lo tenía prevenido;	
	mas, si admirar hubiera	1560
	algo en el mundo, la hermosura fuera	
	de la mujer. Leía	
	una vez, en los libros que tenía,	
	que lo que a Dios mayor estudio debe	
	era el hombre, por ser un mundo breve.	1565
	Mas ya que lo es recelo	
	la mujer, pues ha sido un breve cielo,	
	y más beldad encierra	
	que el hombre, cuanto va de cielo a tierra.	
	Y más si es la que miro.	1570
ROSAURA.	(*Aparte.* El Príncipe está aquí; yo me retiro.)	
SEGISMUNDO.	¡Oye, mujer, detente!	
	No juntes el ocaso y el oriente,	
	huyendo al primer paso;	
	que, juntando el oriente y el ocaso,	1575
	la lumbre y sombra fría,	
	serás sin duda síncopa del día.	
	(*Aparte.* Pero, ¿qué es lo que veo?)	
ROSAURA.	(*Aparte.* Lo mismo que estoy viendo dudo y creo.)	
SEGISMUNDO.	(*Aparte.* Yo he visto esta belleza otra vez.)	1580
ROSAURA.	(*Aparte.* Yo esta pompa, esta grandeza	
	he visto reducida a una estrecha prisión.)	
SEGISMUNDO.	(*Aparte.* Ya hallé mi vida.)	
	Mujer, que aqueste nombre	
	es el mejor requiebro para el hombre,	1585
	¿quién eres que, sin verte,	
	adoración me debes, y de suerte	
	por la fe te conquisto,	
	que me persuado a que otra vez te he visto?	
	¿Quién eres, mujer bella?	1590
ROSAURA.	(*Aparte.* Disimular me importa.) Soy de Estrella	
	una infelice dama.	
SEGISMUNDO.	No digas tal; di el sol, a cuya llama	
	aquella Estrella vive,	
	pues de tus rayos resplandor recibe.	1595
	Yo vi, en reino de olores,	
	que presidía entre comunes flores	
	la deidad de la rosa,	
	y era su emperatriz por más hermosa;	

Yet, if I had to name something truly amazing in the world, it would be the beauty of woman. I once read in my books that what cost God the greatest amount of effort was man, for he is a world writ small. Be that as it may, woman causes me more unease, for she is Heaven writ small and is as superior to man in beauty as Heaven is to earth, especially the one I'm looking at now.

ROSSAURA. *(Aside.)* The prince is here; I shall withdraw.

SIGISMUND. Hey, woman, stop! Don't couple sunset and sunrise with your speedy retreat; for in coupling sunrise and sunset, warmth and cold shadow, you will no doubt syncopate the day.

(Aside.) But what's this I'm seeing?

ROSSAURA. *(Aside.)* I can't believe my own eyes.

SIGISMUND. *(Aside.)* I've seen this beauty before.

ROSSAURA. *(Aside.)* I've seen this splendour, this grandeur reduced to the confines of a narrow cell.

SIGISMUND. *(Aside.)* My life has returned.

[To ROSSAURA.] Woman – for this term is the best compliment a man can pay – who are you, that without recognizing you I recall your affection, and my spirit grasps for you so strongly that I'm convinced I've seen you before? Who are you, beautiful woman?

ROSSAURA. *(Aside.)* I must keep my identity a secret.

[To SIGISMUND.] Just a lowly lady-in-waiting to Princess Stella.

SIGISMUND. You misspeak; you are the sun on whose flame that Stellar beauty lives, for she takes her resplendence from your rays. I have seen, in the scented realm, the deity of the rose rule over the ordinary flowers, empress through her greater beauty; I

yo vi, entre piedras finas,   1600
de la docta academia de sus minas,
preferir el diamante,
y ser su emperador por más brillante;
yo, en esas cortes bellas
de la inquieta república de estrellas,   1605
vi en el lugar primero,
por rey de las estrellas, el lucero;
yo, en esferas perfectas,
llamando el sol a cortes los planetas,
le vi que presidía   1610
como mayor oráculo del día.
Pues ¿cómo, si entre flores, entre estrellas,
piedras, signos, planetas, las más bellas
prefieren, tú has servido
la de menos beldad, habiendo sido,   1615
por más bella y hermosa,
sol, lucero, diamante, estrella y rosa?

(Sale CLOTALDO al paño.)

CLOTALDO.	*(Aparte.* A Segismundo reducir deseo,	
	porque en fin le he crïado. Mas ¿qué veo?)	
ROSAURA.	Tu favor reverencio.	1620
	Respóndate, retórico, el silencio:	
	cuando tan torpe la razón se halla,	
	mejor habla, señor, quien mejor calla.	
SEGISMUNDO.	No has de ausentarte, espera.	
	¿Cómo quieres dejar desa manera	1625
	a escuras mi sentido?	
ROSAURA.	Esta licencia a Vuestra Alteza pido.	
SEGISMUNDO.	Irte con tal violencia	
	no es pedir, es tomarte la licencia.	
ROSAURA.	Pues si tú no la das, tomarla espero.	1630
SEGISMUNDO.	Harás que de cortés pase a grosero,	
	porque la resistencia	
	es veneno crüel de mi paciencia.	
ROSAURA.	Pues cuando ese veneno,	
	de furia, de rigor y saña lleno,	1635
	la paciencia venciera,	
	mi respeto no osara ni pudiera.	
SEGISMUNDO.	Sólo por ver si puedo,	
	harás que pierda a tu hermosura el miedo;	

have seen, in the mines of the learned academy of precious stones, the diamond crowned emperor because of his greater brilliance; I have seen, in the beautiful palaces of the restless constellations, the morning star, first in rank, rule as king; I have seen, in the perfect spheres of heaven, the sun call the planets to court, presiding over them as a great oracle of light. So how is it that flowers, stones, constellations, and planets defer to the most beautiful among them, yet you serve one of lesser beauty while you, ever more beautiful and lovely, are the sun, the morning star, the diamond, and the rose?

(Enter CLOTHOLD, unseen.)

CLOTHOLD.	*(Aside.)* I must restrain Sigismund, for I'm the one, after all, who raised him. But what's this I'm seeing now?
ROSSAURA.	I cherish your kindness, but silence will be my most eloquent response; when reason falters, my lord, the most articulate are those who keep quiet. *[She turns to exit.]*
SIGISMUND.	Do not leave; wait. How can you wish to leave my senses in the dark like that?
ROSSAURA.	I request Your Highness's permission.
SIGISMUND.	To go so abruptly is not a request; it's a demand.
ROSSAURA.	Well, if you don't grant me permission, I'll have no other choice.
SIGISMUND.	You're going to force me from politeness to boorishness, because resistance is a cruel venom to my patience.
ROSSAURA.	Well even if that venom, full of fury, severity, and wrath, were to overcome your patience, it wouldn't dare attack my honour, nor could it.
SIGISMUND.	You'll make me lose the inhibitions your beauty inspires in

	que soy muy inclinado	1640
	a vencer lo imposible. Hoy he arrojado	
	dese balcón a un hombre que decía	
	que hacerse no podía;	
	y así, por ver si puedo, cosa es llana	
	que arrojaré tu honor por la ventana.	1645

CLOTALDO.   (*Aparte*. Mucho se va empeñando.
             ¿Qué he de hacer, cielos, cuando,
             tras un loco deseo,
             mi honor segunda vez a riesgo veo?)

ROSAURA.   No en vano prevenía   1650
             a este reino infeliz tu tiranía
             escándalos tan fuertes
             de delitos, traiciones, iras, muertes.
             Mas ¿qué ha de hacer un hombre,
             que de humano no tiene más que el nombre,   1655
             atrevido, inhumano,
             crüel, soberbio, bárbaro y tirano,
             nacido entre las fieras?

SEGISMUNDO. Porque tú ese baldón no me dijeras
             tan cortés me mostraba,   1660
             pensando que con esto te obligaba.
             Mas, si lo soy hablando deste modo,
             has de decirlo, ¡vive Dios!, por todo.
             ¡Hola, dejadnos solos, y esa puerta
             se cierre, y no entre nadie!

(Vase CLARÍN.)

ROSAURA.   (*Aparte*. Yo soy muerta.)   1665
             ¡Advierte!

SEGISMUNDO. Soy tirano,
             y ya pretendes reducirme en vano.

CLOTALDO.   (*Aparte*. ¡Oh, qué lance tan fuerte!
             Saldré a estorbarlo, aunque me dé la muerte.)
             ¡Señor, atiende, mira!   1670

SEGISMUNDO. Segunda vez me has provocado a ira,
             viejo caduco y loco.
             ¿Mi enojo y mi rigor tienes en poco?
             ¿Cómo hasta aquí has llegado?

CLOTALDO.   De los acentos desta voz llamado,   1675
             a decirte que seas
             más apacible, si reinar deseas;

	me, just to see if I can, for I'm strongly inclined to overcome the impossible. Today I threw a man off that balcony who said it couldn't be done; and thus, have no doubt that I'll throw your honour out the window, just to see if I can.
CLOTHOLD.	*(Aside.)* His rashness knows no bounds. What am I to do, heavens, before such mad desire when I find my honour at risk a second time?
ROSSAURA.	Not in vain were the warnings that this unlucky realm would suffer, at the hands of your tyranny, terrible upheavals of crime, treason, wrath, and death. Yet what is to be expected of a man who is human in name only: reckless, inhuman, cruel, prideful, barbaric, and tyrannical, a man born among beasts?
SIGISMUND.	Precisely so you wouldn't hurl that insult at me, I was polite with you, thinking I could win you over with such measures. But if this is what you call barbaric, then I might as well live up to your insults. *[To BUGLE.]* You there, leave us alone, close the door, and make sure no one comes in.

(Exit BUGLE.)

ROSSAURA.	*(Aside.)* I'm finished! *[To SIGISMUND.]* Beware…
SIGISMUND.	I'm a tyrant, remember? So your attempts to restrain me are in vain.
CLOTHOLD.	*(Aside.)* Oh, what an awful predicament! I must stop him, even if he kills me. *[To SIGISMUND.]* My lord, listen to reason.
SIGISMUND.	This is the second time you've provoked my ire, you decrepit old madman. Do you take my anger and severity lightly? How did you get in here?
CLOTHOLD.	Summoned by the cries of her voice, I'm here to tell you to

| | y no, por verte ya de todos dueño, seas crüel, porque quizá es un sueño. | |
| SEGISMUNDO. | A rabia me provocas cuando la luz del desengaño tocas. Veré, dándote muerte, si es sueño o si es verdad. | 1680 |

(Al ir a sacar la daga, se la tiene CLOTALDO y se arrodilla.)

CLOTALDO.	Yo desta suerte librar mi vida espero.	
SEGISMUNDO.	¡Quita la osada mano del acero!	1685
CLOTALDO.	Hasta que gente venga, que tu rigor y cólera detenga, no he de soltarte.	
ROSAURA.	¡Ay cielos!	
SEGISMUNDO.	Suelta, digo, caduco loco, bárbaro, enemigo, o será desta suerte *(Luchan.)* el darte agora entre mis brazos muerte.	1690
ROSAURA.	¡Acudid todos presto, que matan a Clotaldo!	

(Vase ROSAURA. Sale ASTOLFO a tiempo que cae CLOTALDO a sus pies, y él se pone en medio).

ASTOLFO.	Pues ¿qué es esto, príncipe generoso? ¿Así se mancha acero tan brïoso en una sangre helada? Vuelva a la vaina tu lucida espada.	1695
SEGISMUNDO.	En viéndola teñida en esa infame sangre.	
ASTOLFO.	Ya su vida tomó a mis pies sagrado; y de algo ha de servirme haber llegado.	1700
SEGISMUNDO.	Sírvate de morir, pues desta suerte también sabré vengarme con tu muerte de aquel pasado enojo.	
ASTOLFO.	Yo defiendo mi vida: así la majestad no ofendo.	1705

(Sacan las espadas, y salen el REY BASILIO y ESTRELLA.)

be more pleasant if you desire to rule and that you needn't resort to cruelty to assert yourself over others, because this may be a dream.

SIGISMUND.   You provoke my rage by lecturing me about reality. I'll kill you and test whether this is a dream or reality.

(As he goes to unsheathe his sword, CLOTHOLD detains him and kneels before him.)

CLOTHOLD.   I'm hoping this gesture will spare my life.

SIGISMUND.   Take your brazen hand off my blade.

CLOTHOLD.   Until someone arrives who can restrain your severity and quick temper, I shall not let you go.

ROSSAURA.   Good heavens!

SIGISMUND.   Let go I say, you decrepit madman, you barbaric fiend, or... *(They fight.)* ...I'll kill you with my bare hands.

ROSSAURA.   Come quickly, everyone, he's killing Clothold! *(Exit.)*

(As AISTULF enters, CLOTHOLD falls at his feet, and the duke steps between the two antagonists.)

AISTULF.   What's all this about, gentle prince? You would tarnish your valiant blade with an old man's blood? Return your illustrious sword to its sheath.

SIGISMUND.   As soon as I've drenched it in his contemptible blood.

AISTULF.   His life has sought refuge at my feet; I must give some purpose to my arrival.

SIGISMUND.   Let death be your purpose; that way I can also avenge your earlier insolence.

AISTULF.   I act in self-defence, not lese-majesty.

(They unsheathe their swords. Enter VASILY and STELLA.)

CLOTALDO.	¡No le ofendas, señor!
BASILIO.	Pues ¿aquí espadas?
ESTRELLA.	(*Aparte.* Astolfo es. ¡Ay de mí, penas airadas!)
BASILIO.	Pues, ¿qué es lo que ha pasado?
ASTOLFO.	Nada, señor, habiendo tú llegado.

(Envainan.)

SEGISMUNDO.	Mucho, señor, aunque hayas tú venido.	1710
	Yo a ese viejo matar he pretendido.	
BASILIO.	¿Respeto no tenías	
	a estas canas?	
CLOTALDO.	Señor, ved que son mías;	
	que no importa veréis.	
SEGISMUNDO.	Acciones vanas,	
	querer que tenga yo respeto a canas;	1715
	pues aun ésas podría	
	ser que viese a mis plantas algún día;	
	porque aún no estoy vengado	
	del modo injusto con que me has crïado.	

(Vase.)

BASILIO.	Pues antes que lo veas,	1720
	volverás a dormir adonde creas	
	que cuanto te ha pasado,	
	como fue bien del mundo, fue soñado.	

(Vanse el REY y CLOTALDO. Quedan ESTRELLA y ASTOLFO.)

ASTOLFO.	¡Qué pocas veces el hado	
	que dice desdichas miente,	1725
	pues es tan cierto en los males	
	cuanto dudoso en los bienes!	
	¡Qué buen astrólogo fuera,	
	si siempre casos crüeles	
	anunciara, pues no hay duda	1730
	que ellos fueran verdad siempre!	
	Conocerse esta experiencia	
	en mí y Segismundo puede,	
	Estrella, pues en los dos	
	hizo muestras diferentes.	1735
	En él previno rigores,	
	soberbias, desdichas, muertes,	
	y en todo dijo verdad,	
	porque todo, al fin, sucede.	

CLOTHOLD.	Don't hurt him, my lord.
VASILY.	What's this? Swords drawn in the palace?
STELLA.	*(Aside.)* It's Aistulf! Oh miserable me, what cruel torment!
VASILY.	What's going on?
AISTULF.	Nothing, my lord, now that you're here.

(They sheathe their swords.)

SIGISMUND.	A great deal, my lord, despite your arrival. I tried to kill that old man.
VASILY.	You would show no respect for his grey hair?
CLOTHOLD.	Don't fret, my lord; my grey hair is unimportant.
SIGISMUND.	It is in vain to hope that I show respect for grey hair; why, I might even see yours *[gesturing at VASILY]* at my feet one day, because I still haven't had my revenge for the unjust manner in which you raised me. *(Exit.)*
VASILY.	Well before you reach that point, you'll return to sleep in a place where you'll believe that all that has happened to you, since it was of this world, was a dream.

(Exit VASILY and CLOTHOLD. STELLA and AISTULF remain onstage.)

AISTULF.	How seldom fate errs in predicting misfortune, for it is as accurate in foretelling evil as it is inaccurate in foretelling good. What an excellent astrologer it would be if it made only cruel predictions, for there's no doubt that they would always come true! This theory, Stella, is confirmed in the case of both Sigismund and myself, for in each of us there was a different prediction. In Sigismund's case, it foresaw severity, excessive pride, misfortune, and death, and it was right in each instance because it's all happening. But in my

| | Pero en mí – que al ver, señora, | 1740 |

Pero en mí – que al ver, señora,   1740
esos rayos excelentes,
de quien el sol fue una sombra
y el cielo un amago breve – ,
que me previno venturas,
trofeos, aplausos, bienes,   1745
dijo mal y dijo bien,
pues sólo es justo que acierte
cuando amaga con favores
y ejecuta con desdenes.

ESTRELLA.   No dudo que esas finezas   1750
son verdades evidentes,
mas serán por otra dama,
cuyo retrato pendiente
trujistes al cuello cuando
llegastis, Astolfo, a verme;   1755
y, siendo así, esos requiebros
ella sola los merece.
Acudid a que ella os pague,
que no son buenos papeles
en el consejo de amor   1760
las finezas ni las fees
que se hicieron en servicio
de otras damas y otros reyes.

(Sale ROSAURA al paño.)

ROSAURA.   (*Aparte.* ¡Gracias a Dios que han llegado
ya mis desdichas crüeles   1765
al término suyo, pues
quien esto ve nada teme!)

ASTOLFO.   Yo haré que el retrato salga
del pecho, para que entre
la imagen de tu hermosura: 1770
donde entra Estrella, no tiene
lugar la sombra… (*Aparte.* ni Estrella
donde el sol). Voy a traerle.
(*Aparte.* Perdona, Rosaura hermosa,
este agravio, porque, ausentes,   1775
no se guardan más fe que ésta
los hombres y las mujeres.)

(Vase.)

case – where, upon seeing, my lady, your exquisite brilliance, of which the sun is but a shadow and Heaven a meagre imitation, it predicted good fortune, trophies, acclaim, and wealth – it spoke incorrectly but also correctly, for it can only be correct when it promises kindness and delivers contempt.

STELLA.
I'm sure that your compliments are heartfelt; yet I suspect they're intended for another lady, whose portrait you were wearing in the locket around your neck when you first came to see me, Aistulf. That being the case, she alone deserves your flattery; go to her to claim your reward, for insincere compliments and misrepresentations are no more valid in love's court than they are in the king's.

(Enter ROSSAURA, hidden.)

ROSSAURA.
(Aside.) Thank God my cruel misfortunes are finally coming to an end, for anyone who suffers through this is prepared for anything!

AISTULF.
I'll banish the locket's picture from my breast to make way for your beautiful image. Where Stella is present, shadows have no place...

(Aside.) ...nor do Stellar glimmers in the presence of the sun.

[To STELLA.] I'll go and get the locket.

(Aside.) Forgive me, lovely Rossaura, for this offence, but men and women are no more faithful than this when they're apart. *(Exit.)*

ROSAURA.	(*Aparte.* Nada he podido escuchar,
	temerosa que me viese.)
ESTRELLA.	Astrea.
ROSAURA.	Señora mía. 1780
ESTRELLA.	Heme holgado que tú fueses
	la que llegaste hasta aquí,
	porque de ti solamente
	fiara un secreto.
ROSAURA.	Honras,
	señora, a quien te obedece. 1785
ESTRELLA.	En el poco tiempo, Astrea,
	que ha que te conozco, tienes
	de mi voluntad las llaves.
	Por esto, y por ser quien eres,
	me atrevo a fiar de ti 1790
	lo que aun de mí muchas veces
	recaté.
ROSAURA.	Tu esclava soy.
ESTRELLA.	Pues, para decirlo en breve,
	mi primo Astolfo – bastara
	que mi primo te dijese, 1795
	porque hay cosas que se dicen
	con pensarlas solamente –
	ha de casarse conmigo,
	si es que la fortuna quiere
	que con una dicha sola 1800
	tantas desdichas descuente.
	Pesóme que, el primer día,
	echado al cuello trujese
	el retrato de una dama.
	Habléle en él cortésmente; 1805
	es galán y quiere bien;
	fue por él, y ha de traerle
	aquí. Embarázame mucho
	que él a mí a dármele llegue.
	Quédate aquí y, cuando venga, 1810
	le dirás que te le entregue
	a ti. No te digo más;
	discreta y hermosa eres;
	bien sabrás lo que es amor.

(Vase.)

ROSSAURA.	*(Aside.)* I was so worried he'd see me that I didn't catch anything they said.
STELLA.	Astraea?
ROSSAURA.	My lady?
STELLA.	I'm glad it's you, because you're the only one I can trust with a secret.
ROSSAURA.	You're too kind, my lady, to one who serves you.
STELLA.	In the short time I've known you, Astraea, you've earned the keys to my conscience; for this reason, and because of who you are, I'm going to trust you with a secret that I'm not even comfortable with myself.
ROSSAURA.	I am your slave.
STELLA.	Well, to make a long story short, my first cousin Aistulf – *first* in more ways than one, if you know what I mean – is to marry me, if in fact fortune decides to remedy so much adversity with a single act of joy. I was distressed that the first day I saw him he was wearing the portrait of another lady around his neck. I spoke to him about it politely; he's a gallant and sincere lover, so he went to get the locket and is going to bring it here. But I feel awkward accepting it from him directly. Stay here, and when he comes, tell him to hand it over to you. I'll say no more; you're discreet and beautiful – surely you know what it means to be in love. *(Exit.)*

ROSAURA.   ¡Ojalá no lo supiese!   1815
¡Válgame el cielo! ¿Quién fuera
tan atenta y tan prudente
que supiera aconsejarse
hoy en ocasión tan fuerte?
¿Habrá persona en el mundo   1820
a quien el cielo inclemente
con más desdichas combata
y con más pesares cerque?
¿Qué haré en tantas confusiones,
donde imposible parece   1825
que halle razón que me alivie
ni alivio que me consuele?
Desde la primer desdicha
no hay suceso ni accidente
que otra desdicha no sea;   1830
que unas a otras suceden,
herederas de sí mismas.
A la imitación del fénix,
unas de las otras nacen,
viviendo de lo que mueren;   1835
y siempre de sus cenizas
está el sepulcro caliente.
Que eran cobardes, decía
un sabio, por parecerle
que nunca andaba una sola;   1840
yo digo que son valientes,
pues siempre van adelante,
y nunca la espalda vuelven.
Quien las llevare consigo,
a todo podrá atreverse,   1845
pues en ninguna ocasión
no haya miedo que le dejen.
Dígalo yo, pues en tantas
como a mi vida suceden,
nunca me he hallado sin ellas,   1850
ni se han cansado hasta verme
herida de la fortuna,
en los brazos de la muerte.
¡Ay de mí! ¿Qué debo hacer
hoy en la ocasión presente?   1855
Si digo quién soy, Clotaldo,

ROSSAURA.   If only I didn't! Heaven help me! What woman is careful and prudent enough to figure a way out of such a dilemma? Can there be anyone else in the world that the merciless stars assail with more misfortune and besiege with more sorrow? What shall I do amid such confusion, where it seems impossible to find a solution that comforts me or a comfort that consoles me? Since the first misfortune, every event or blunder has turned into another, for they succeed one another like heirs. In imitation of the phoenix, they breed one another, living on what kills them; and their urn is always alive with their ashes. Misfortunes are cowardly, a philosopher once said, because they never seem to walk alone; but I say they're courageous, since they always push forward and never look back. Whoever is escorted by misfortunes can aim for the stars, for he never need fear that they will abandon him. I can say so because so many have occurred in my life that I've never found myself without them, and they never give up until they find me, wounded by fortune or in the arms of death. Oh, miserable me! What shall I do in these circumstances? If I reveal my identity, Clothold, to whose protection and honour

a quien mi vida le debe
este amparo y este honor,
conmigo ofenderse puede;
pues me dice que, callando,   1860
honor y remedio espere.
Si no he de decir quién soy
a Astolfo, y él llega a verme,
¿cómo he de disimular?
Pues, aunque fingirlo intenten   1865
la voz, la lengua y los ojos,
les dirá el alma que mienten.
¿Qué haré? Mas ¿para qué estudio
lo que haré, si es evidente
que, por más que lo prevenga,   1870
que lo estudie y que lo piense,
en llegando la ocasión
ha de hacer lo que quisiere
el dolor, porque ninguno
imperio en sus penas tiene?   1875
Y pues a determinar
lo que ha de hacer no se atreve
el alma, llegue el dolor
hoy a su término, llegue
la pena a su extremo, y salga   1880
de dudas y pareceres
de una vez; pero hasta entonces,
¡valedme, cielos, valedme!

(Sale ASTOLFO con el retrato.)

ASTOLFO.	Éste es, señora, el retrato;
	mas ¡ay Dios!
ROSAURA.	¿Qué se suspende 1885
	Vuestra Alteza? ¿Qué se admira?
ASTOLFO.	De oírte, Rosaura, y verte.
ROSAURA.	¿Yo Rosaura? Hase engañado
	Vuestra Alteza, si me tiene
	por otra dama; que yo 1890
	soy Astrea, y no merece
	mi humildad tan grande dicha
	que esa turbación le cueste.
ASTOLFO.	Basta, Rosaura, el engaño;
	porque el alma nunca miente 1895

I owe my life, might be offended, for he has asked me to keep quiet while I await his remedy to my dishonour. But if I don't reveal my identity, how can I keep up the charade if Aistulf recognizes me? For even if I attempt to disguise myself with my voice, my speech, and my eyes, my soul will expose them as liars. What shall I do? But why reflect on what to do, when it's evident that, no matter how I prepare, reflect, and think, when the moment arrives, my grief will do as it sees fit? For no one is master of his sorrow. And since my soul dares not determine a course of action, let my grief culminate today and let my sorrow reach its extreme, but let me be freed of doubting and guessing once and for all. But until then, give me strength, heavens, give me strength!

(Enter AISTULF with the locket.)

AISTULF.	Here's the locket, my lady…but…Oh, God!
ROSSAURA.	What's the matter, my lord? What's got you so shocked?
AISTULF.	Hearing your voice, Rossaura, and seeing you here.
ROSSAURA.	Rossaura? You are mistaken, my lord, if you take me for another lady; for I am Astraea, and my humble station is not worthy of the joy caused by your confused affection.
AISTULF.	Enough with the deception, Rossaura, for the soul never lies;

| | y, aunque como a Astrea te mire, | |
| | como a Rosaura te quiere. | |

ROSAURA.   No he entendido a Vuestra Alteza,
            y así no sé responderle.
            Sólo lo que yo diré   1900
            es que Estrella, que lo puede
            ser de Venus, me mandó
            que en esta parte le espere,
            y de la suya le diga
            que aquel retrato me entregue   1905
            – que está muy puesto en razón – ,
            y yo misma se lo lleve.
            Estrella lo quiere así,
            porque, aun las cosas más leves,
            como sean en mi daño,   1910
            es Estrella quien las quiere.

ASTOLFO.   Aunque más esfuerzos hagas,
            ¡oh, qué mal, Rosaura, puedes
            disimular! Di a los ojos
            que su música concierten   1915
            con la voz; porque es forzoso
            que desdiga y que disuene
            tan destemplado instrumento
            que ajustar y medir quiere
            la falsedad de quien dice   1920
            con la verdad de quien siente.

ROSAURA.   Ya digo que sólo espero
            el retrato.

ASTOLFO.   Pues que quieres
            llevar al fin el engaño,
            con él quiero responderte.   1925
            Dirásle, Astrea, a la Infanta
            que yo la estimo de suerte
            que, pidiéndome un retrato,
            poca fineza parece
            enviársele, y así,   1930
            porque le estime y le precie,
            le envío el original;
            y tú llevársele puedes,
            pues ya le llevas contigo
            como a ti misma te lleves.   1935

and though mine may look upon you as Astraea, it loves you as Rossaura.

ROSSAURA. I don't understand, my lord, so I don't know how to respond. All I can say is that Stella – who is at least as Stellar as Venus – has ordered me to wait here for you and to ask you, on her behalf, to hand over that locket and to take it to her myself. It is a most reasonable request. Stella wishes it thus, for even the tiniest things, if they work to my disadvantage, are Stellar in design.

AISTULF. Try as you might, Rossaura, you're a most unconvincing liar! Tell your eyes to harmonize their music to your voice; for such a cacophonous instrument must stutter and falter in attempting to adjust and calibrate the falsehoods of the speaker to the truth of his sentiments.

ROSSAURA. I repeat that I'm here only for the locket.

AISTULF. Well, since you insist on carrying on with this charade, I'll reply in kind. You may tell the princess, Astraea, that I hold her in such esteem that, when she asks me for a portrait, I consider it in poor taste to send it to her; rather, that she may treasure and revere it, I'll send her the original. And you may take it to her, for you carry it in yourself – when you're not beside yourself.

ROSAURA.   Cuando un hombre se dispone,
                   restado, altivo y valiente,
                   a salir con una empresa,
                   aunque por trato le entreguen
                   lo que valga más, sin ella   1940
                   necio y desairado vuelve.
                   Yo vengo por un retrato,
                   y aunque un original lleve
                   que vale más, volveré
                   desairada, y así, déme   1945
                   Vuestra Alteza ese retrato,
                   que sin él no he de volverme.
ASTOLFO.   Pues ¿cómo, si no he de darle,
                   le has de llevar?
ROSAURA.   Desta suerte.
                   ¡Suéltale, ingrato!
ASTOLFO.   Es en vano.   1950
ROSAURA.   ¡Vive Dios, que no ha de verse
                   en manos de otra mujer!
ASTOLFO.   Terrible estás.
ROSAURA.   Y tú aleve.
ASTOLFO.   Ya basta, Rosaura mía.
ROSAURA.   ¿Yo tuya, villano? ¡Mientes!   1955

(Sale ESTRELLA.)

ESTRELLA.   ¡Astrea, Astolfo! ¿Qué es esto?
ASTOLFO.   (*Aparte.* Aquésta es Estrella.)
ROSAURA.   (*Aparte.* Déme,
                   para cobrar mi retrato,
                   ingenio el amor.) Si quieres
                   saber lo que es, yo, señora,   1960
                   te lo diré.
ASTOLFO.   (*Aparte.* ¿Qué pretendes?)
ROSAURA.   Mandásteme que esperase
                   aquí a Astolfo y le pidiese
                   un retrato de tu parte;
                   quedé sola y, como vienen   1965
                   de unos discursos a otros
                   las noticias fácilmente,
                   viéndote hablar de retratos,
                   con su memoria, acordéme
                   de que tenía uno mío   1970

ROSSAURA.	When a determined, proud, and courageous man agrees to undertake a mission, if he returns without reaching the goal – even if he acquires something more valuable in the process – he faces ridicule and humiliation. I'm here for a portrait, and even if I take back an original of greater worth, I'll be ridiculed. Give me the locket, my lord, for I shall not return without it.
AISTULF.	Well how do you expect to take it if I don't give it to you?
ROSSAURA.	Like this! *[She grabs for the locket.]* Give it to me, you ingrate!
AISTULF.	Your efforts are in vain.
ROSSAURA.	By God, it's not for another woman's hands!
AISTULF.	You're ferocious today.
ROSSAURA.	And you're a two-timing scoundrel!
AISTULF.	That's enough, my Rossaura.
ROSSAURA.	I'm not your Rossaura, you swine!

([They continue struggling.] Enter STELLA.)

STELLA.	Astraea, Aistulf, what's going on here?
AISTULF.	*(Aside.)* Oh no, it's Stella!
ROSSAURA.	*(Aside.)* May love grant me the ingenuity to get my locket back. *(To STELLA.)* If you wish to know what's going on, my lady, I'll tell you.
AISTULF.	*(Aside [to ROSSAURA].)* What do you think you're doing?
ROSSAURA.	You ordered me to wait here for Aistulf and to ask him for a locket on your behalf. I was left alone, and as related topics associate freely in the mind, your talk of lockets reminded me that I was carrying one of my own in my sleeve. I decided

en la manga. Quise verle,
porque una persona sola
con locuras se divierte;
cayóseme de la mano
al suelo; Astolfo, que viene   1975
a entregarte el de otra dama,
le levantó, y tan rebelde
está en dar el que le pides
que, en vez de dar uno, quiere
llevar otro. Pues el mío   1980
aun no es posible volverme
con ruegos y persuasiones,
colérica y impaciente
yo se le quise quitar.
Aquél que en la mano tiene   1985
es mío; tú lo verás
con ver si se me parece.

ESTRELLA.   ¡Soltad, Astolfo, el retrato!

(Quítasele.)

ASTOLFO.   ¡Señora!
ESTRELLA.   No son crüeles
a la verdad los matices.   1990
ROSAURA.   ¿No es mío?
ESTRELLA.   ¿Qué duda tiene?
ROSAURA.   Di que ahora te entregue el otro.
ESTRELLA.   Toma tu retrato, y vete.
ROSAURA.   (*Aparte.* Yo he cobrado mi retrato;
venga ahora lo que viniere.   1995

(Vase.)

ESTRELLA.   Dadme ahora el retrato vos
que os pedí, que, aunque no piense
veros ni hablaros jamás,
no quiero, no, que se quede
en vuestro poder, siquiera   2000
porque yo tan neciamente
lo he pedido.
ASTOLFO.   (*Aparte.* ¿Cómo puedo
salir de lance tan fuerte?)
Aunque quiera, hermosa Estrella

to look at it, for people always entertain themselves with nonsense when they're alone. I accidentally dropped it on the floor, and Aistulf, who'd just arrived to give you the other lady's locket, picked it up; and not only is he unwilling to hand over the one you'd asked him for, but he also wants to take mine. And since he wouldn't give it back even though I begged and beseeched him, I grew angry and impatient and tried to take it back by force. That one he holds in his hand now is mine; you'll know as soon as you see the resemblance it bears to me.

STELLA.   Give me the locket, Aistulf. *(She takes it from him.)*
AISTULF.   My lady!
STELLA.   A faithful copy of the original.
ROSSAURA.   So you agree it's mine?
STELLA.   Could there be any doubt?
ROSSAURA.   Now tell him to give you the other one.
STELLA.   Take your locket and go.
ROSSAURA.   *(Aside.)* At least I got my locket back. The rest is their problem. *(Exit.)*

STELLA.   Now give me the locket I asked you for; for though I shall never look at you or speak to you again, I don't want it to remain in your power – no – if only because I so foolishly asked you for it.

AISTULF.   *(Aside.)* How can I get myself out of this one?
               [To STELLA.] Although I should like, beautiful Stella, to

	servirte y obedecerte,	2005
	no podré darte el retrato	
	que me pides, porque...	
ESTRELLA.	Eres	
	villano y grosero amante.	
	No quiero que me le entregues;	
	porque yo tampoco quiero,	2010
	con tomarle, que me acuerdes	
	de que yo te le he pedido.	

(Vase.)

ASTOLFO.	¡Oye, escucha, mira, advierte!	
	¡Válgate Dios por Rosaura!	
	¿Dónde, cómo o de qué suerte	2015
	hoy a Polonia has venido	
	a perderme y a perderte?	

(Vase.)

Escena 2

(Descúbrese SEGISMUNDO como al principio, con pieles y cadena, durmiendo en el suelo. Salen CLOTALDO, CLARÍN y los dos criados.)

CLOTALDO.	Aquí le habéis de dejar,	
	pues hoy su soberbia acaba	
	donde empezó.	
CRIADO 1.	Como estaba,	2020
	la cadena vuelvo a atar.	
CLARÍN.	No acabes de despertar,	
	Segismundo, para verte	
	perder, trocada, la suerte,	
	siendo tu gloria fingida	2025
	una sombra de la vida	
	y una llama de la muerte.	
CLOTALDO.	A quien sabe discurrir	
	así, es bien que se prevenga	
	una estancia donde tenga	2030
	harto lugar de argüir.	
	Éste es el que habéis de asir	
	y en ese cuarto encerrar.	
CLARÍN.	¿Por qué a mí?	

	serve and obey you, I can't give you the locket you request because…
STELLA.	You're a swine and a boorish suitor! Keep it, for I wouldn't want to be reminded, in accepting it, that I ever asked you for anything! *(Exit.)*
AISTULF.	Wait…listen…look…I…! Goddamn you, Rossaura! Where, how, and why did you turn up in Poland today? You're going to destroy yourself and me with you! *(Exit.)*

Scene 2

([The tower.] SIGISMUND, bound in chains and dressed in animal skins as at the beginning of the play, is revealed asleep on the floor. Enter CLOTHOLD, BUGLE, and two SERVANTS.)

CLOTHOLD.	*(To the SERVANTS.)* Leave him here, and his excessive pride will end today where it began.
SERVANT 1.	I've secured the chain as before.
BUGLE.	Better not to wake up, Sigismund; you'll only find yourself destroyed, your fate reversed, your false grandeur reduced to a shadow of life and a glow of death.
CLOTHOLD.	Anyone who speaks so glibly should have a nice place in which to debate himself at length. *[To the SERVANTS.]* Seize this man and lock him away in that room.
BUGLE.	Why me?

CLOTALDO.	Porque ha de estar	
	guardado en prisión tan grave	2035
	Clarín que secretos sabe,	
	donde no pueda sonar.	
CLARÍN.	¿Yo, por dicha, solicito	
	dar muerte a mi padre? No.	
	¿Arrojé del balcón yo	2040
	al Ícaro de poquito?	
	¿Yo muero ni resucito?	
	¿Yo sueño o duermo? ¿A qué fin	
	me encierran?	
CLOTALDO.	Eres Clarín.	
CLARÍN.	Pues ya digo que seré	2045
	corneta, y que callaré,	
	que es instrumento rüin.	

(Llévanle. Sale el REY BASILIO rebozado.)

BASILIO.	¿Clotaldo?	
CLOTALDO.	¡Señor! ¿Así	
	viene Vuestra Majestad?	
BASILIO.	La necia curiosidad	2050
	de ver lo que pasa aquí	
	a Segismundo, ¡ay de mí!,	
	deste modo me ha traído.	
CLOTALDO.	Mírale allí reducido	
	a su miserable estado.	2055
BASILIO.	¡Ay, príncipe desdichado,	
	y en triste punto nacido!	
	Llega a despertarle ya,	
	que fuerza y vigor perdió	
	esos lotos que bebió.	2060
CLOTALDO.	Inquieto, señor, está,	
	y hablando.	
BASILIO.	¿Qué soñará	
	agora? Escuchemos, pues.	
SEGISMUNDO.	*(En sueños.)* Piadoso príncipe es	
	el que castiga tiranos.	2065
	¡Muera Clotaldo a mis manos!	
	¡Bese mi padre mis pies!	
CLOTALDO.	Con la muerte me amenaza.	
BASILIO.	A mí, con rigor y afrenta.	
CLOTALDO.	Quitarme la vida intenta.	2070

CLOTHOLD.	Because a Bugle with so many secrets must be kept locked away in a harsh prison, where it can't sound off.
BUGLE.	Have I, by chance, tried to kill my father? No. Am I the one who threw little Icarus off the balcony? Is my death or rebirth the issue? Does my dreaming or sleeping matter? What's your purpose in locking me up?
CLOTHOLD.	You're Bugle.
BUGLE.	Well I'll call myself Horn from now on, and I'll keep quiet, as befits those with horns.

(They take him away. Enter King VASILY, his face hidden behind a cloak.)

VASILY.	Clothold?
CLOTHOLD.	My lord! Why does Your Majesty come in disguise?
VASILY.	A foolish curiosity to see what happens with Sigismund – Oh, miserable me! – has brought me here in this fashion.
CLOTHOLD.	Behold him there, reduced to his miserable state.
VASILY.	Oh, unfortunate prince, born at such a sad moment! *[To CLOTHOLD.]* Go wake him now, for the lotus he drank should be wearing off.
CLOTHOLD.	He is restless, my lord, and talking in his sleep.
VASILY.	What could he be dreaming now? Let's listen.
SIGISMUND.	*(In his sleep.)* Faithful is the prince who punishes tyrants. Clothold shall die by my hands! My father shall kiss my feet!
CLOTHOLD.	He threatens me with death.
VASILY.	And me with severity and disrespect.
CLOTHOLD.	He means to take my life.

BASILIO.	Rendirme a sus plantas traza.
SEGISMUNDO.	*(En sueños.)* ¡Salga a la anchurosa plaza
	del gran teatro del mundo
	este valor sin segundo!
	Porque mi venganza cuadre, 2075
	¡vean triunfar de su padre
	al príncipe Segismundo!
	(Despierta.)
	Mas, ¡ay de mí!, ¿dónde estoy?
BASILIO.	*(Aparte a CLOTALDO.* Pues a mí no me ha de ver.
	Ya sabes lo que has de hacer. 2080
	Desde allí a escucharte voy.)

(Retírase.)

SEGISMUNDO.	¿Soy yo, por ventura? ¿Soy
	el que preso y aherrojado
	llego a verme en tal estado?
	¿No sois mi sepulcro vos, 2085
	torre? Sí. ¡Válgame Dios,
	qué de cosas he soñado!
CLOTALDO.	*(Aparte.* A mí me toca llegar
	a hacer la deshecha ahora.)
	¿Es ya de despertar hora? 2090
SEGISMUNDO.	Sí, hora es ya de despertar.
CLOTALDO.	¿Todo el día te has de estar
	durmiendo? ¿Desde que yo
	al águila que voló
	con tarda vista seguí, 2095
	y te quedaste tú aquí,
	nunca has despertado?
SEGISMUNDO.	No,
	ni aun agora he despertado;
	que, según, Clotaldo, entiendo,
	todavía estoy durmiendo 2100
	y no estoy muy engañado;
	porque si ha sido soñado
	lo que vi palpable y cierto,
	lo que veo será incierto;
	y no es mucho que, rendido, 2105
	pues veo estando dormido,
	que sueñe estando despierto.
CLOTALDO.	Lo que soñaste me di.

VASILY.	He schemes to subjugate me at his feet.
SIGISMUND.	*(In his sleep.)* On the broad public square that is the great stage of the world, my unequalled valour shall be the star. For my vengeance to take shape, all must watch Prince Sigismund triumph over his father. *(He awakens.)* But – Oh, miserable me! – where am I?
VASILY.	*(Aside to CLOTHOLD.)* He mustn't see me. You know what to do. I'll listen from over there. *(He withdraws from the prince's view.)*
SIGISMUND.	Is this really me? Am I the one I see reduced to this state, a chained captive? Are you not my grave, tower? Yes. Good god, what a torrent of dreams!
CLOTHOLD.	*(Aside.)* It's up to me to pull off the deception. *[To SIGISMUND.]* Is it finally time to wake up?
SIGISMUND.	Yes, it's finally time to wake up.
CLOTHOLD.	Must you spend all day sleeping? You haven't woken up since I left to follow the flight of that majestic eagle while you stayed put?
SIGISMUND.	No, nor am I awake now, for as I see it, Clothold, I'm still sleeping. My reasoning is sound because, if what seemed so palpable and true to me was only a dream, then what I'm seeing now mustn't be trusted. And it's no surprise that, if I can see in my sleep, exhaustion should lead me to dream while awake.
CLOTHOLD.	Tell me what you dreamed.

SEGISMUNDO.   Supuesto que sueño fue,
                     no diré lo que soñé;   2110
                     lo que vi, Clotaldo, sí.
                     Yo desperté y yo me vi,
                     ¡qué crueldad tan lisonjera!,
                     en un lecho que pudiera,
                     con matices y colores,   2115
                     ser el catre de las flores
                     que tejió la Primavera.
                     Aquí mil nobles, rendidos
                     a mis pies, nombre me dieron
                     de su príncipe y sirvieron   2120
                     galas, joyas y vestidos.
                     La calma de mis sentidos
                     tú trocaste en alegría
                     diciendo la dicha mía:
                     que, aunque estoy desta manera,   2125
                     príncipe en Polonia era.
CLOTALDO.   ¡Buenas albricias tendría!
SEGISMUNDO.   No muy buenas: por traidor,
                     con pecho atrevido y fuerte,
                     dos veces te daba muerte.   2130
CLOTALDO.   ¿Para mí tanto rigor?
SEGISMUNDO.   De todos era señor
                     y de todos me vengaba.
                     Sólo a una mujer amaba;
                     que fue verdad, creo yo,   2135
                     en que todo se acabó
                     y esto sólo no se acaba.

(Vase el REY.)

CLOTALDO.   (*Aparte.* Enternecido se ha ido el Rey
                     de haberle escuchado.)
                     Como habíamos hablado   2140
                     de aquella águila, dormido,
                     tu sueño imperios han sido;
                     mas en sueños fuera bien
                     entonces honrar a quien
                     te crió en tantos empeños,   2145
                     Segismundo, que aun en sueños
                     no se pierde el hacer bien.

(Vase.)

SIGISMUND.   Even assuming it was a dream, I won't say what I dreamed, Clothold, but rather what I saw, yes. I awoke to find myself – What cruel flattery! – upon a bed that could have been, with a bit of detail and colour, a bed of flowers woven by Spring, where a thousand noblemen, bowing at my feet, called me their prince and adorned me in fine clothes and precious stones. You turned the numbness of my senses into happiness by announcing the good news; for, although this is my lot here, there I was Prince of Poland.

CLOTHOLD.   You must have given me a handsome reward.

SIGISMUND.   Not really. With a valiant and mighty spirit, I twice tried to kill you for your treason.

CLOTHOLD.   Such severity toward me?

SIGISMUND.   I was lord over all, and I wanted revenge on everyone. My only love was for a woman, and I believe it was real because, while everything else has vanished, it alone has remained with me.

(Exit the KING.)

CLOTHOLD.   *(Aside.)* The king has left, filled with pity at the prince's remarks.
              [To SIGISMUND.] Because we had spoken about that eagle, when you slept you dreamt of empire. But in your dreams it would be fitting, Sigismund, to show more respect to he who raised you with such care; for even in dreams doing what's right mustn't be overlooked.

(Exit.)

SEGISMUNDO. Es verdad; pues reprimamos
              esta fiera condición,
              esta furia, esta ambición   2150
              por si alguna vez soñamos.
              Y sí haremos, pues estamos
              en mundo tan singular
              que el vivir sólo es soñar,
              y la experiencia me enseña   2155
              que el hombre que vive sueña
              lo que es hasta despertar.
              Sueña el rey que es rey, y vive
              con este engaño mandando,
              disponiendo y gobernando;   2160
              y este aplauso, que recibe
              prestado, en el viento escribe
              y en cenizas le convierte
              la muerte: ¡desdicha fuerte!
              ¡Que hay quien intente reinar   2165
              viendo que ha de despertar
              en el sueño de la muerte!
              Sueña el rico en su riqueza,
              que más cuidados le ofrece;
              sueña el pobre que padece   2170
              su miseria y su pobreza;
              sueña el que a medrar empieza;
              sueña el que afana y pretende;
              sueña el que agravia y ofende;
              y en el mundo, en conclusión,   2175
              todos sueñan lo que son,
              aunque ninguno lo entiende.
              Yo sueño que estoy aquí
              destas prisiones cargado,
              y soñé que en otro estado   2180
              más lisonjero me vi.
              ¿Qué es la vida?: un frenesí.
              ¿Qué es la vida?: una ilusión,
              una sombra, una ficción;
              y el mayor bien es pequeño,   2185
              que toda la vida es sueño,
              y los sueños, sueños son.

SIGISMUND. This is true. So we must repress this savage character, this fury, this ambition, in case we dream again. And we no doubt shall, for we live in such a singular world that living is no more than dreaming; and experience teaches me that the man who lives dreams what he is until waking. The king dreams he's king, and he lives under this deception commanding, planning, and governing; and his acclaim, which he receives on loan, he scribbles on the wind, where death turns it to ash. What grave misfortune! To think that anyone should try to govern knowing that he will awaken in the sleep of death! The rich man dreams of his riches, which bring him more worries; the poor man dreams he suffers in misery and poverty; the man who improves his lot dreams; the man who toils and solicits dreams; the man who insults and offends dreams. And in this world, in short, everyone dreams what he is though no one realizes it. I dream that I'm here, weighed down by these chains, and I dreamt that I found myself in another, more flattering state. What is life? A frenzy. What is life? An illusion, a shadow, a fiction; and the greatest good is fleeting, for all life is a dream, and even dreams are but dreams.

ACTO 3

Escena 1
(Sale CLARÍN.)

CLARÍN.   En una encantada torre,
por lo que sé, vivo preso.
¿Qué me harán por lo que ignoro,   2190
si por lo que sé me han muerto?
¡Que un hombre con tanta hambre
viniese a morir viviendo!
Lástima tengo de mí.
Todos dirán: «bien lo creo»;   2195
y bien se puede creer,
pues para mí este silencio
no conforma con el nombre
Clarín, y callar no puedo.
Quien me hace compañía   2200
aquí – si a decirlo acierto –
son arañas y ratones:
¡miren qué dulces jilgueros!
De los sueños desta noche
la triste cabeza tengo   2205
llena de mil chirimías,
de trompetas y embelecos,
de procesiones, de cruces,
de disciplinantes; y éstos,
unos suben, otros bajan;   2210
unos se desmayan viendo
la sangre que llevan otros.
Mas yo, la verdad diciendo,
de no comer me desmayo,
que en esta prisión me veo   2215
donde ya todos los días
en el filósofo leo
Nicomedes, y las noches
en el concilio Niceno.
Si llaman santo al callar,   2220
como en calendario nuevo,
San Secreto es para mí,

ACT 3

Scene 1

([The tower.] Enter BUGLE.)

BUGLE.　　　In a haunted tower, because of what I know, I'm being held captive. What will they do to me for my ignorance if they axe me for my knowledge? To think that a fellow should be sentenced to a life of starving to death! I feel sorry for myself! Everyone will say, "I can believe it," and I'm sure they can, for in my opinion this silence doesn't befit the name Bugle, and I can't keep my mouth shut. My company here, if I can bring myself to say it, are spiders and mice: what lovely goldfinches! My dreams last night filled my poor head with shawms, trumpets, and tomfoolery; and with processions, crucifixes, and penitents marching up and down and fainting at the sight of one another's blood. Yet I, to tell the truth, am fainting from hunger, for this prison's favourite philosopher is Empty-Plato and its only creed is the Frail-Mary. If silence be considered saintly, then Saint Secret is my man, for I fast

pues le ayuno y no le huelgo;
aunque está bien merecido
el castigo que padezco,   2225
pues callé, siendo crïado,
que es el mayor sacrilegio.

(Ruido de cajas y gente, y dicen dentro.)

SOLDADO 1.   Ésta es la torre en que está.
               ¡Echad la puerta en el suelo!
               ¡Entrad todos!
CLARÍN.   ¡Vive Dios!   2230
               Que a mí me buscan es cierto,
               pues que dicen que aquí estoy.
               ¿Qué me querrán?

(Salen los soldados que pudieren.)

SOLDADO 1.   ¡Entrad dentro!
SOLDADO 2.   Aquí está.
CLARÍN.   No está.
TODOS.   ¡Señor!
CLARÍN.   ¿Si vienen borrachos éstos?   2235
SOLDADO 2.   Tú nuestro príncipe eres;
               ni admitimos ni queremos
               sino al señor natural,
               y no príncipe extranjero.
               A todos nos da los pies.   2240
TODOS.   ¡Viva el gran príncipe nuestro!
CLARÍN.   (*Aparte.* ¡Vive Dios, que va de veras!
               ¿Si es costumbre en este reino
               prender uno cada día
               y hacerle príncipe, y luego   2245
               volverle a la torre? Sí,
               pues cada día lo veo.
               Fuerza es hacer mi papel.)
SOLDADOS.   Danos tus plantas.
CLARÍN.   No puedo,
               porque las he menester   2250
               para mí, y fuera defeto
               ser príncipe desplantado.
SOLDADO 2.   Todos a tu padre mesmo
               le dijimos que a ti sólo
               por príncipe conocemos,   2255
               no al de Moscovia.

in his honour and never feast! But the punishment I suffer is well deserved, for I'm a servant who kept his mouth shut, which is the greatest sacrilege.

(A sound of drums and people is heard, and a voice speaks from offstage.)

SOLDIER 1.   This is the tower he's in. Knock down the door; everybody in!

BUGLE.   By God! They must be looking for me, for they say I'm in here! What can they want with me?

(Enter as many SOLDIERS as possible.)

SOLDIER 1.   Inside, inside.

SOLDIER 2.   *[Pointing to BUGLE.]* Here he is.

BUGLE.   No he isn't.

SOLDIERS.   My lord...

BUGLE.   *[Aside.]* Are these guys drunk or what?

SOLDIER 2.   You are our prince; we don't want and won't accept anyone but our rightful lord, not a foreign prince. Give us all your feet, that we may bow before them.

SOLDIERS.   Long live our great prince!

BUGLE.   *(Aside.)* By God, it's for real! Can it be a custom of this kingdom to take a new prisoner each day, make him prince, and then return him to the tower? Apparently, for I've seen it happen twice now. I'll have to play my role.

SOLDIERS.   Give us the soles of your feet. *[They kneel to kiss his feet.]*

BUGLE.   I can't because I need them for myself, and I wouldn't do you much good as a desolated prince.

SOLDIER 2.   We all told your father himself that we recognize only you as our prince, not the Muscovite.

CLARÍN.   ¿A mi padre
                   le perdistis el respeto?
                   Sois unos tales por cuales.
SOLDADO 1.   Fue lealtad de nuestros pechos.
CLARÍN.   Si fue lealtad, yo os perdono.   2260
SOLDADO 2.   Sal a restaurar tu imperio.
                   ¡Viva Segismundo!
TODOS.   ¡Viva!
CLARÍN.   (*Aparte.* ¿Segismundo dicen? ¡Bueno!
                   Segismundos llaman todos
                   los príncipes contrahechos.)   2265

(Sale SEGISMUNDO.)

SEGISMUNDO.   ¿Quién nombra aquí a Segismundo?
CLARÍN.   (*Aparte.* ¿Mas que soy príncipe huero?)
SOLDADO 2.   ¿Quién es Segismundo?
SEGISMUNDO.   Yo.
SOLDADO 2.   Pues ¿cómo, atrevido y necio,
                   tú te hacías Segismundo?   2270
CLARÍN.   ¿Yo Segismundo? Eso niego,
                   que vosotros fuistis quien
                   me segismundasteis. Luego
                   vuestra ha sido solamente
                   necedad y atrevimiento.   2275
SOLDADO 1.   Gran príncipe Segismundo
                   – que las señas que traemos
                   tuyas son, aunque por fe
                   te aclamamos señor nuestro – ,
                   tu padre, el gran rey Basilio,   2280
                   temeroso que los cielos
                   cumplan un hado que dice
                   que ha de verse, a tus pies puesto,
                   vencido de ti, pretende
                   quitarte acción y derecho   2285
                   y dársela a Astolfo, duque
                   de Moscovia. Para esto
                   juntó su corte, y el vulgo,
                   penetrando ya y sabiendo
                   que tiene rey natural,   2290
                   no quiere que un extranjero
                   venga a mandarle; y así,
                   haciendo noble desprecio

BUGLE.	You talked back to my father? You're a bunch of lowlifes!
SOLDIER 1.	It was the loyalty of our hearts speaking.
BUGLE.	If it was loyalty, then I forgive you.
SOLDIER 2.	Come forth and restore your rule. Long live Sigismund!
ALL.	Long live Sigismund!
BUGLE.	*(Aside.)* Why do they call me Sigismund? It must be the name they reserve for all their bogus princes.

Enter SIGISMUND.

SIGISMUND.	Who calls Sigismund's name?
BUGLE.	*(Aside.)* Is my time as prince already up?
SOLDIER 2.	Which of you is Sigismund?
SIGISMUND.	I am.
SOLDIER 2.	*[To BUGLE.]* You impudent fool! How dare you call yourself Sigismund?
BUGLE.	Me, call myself Sigismund? I deny that charge. You're the ones who Sigismunded me, so you're the impudent fools.
SOLDIER 1.	Great Prince Sigismund – your appearance confirms your identity, though our faith has already affirmed you as our lord – your father, the great King Vasily, fearful lest the stars fulfil a prediction that says he will end up at your feet, vanquished by your might, is attempting to deny you your rightful authority and give it to Aistulf, Duke of Muscovy. For this purpose he convened his court, and the masses, learning of the events and realizing that they have a natural-born prince, refuse to be ruled by a foreigner. And thus, nobly overlooking

de la inclemencia del hado,
te ha buscado donde preso   2295
vives para que, valido
de sus armas y saliendo
desta torre a restaurar
tu imperial corona y cetro,
se la quites a un tirano.   2300
Sal, pues; que en ese desierto
ejército numeroso
de bandidos y plebeyos
te aclama. La libertad
te espera. Oye sus acentos.   2305

VOCES.   ¡Viva Segismundo, viva!
SEGISMUNDO. (*Aparte.* ¿Otra vez – ¡qué es esto, cielos! –
queréis que sueñe grandezas
que ha de deshacer el tiempo?
¿Otra vez queréis que vea,   2310
entre sombras y bosquejos,
la majestad y la pompa
desvanecida del viento?
¿Otra vez queréis que toque
el desengaño o el riesgo   2315
a que el humano poder
nace humilde y vive atento?
Pues no ha de ser, no ha de ser.
Miradme otra vez sujeto
a mi fortuna. Y pues sé   2320
que toda esta vida es sueño,
¡idos, sombras, que fingís
hoy a mis sentidos muertos
cuerpo y voz, siendo verdad
que ni tenéis voz ni cuerpo;   2325
que no quiero majestades
fingidas; pompas no quiero!
Fantásticas ilusiones
que al soplo menos ligero
del aura han de deshacerse,   2330
bien como el florido almendro
que, por madrugar sus flores
sin aviso y sin consejo,
al primer soplo se apagan,
marchitando y desluciendo   2335

the inclemency of fate, they've come looking for you where you're held prisoner so that, aided by their weapons, you may break out of this tower and recover your imperial crown and sceptre, stripping them from a tyrant. Come forth, then, for on that barren mount a numerous army of outlaws and peasants salutes you. Freedom awaits you; listen to its chant.

VOICES. *[Offstage.]* Long live Sigismund! Long live the prince!

SIGISMUND. *(Aside.)* What's happening, heavens? Do you wish me to dream again of greatness that will be undone by time? Am I to glimpse again the shadowy outlines of majesty and pomp that will be swept away by the wind? Must I come to grips with the truth again, that human power is born of jeopardy and lives in uncertainty? It shall not be; it shall not be. Here I am, again a prisoner of my fortune. And since I know that this life is all a dream, be gone shadows, you who today give body and voice to my deadened senses, when truth holds that you have neither body nor voice. For I don't want counterfeit majesty and pomp, no. Fanciful illusions that unravel at the slightest touch of the breeze – just like the budding almond tree whose flowers, without warning or counsel, bloom early and expire at the first cold wind, withering and tarnishing the

de sus rosados capillos
belleza, luz y ornamento,
ya os conozco, ya os conozco,
y sé que os pasa lo mesmo
con cualquiera que se duerme.   2340
Para mí no hay fingimientos,
que, desengañado ya,
sé bien que la vida es sueño.)

SOLDADO 2.   Si piensas que te engañamos,
vuelve a ese monte soberbio   2345
los ojos, para que veas
la gente que aguarda en ellos
para obedecerte.

SEGISMUNDO.   Ya
otra vez vi aquesto mesmo
tan clara y distintamente   2350
como agora lo estoy viendo,
y fue sueño.

SOLDADO 1.   Cosas grandes
siempre, gran señor, trujeron
anuncios; y esto sería,
si lo soñaste primero.   2355

SEGISMUNDO.   Dices bien: anuncio fue.
(*Aparte.* Y caso que fuese cierto,
pues que la vida es tan corta,
soñemos, alma, soñemos
otra vez; pero ha de ser   2360
con atención y consejo
de que hemos de despertar
deste gusto al mejor tiempo;
que, llevándolo sabido,
será el desengaño menos;   2365
que es hacer burla del daño
adelantarle el consejo.
Y con esta prevención
de que, cuando fuese cierto,
es todo el poder prestado   2370
y ha de volverse a su dueño,
atrevámonos a todo.)
Vasallos, yo os agradezco
la lealtad. En mí lleváis
quien os libre, osado y diestro,   2375

beauty, brightness, and colour of their rosy buds – I see you, I recognize you, and I know you play the same game with everyone who falls asleep. I won't be fooled this time, for I've learned the truth and know that life is a dream.

SOLDIER 2. If you think we're deceiving you, turn your gaze toward that defiant mountainside and you'll see the people who wait there to obey your command.

SIGISMUND. I've seen this before as clearly and distinctly as I'm seeing it now, and it was a dream.

SOLDIER 1. Great things, my lord, are always foreshadowed, which explains how you could have dreamt this moment.

SIGISMUND. You speak convincingly: it was a foreshadowing.

(Aside.) And in case that be true, since life is so short, let's dream, my soul, let's dream again. But we must do so with vigilance and with the awareness that we may awaken from this delight at the best moment; if we keep that in mind, the truth will sting less, for to be prepared for harm is to avoid it. And with the caveat that, even if this is not a dream, all power is on loan and must be returned to its owner, let us stop at nothing.

[To the SOLDIERS.] Vassals, I appreciate your loyalty. You may count on my boldness and skill to liberate you from

de extranjera esclavitud.
Tocad al arma, que presto
veréis mi inmenso valor.
Contra mi padre pretendo
tomar armas y sacar   2380
verdaderos a los cielos:
presto he de verle a mis plantas.
(*Aparte.* Mas, si antes desto despierto,
¿no será bien no decirlo,
supuesto que no he de hacerlo?)   2385

TODOS.   ¡Viva Segismundo, viva!

(Sale CLOTALDO.)

CLOTALDO.   ¿Qué alboroto es éste, cielos?
SEGISMUNDO.   ¡Clotaldo!
CLOTALDO.   Señor! (*Aparte.* En mí
su crueldad prueba.)
CLARÍN.   (*Aparte.* Yo apuesto
que le despeña del monte.)   2390

(Vase.)

CLOTALDO.   A tus reales plantas llego,
ya sé que a morir.
SEGISMUNDO.   Levanta,
levanta, padre, del suelo;
que tú has de ser norte y guía
de quien fíe mis aciertos;   2395
que ya sé que mi crianza
a tu mucha lealtad debo.
Dame los brazos.
CLOTALDO.   ¿Qué dices?
SEGISMUNDO.   Que estoy soñando y que quiero
obrar bien; pues no se pierde   2400
obrar bien, aun entre sueños.
CLOTALDO.   Pues, señor, si el obrar bien
es ya tu blasón, es cierto
que no te ofenda el que yo
hoy solicite lo mesmo.   2405
A tu padre has de hacer guerra;
yo aconsejarte no puedo
contra mi Rey, ni valerte.
A tus plantas estoy puesto:
dame la muerte.

slavery to a foreigner. Sound the call to arms, and shortly you will see my immense valour in action. I aim to take arms against my father and prove the stars true; soon I shall have him at my feet.

(Aside.) Yet, in case I should wake up before then, wouldn't it be better to avoid making promises that I can't keep?

ALL.   *[Offstage.]* Long live Sigismund! Long live the prince!

(Enter CLOTHOLD.)

CLOTHOLD.	What's all this commotion, heavens?
SIGISMUND.	Clothold.
CLOTHOLD.	My lord…
	(Aside.) My life will be the test of his cruelty.
BUGLE.	*(Aside.)* I'll bet he throws him off the mountain. *(Exit.)*
CLOTHOLD.	I come before your royal feet, certain of my death. *[He kneels before the prince.]*
SIGISMUND.	On your feet, father, on your feet; you will be the compass and guide to whom I entrust my accomplishments, for I know I owe my upbringing to your great loyalty. Let me embrace you.
CLOTHOLD.	What are you saying?
SIGISMUND.	That I'm dreaming, and that I wish to do what's right; for good works mustn't be overlooked, even in dreams.
CLOTHOLD.	Well, my lord, if doing what's right is now your motto, then you won't be offended if I appeal to it today. You would wage war against your father; I cannot counsel you or come to your aid against my king. I am at your mercy; kill me.

SEGISMUNDO.	¡Villano,	2410
	traidor, ingrato! (*Aparte*. Mas, ¡cielos!,	
	reportarme me conviene,	
	que aún no sé si estoy despierto.)	
	Clotaldo, vuestro valor	
	os envidio y agradezco.	2415
	Idos a servir al Rey,	
	que en el campo nos veremos.	
	Vosotros, tocad el arma.	
CLOTALDO.	Mil veces tus plantas beso.	

(Vase.)

SEGISMUNDO.	A reinar, fortuna, vamos.	2420
	No me despiertes, si duermo;	
	y si es verdad, no me duermas.	
	Mas sea verdad o sueño,	
	obrar bien es lo que importa.	
	Si fuere verdad, por serlo;	2425
	si no, por ganar amigos	
	para cuando despertemos.	

(Vanse, y tocan el arma.)

Escena 2
(Salen el REY BASILIO y ASTOLFO.)

BASILIO.	¿Quién, Astolfo, podrá parar, prudente,	
	la furia de un caballo desbocado?	
	¿Quién detener de un río la corriente	2430
	que corre al mar, soberbio y despeñado?	
	¿Quién un peñasco suspender, valiente,	
	de la cima de un monte, desgajado?	
	Pues todo fácil de parar ha sido,	
	y un vulgo no, soberbio y atrevido.	2435
	Dígalo en bandos el rumor partido,	
	pues se oye resonar en lo profundo	
	de los montes el eco repetido,	
	unos «¡Astolfo!» y otros «¡Segismundo!».	
	El dosel de la jura, reducido	2440
	a segunda intención, a honor segundo,	
	teatro funesto es, donde importuna	
	representa tragedias la fortuna.	

SIGISMUND.   Swine! Traitor! Ingrate!
                  (Aside.) But heavens! It behoves me to exercise restraint, for
                  I still don't know if I'm awake.
                  [To CLOTHOLD.] Clothold, I envy and appreciate your
                  valour. Go and serve the king, and we'll meet again on the
                  battlefield. *[To his SOLDIERS.]* Sound the call to arms.
CLOTHOLD.   *[Rising.]* I kiss your feet a thousand times. *(Exit.)*
SIGISMUND.   Off we go, fortune, to claim my throne. Don't wake me if I'm
                  sleeping, and don't lull me to sleep if it's real. Yet, whether
                  it's reality or a dream, doing what's right is what matters. If
                  it's reality, then for the sake of reality; if it's a dream, then for
                  the purpose of winning friends for when we awake. *(Exit all
                  amid the call to arms.)*

Scene 2

([The palace.] Enter VASILY and AISTULF.)

VASILY.   Who, Aistulf, is wise enough to curb the fury of a runaway
                  horse? Who can detain the current of a defiant river in its
                  downhill rush to the sea? Who is valiant enough to stop a
                  boulder that has broken free of the mountaintop? Well that's
                  all easy in comparison to halting a defiant and reckless mob.
                  The proof is in the clashing cries of Poland's rival parties,
                  which penetrate the innermost mountains with thunderous
                  echoes of "Long live Aistulf!" or "Long live Sigismund!"
                  The coronation site, fallen prey to wayward aspirations
                  and hidden loyalties, has become a gloomy theatre where
                  importunate fortune stages her tragedies.

ASTOLFO.	Suspéndase, señor, el alegría;
	cese el aplauso y gusto lisonjero 2445
	que tu mano feliz me prometía;
	que si Polonia — a quien mandar espero —
	hoy se resiste a la obediencia mía,
	es porque la merezca yo primero.
	Dadme un caballo y, de arrogancia lleno, 2450
	rayo descienda el que blasona trueno.

(Vase.)

BASILIO.	Poco reparo tiene lo infalible,
	y mucho riesgo lo previsto tiene.
	Si ha de ser, la defensa es imposible,
	que quien la excusa más, más la previene. 2455
	¡Dura ley! ¡Fuerte caso! ¡Horror terrible!
	Quien piensa que huye el riesgo, al riesgo viene.
	Con lo que yo guardaba me he perdido;
	yo mismo, yo, mi patria he destrüido.

(Sale ESTRELLA.)

ESTRELLA.	Si tu presencia, gran señor, no trata 2460
	de enfrenar el tumulto sucedido
	— que de uno en otro bando se dilata
	por las calles y plazas, dividido — ,
	verás tu reino, en ondas de escarlata,
	nadar entre la púrpura, teñido 2465
	de su sangre; que ya, con triste modo,
	todo es desdichas, y tragedias todo.
	Tanta es la ruina de tu imperio, tanta
	la fuerza del rigor duro y sangriento
	que visto admira y escuchado espanta. 2470
	El sol se turba y se embaraza el viento;
	cada piedra un pirámide levanta
	y cada flor construye un monumento;
	cada edificio es un sepulcro altivo,
	cada soldado un esqueleto vivo. 2475

(Sale CLOTALDO.)

CLOTALDO.	¡Gracias a Dios que vivo a tus pies llego!
BASILIO.	¡Clotaldo! Pues ¿qué hay de Segismundo?
CLOTALDO.	Que el vulgo, monstruo despeñado y ciego,
	la torre penetró, y de lo profundo

AISTULF.	We must suspend the celebration and postpone the applause and flattering delights that your fortunate hand promised me; for if Poland, which I hope to rule, today refuses obedience to me, it is to make me earn it first. Give me a horse, and let him who boasts with thunder descend like lightning, full of arrogance. *(Exit.)*
VASILY.	The inevitable has little remedy, and the foreseen carries considerable risk; if it's meant to be, there's no defence against it, for he who most tries to avoid it most precipitates its arrival. What harsh logic! What awful circumstances! What tremendous horror! He who believes he's running from danger ends up running into it. In trying to avoid it, I have ruined myself. I, and I alone, have destroyed my fatherland.

(Enter STELLA.)

STELLA.	If you do not act, your majesty, to put a stop to the chaos that has broken out and, spreading from one side to the next, polarizes streets and squares, you will soon find your kingdom swimming in waves of scarlet, dyed in the crimson of its own blood; sadly, misfortune and tragedy are already widespread. Such is the ruin of your empire, such the might of harsh and bloody inclemency that it amazes the eyes and alarms the ears. The sun is startled and the wind falters; the rocks form tombstones and the flowers cluster on gravesites; every building is a mausoleum and every soldier, a living skeleton.

(Enter CLOTHOLD.)

CLOTHOLD.	Thank God I've made it here alive!
VASILY.	Clothold, what can you tell us of Sigismund?
CLOTHOLD.	A monstrous mob, reckless and blind, has broken into the

	della sacó su príncipe, que luego	2480
	que vio segunda vez su honor segundo,	
	valiente se mostró, diciendo, fiero,	
	que ha de sacar al cielo verdadero.	
BASILIO.	Dadme un caballo, porque yo en persona	
	vencer valiente a un hijo ingrato quiero;	2485
	y en la defensa ya de mi corona,	
	lo que la ciencia erró venza el acero.	

(Vase.)

ESTRELLA.	Pues yo, al lado del sol, seré Belona.	
	Poner mi nombre junto al tuyo espero,	
	que he de volar sobre rendidas alas	2490
	a competir con la deidad de Palas.	

(Vase ESTRELLA, y tocan al arma. Sale ROSAURA y detiene a CLOTALDO.)

ROSAURA.	Aunque el valor que se encierra	
	en tu pecho desde allí	
	dé voces, óyeme a mí;	
	que yo sé que todo es guerra.	2495
	Ya sabes que yo llegué,	
	pobre, humilde y desdichada,	
	a Polonia y, amparada	
	de tu valor, en ti hallé	
	piedad. Mandásteme, ¡ay cielos!,	2500
	que disfrazada viviese	
	en palacio, y pretendiese,	
	disimulando mis celos,	
	guardarme de Astolfo. En fin	
	él me vio, y tanto atropella	2505
	mi honor que, viéndome, a Estrella	
	de noche habla en un jardín.	
	Déste la llave he tomado,	
	y te podrá dar lugar	
	de que en él puedas entrar	2510
	a dar fin a mi cuidado.	
	Aquí, altivo, osado y fuerte,	
	volver por honor podrás,	
	pues que ya resuelto estás	
	a vengarme con su muerte.	2515
CLOTALDO.	Verdad es que me incliné,	
	desde el punto que te vi,	

tower and liberated the prince from its depths. Finding his power seconded a second time, he became valiant, proclaiming fiercely that he will prove the stars right.

VASILY.
Give me a horse, for I wish valiantly to defeat my ungrateful son in person. In defence of my crown, may steel triumph where knowledge has failed. *(Exit.)*

STELLA.
And I, flanking the sun, shall act as Bellona. I hope to write my name next to yours *[Gesturing toward VASILY as he exits]*, for on obedient wings I shall fly in competition with the deity of Pallas. *(Exit amid the call to arms.)*

(Enter ROSSAURA, who detains CLOTHOLD.)

ROSSAURA.
I realize that we're in the midst of war; but even if your valour is bursting in your breast, hear me out. You know that I arrived in Poland poor, humble, and unfortunate, and that, aided by your valour, I found mercy in your person. You ordered me – Oh, heavens! – to live in disguise in the palace and to attempt, concealing my jealousy, to keep away from Aistulf. But he saw me in the end, and so recklessly does he trample my honour that he speaks to Stella in front of me every night in the garden. I've stolen the key, with which I can provide the means for you to enter the garden and put an end to my troubles. There, with bluster, daring, and might, you can restore my honour since you are already resolved to avenge me with his death.

CLOTHOLD.
It's true that from the moment I first saw you, Rossaura,

a hacer, Rosaura, por ti
— testigo tu llanto fue —
cuanto mi vida pudiese.   2520
Lo primero que intenté
quitarte aquel traje fue,
porque, si Astolfo te viese,
te viese en tu propio traje,
sin juzgar a liviandad   2525
la loca temeridad
que hace del honor ultraje.
En este tiempo trazaba
cómo cobrar se pudiese
tu honor perdido, aunque fuese   2530
— ¡tanto tu honor me arrestaba! —
dando muerte a Astolfo. ¡Mira
qué caduco desvarío!
Si bien, no siendo rey mío,
ni me asombra ni me admira.   2535
Darle pensé muerte cuando
Segismundo pretendió
dármela a mí, y él llegó,
su peligro atropellando,
a hacer en defensa mía   2540
muestras de su voluntad
que fueron temeridad,
pasando de valentía.
Pues, ¿cómo yo agora, advierte,
teniendo alma agradecida,   2545
a quien me ha dado la vida
le tengo que dar la muerte?
Y así, entre dos repartidos
el efeto y el cuidado,
viendo que a ti te la he dado,   2550
y que dél la he recibido,
no sé a qué parte acudir,
no sé qué parte ayudar:
si a ti me obligué con dar,
dél lo estoy con recibir.   2555
Y así, en la acción que se ofrece,
nada a mi amor satisface,
porque soy persona que hace
y persona que padece.

I was moved to do for you – as your sobs bore witness – whatever my life allowed. The first thing I did was to get you to change that outfit you were wearing so that, if Aistulf were to see you, he'd see you in your own clothes and not take for indecency the mad temerity that besmirches honour. I've since been trying to determine how to recover your lost honour even if it meant – so much does your honour preoccupy me – killing Aistulf. What wayward madness! Although, given that he's not my king, I am neither cowed nor awed by him. I was planning to kill him when Sigismund tried to kill me, and then he arrived and, overlooking the danger to himself, demonstrated a degree of altruism in my defence that went past courage to temerity. So tell me, how am I now to kill the person who saved my life, when my soul is full of gratitude? And thus, torn between the effect of his action and my obligation to you, having given you life and received it from him, I don't know which party to go to or to help; for to you I'm bound on account of giving, and to him I'm bound on account of receiving. And thus, in the matter at hand, nothing satisfies my loving nature because my active and passive sides are in conflict.

ROSAURA.   No tengo que prevenir   2560
                que, en un varón singular,
                cuanto es noble acción el dar
                es bajeza el recibir.
                Y este principio asentado,
                no has de estarle agradecido,   2565
                supuesto que, si él ha sido
                el que la vida te ha dado
                y tú a mí, evidente cosa
                es que él forzó tu nobleza
                a que hiciese una bajeza   2570
                y yo una acción generosa:
                luego estás dél ofendido,
                luego estás de mí obligado,
                supuesto que a mí me has dado
                lo que dél has recibido;   2575
                y así, debes acudir
                a mi honor en riesgo tanto,
                pues yo le prefiero cuanto
                va de dar a recibir.
CLOTALDO.   Aunque la nobleza vive   2580
                de la parte del que da,
                el agradecerla está
                de parte del que recibe.
                Y pues ya dar he sabido,
                ya tengo con nombre honroso   2585
                el nombre de generoso:
                déjame el de agradecido,
                pues le puedo conseguir
                siendo agradecido cuanto
                liberal, pues honra tanto   2590
                el dar como el recibir.
ROSAURA.   De ti recibí la vida,
                y tú mismo me dijiste,
                cuando la vida me diste,
                que la que estaba ofendida   2595
                no era vida; luego yo
                nada de ti he recibido,
                pues muerte, no vida, ha sido
                la que tu mano me dio.
                Y si debes ser primero   2600
                liberal que agradecido

ROSSAURA.   I needn't remind you that, in men of distinction, receiving is as base an action as giving is noble. Accepting this principle, you have no reason to be grateful to him given that, if he gave you life and you gave me life, it's obvious that he forced your noble nature to commit a base act while I facilitated its generosity. Therefore you should consider yourself offended by him and indebted to me, for you have given to me what you have received from him. And thus you should attend to my honour, which is at great risk, for it gives me precedence in the conflict between giving and receiving.

CLOTHOLD.   Although nobility lives from giving, gratitude for noble actions corresponds to those who receive. And as I have not held back in giving, I have become known as generous in addition to noble. Let me be known also as grateful, for I can be grateful and generous simultaneously, for giving and receiving are equally honourable.

ROSSAURA.   You gave me life and, in doing so, said yourself that a life lived in dishonour is no life. Therefore I have received nothing from you, for your hand has dispensed death, not life. And if you must be generous before being grateful – as you yourself

	– como de ti mismo he oído – ,	
	que me des la vida espero,	
	que no me la has dado; y pues	
	el dar engrandece más,	2605
	sé antes liberal; serás	
	agradecido después.	
CLOTALDO.	Vencido de tu argumento,	
	antes liberal seré.	
	Yo, Rosaura, te daré	2610
	mi hacienda, y en un convento	
	vive; que está bien pensado	
	el medio que solicito,	
	pues, huyendo de un delito,	
	te recoges a un sagrado;	2615
	que cuando, tan dividido,	
	el reino desdichas siente,	
	no he de ser quien las aumente,	
	habiendo noble nacido.	
	Con el remedio elegido,	2620
	soy con el reino leal,	
	soy contigo liberal,	
	con Astolfo agradecido;	
	y así escogerle te cuadre,	
	quedándose entre los dos,	2625
	que no hiciera, ¡vive Dios!,	
	más cuando fuera tu padre.	
ROSAURA.	Cuando tú mi padre fueras,	
	sufriera esa injuria yo;	
	pero no siéndolo, no.	2630
CLOTALDO.	Pues ¿qué es lo que hacer esperas?	
ROSAURA.	Matar al Duque.	
CLOTALDO.	Una dama	
	que padre no ha conocido	
	¿tanto valor ha tenido?	
ROSAURA.	Sí.	
CLOTALDO.	¿Quién te alienta?	
ROSAURA.	Mi fama.	2635
CLOTALDO.	Mira que a Astolfo has de ver...	
ROSAURA.	Todo mi honor lo atropella.	
CLOTALDO.	...tu rey y esposo de Estrella.	
ROSAURA.	¡Vive Dios que no ha de ser!	

	have said – I expect you to give me my life, which you have yet to do; and, since giving is more ennobling, be generous first, and you will be grateful later.
CLOTHOLD.	Your reasoning has convinced me, and I shall be generous first. I shall, Rossaura, give you my inheritance, with which you may retire to a convent. The solution I am suggesting is well considered, since in fleeing from a crime you will take refuge in a sanctuary. For when a divided kingdom is burdened with misfortunes, I don't wish to multiply them, for I was born noble. With this remedy I can be loyal to my country, generous to you, and grateful to Aistulf. It behoves you to accept this remedy, which we'll keep between the two of us, for I wouldn't do anything more even if – By God! – I were your father.
ROSSAURA.	If you were my father, I would accept this insult; but as you're not, I won't.
CLOTHOLD.	Well, then what is it you plan to do?
ROSSAURA.	Kill the duke.
CLOTHOLD.	Can a lady who never knew her father have such courage?
ROSSAURA.	Yes.
CLOTHOLD.	Who drives you?
ROSSAURA.	My reputation.
CLOTHOLD.	Beware that Aistulf is about to become…
ROSSAURA.	He tramples over all my honour.
CLOTHOLD.	…your king and Stella's husband.
ROSSAURA.	By God, it shall not happen!

CLOTALDO.	Es locura.
ROSAURA.	Ya lo veo.
CLOTALDO.	Pues véncela.
ROSAURA.	No podré.
CLOTALDO.	Pues perderás...
ROSAURA.	Ya lo sé.
CLOTALDO.	...vida y honor.
ROSAURA.	Bien lo creo.
CLOTALDO.	¿Qué intentas?
ROSAURA.	Mi muerte.
CLOTALDO.	Mira
	que eso es despecho.
ROSAURA.	Es honor.
CLOTALDO.	Es desatino.
ROSAURA.	Es valor.
CLOTALDO.	Es frenesí.
ROSAURA.	Es rabia, es ira.
CLOTALDO.	En fin, ¿que no se da medio
	a tu ciega pasión?
ROSAURA.	No.
CLOTALDO.	¿Quién ha de ayudarte?
ROSAURA.	Yo.
CLOTALDO.	¿No hay remedio?
ROSAURA.	No hay remedio.
CLOTALDO.	Piensa bien si hay otros modos.
ROSAURA.	Perderme de otra manera.

2640

2645

2650

(Vase.)

CLOTALDO.	Pues has de perderte, espera,
	hija, y perdámonos todos.

2655

(Vase.)

Escena 3

(Tocan y salen, marchando, SOLDADOS., CLARÍN y SEGISMUNDO, vestido de pieles.)

SEGISMUNDO.	Si este día me viera
	Roma, en los triunfos de su edad primera,
	¡oh, cuánto se alegrara,
	viendo lograr una ocasión tan rara
	de tener una fiera

2660

CLOTHOLD.	This is madness.
ROSSAURA.	I know.
CLOTHOLD.	You must overcome it.
ROSSAURA.	I cannot.
CLOTHOLD.	You'll lose…
ROSSAURA.	I know.
CLOTHOLD.	… life and honour.
ROSSAURA.	I know.
CLOTHOLD.	What do you want?
ROSSAURA.	My death.
CLOTHOLD.	Beware, that's sacrilege.
ROSSAURA.	It's honour.
CLOTHOLD.	It's folly.
ROSSAURA.	It's valour.
CLOTHOLD.	It's frenzy.
ROSSAURA.	It's rage, it's wrath.
CLOTHOLD.	So there's no compromising with your obsession?
ROSSAURA.	No.
CLOTHOLD.	Who will assist you?
ROSSAURA.	I'll assist myself.
CLOTHOLD.	There's no solution?
ROSSAURA.	There's no solution.
CLOTHOLD.	Think well; there must be another way.
ROSSAURA.	Only another form of self-destruction. *(Exit.)*
CLOTHOLD.	Well, since you're bent on destroying yourself, wait for me, my daughter, and we'll go down together. *(Exit.)*

Scene 3

([A wilderness area, somewhere between the palace and the tower.] Amid the call to arms, SOLDIERS, BUGLE, and SIGISMUND march out, the latter dressed in animal skins.)

SIGISMUND.	If Rome at the height of her youthful vigour could see me today, how thrilled she would be at the rare chance to have

que sus grandes ejércitos rigiera,
a cuyo altivo aliento
fuera poca conquista el firmamento!
Pero el vuelo abatamos,
espíritu; no así desvanezcamos   2665
aqueste aplauso incierto,
si ha de pesarme, cuando esté despierto,
de haberlo conseguido
para haberlo perdido;
pues mientras menos fuere,   2670
menos se sentirá si se perdiere.

(Dentro, un clarín.)

CLARÍN.   En un veloz caballo
                 – perdóname, que fuerza es el pintallo
                 en viniéndome a cuento – ,
                 en quien un mapa se dibuja atento   2675
                 – pues el cuerpo es la tierra,
                 el fuego el alma que en el pecho encierra,
                 la espuma el mar, el aire su suspiro – ,
                 en cuya confusión un caos admiro,
                 – pues en el alma, espuma, cuerpo, aliento,   2680
                 monstruo es de fuego, tierra, mar y viento – ,
                 de color remendado,
                 rucio y, a su propósito, rodado,
                 del que bate la espuela
                 y, en vez de correr, vuela,   2685
                 a tu presencia llega
                 airosa una mujer.
SEGISMUNDO.   Su luz me ciega.
CLARÍN.   *(Aparte.* ¡Vive Dios que es Rosaura!)

(Vase.)

SEGISMUNDO.   El cielo a mi presencia la restaura.

(Sale ROSAURA, con vaquero, espada y daga.)

ROSAURA.   Generoso Segismundo,   2690
                 cuya majestad heroica
                 sale al día de sus hechos
                 de la noche de sus sombras
                 – y como el mayor planeta,
                 que en los brazos de la aurora   2695

her mighty armies led by a beast whose insolent bravado strikes at the firmament itself! But let's come down to earth, my spirit, lest we shatter this tenuous glory, for I'll only be disappointed, upon waking, at having achieved so much only to lose it; for the lesser the glory, the less its loss will be felt.

(A bugle sounds offstage.)

BUGLE.   We are approached by a swift horse – forgive me, for it demands careful description – upon whom a careful map is drawn in which its body is earth, fire is the soul trapped in its chest, its spittle is the sea, and the air is its breath; the motley figure inspires chaos, for its soul, spittle, body, and breath form a monstrosity of fire, earth, sea, and wind. Upon its coarse coat of dapple grey sits a gallant woman who digs in the spurs and bids it fly rather than gallop toward your presence.

SIGISMUND.   I'm blinded by her aura.

BUGLE.   *(Aside.)* By God, it's Rossaura! *(Exit.)*

SIGISMUND.   Heaven has restored her to my presence.

(Enter ROSSAURA with a splendid cloak, a sword, and a dagger.)

ROSSAURA.   Generous Sigismund, whose heroic majesty emerges into the light of its deeds from the darkness of its shadows: may your rise in the world, shining sun of Poland, imitate the greatest of heavenly bodies, which, in the arms of dawn, recovers

se restituye luciente
a las flores y a las rosas,
y sobre mares y montes,
cuando coronado asoma,
luz esparce, rayos brilla,   2700
cumbres baña, espumas borda – ,
así amanezcas al mundo,
luciente sol de Polonia,
que a una mujer infelice,
que hoy a tus plantas se arroja,   2705
ampares por ser mujer
y desdichada: dos cosas
que, para obligar a un hombre
que de valiente blasona,
cualquiera de las dos basta,   2710
de las dos cualquiera sobra.
Tres veces son las que ya
me admiras, tres las que ignoras
quién soy, pues las tres me has visto
en diverso traje y forma.   2715
La primera me creíste
varón en la rigurosa
prisión donde fue tu vida
de mis desdichas lisonja.
La segunda me admiraste   2720
mujer, cuando fue la pompa
de tu majestad un sueño,
una fantasma, una sombra.
La tercera es hoy que, siendo
monstruo de una especie y otra,   2725
entre galas de mujer,
armas de varón me adornan.
Y por que, compadecido,
mejor mi amparo dispongas,
es bien que de mis sucesos   2730
trágicas fortunas oigas.
De noble madre nací
en la corte de Moscovia,
que, según fue desdichada,
debió de ser muy hermosa.   2735
En ésta puso los ojos

its shining throne before flowers and roses and, stepping out newly crowned, spreads its light and casts its rays over oceans and mountains, bathing high peaks and adorning frothy waves. Take pity on this unlucky woman who today throws herself at your feet; being both unfortunate and a woman, she has two reasons to expect charity from a man who prides himself on his valour, either of which is enough, both of which are more than enough. Three times now you have beheld me with awe, three times without knowing who I am, for on each occasion you've seen me in different attire and character. The first time was in your cruel prison, where you took me for a man and your life played flattery to my misfortunes. The second time – when your majestic splendour was but a dream, a ghost, a shadow – you beheld me as a woman. The third time is today, where I, a monstrous hybrid, am adorned in the fine clothes of a woman and the arms of a man. And so that pity may move you to come to my aid, listen to the tragic story of my life. I was born at court in Muscovy to a noble mother who, to judge from her misfortunes, must have been very beautiful. She caught the eye of a treacherous

un traidor, que no le nombra
mi voz por no conocerle,
de cuyo valor me informa
el mío; pues, siendo objeto   2740
de su idea, siento agora
no haber nacido gentil,
para persuadirme, loca,
a que fue algún dios de aquellos
que en metamorfosis lloran   2745
– lluvia de oro, cisne y toro –
Danae, Leda y Europa.
Cuando pensé que alargaba,
citando aleves historias,
el discurso, hallo que en él   2750
te he dicho en razones pocas
que mi madre, persuadida
a finezas amorosas,
fue, como ninguna, bella,
y fue infeliz como todas.   2755
Aquella necia disculpa
de fe y palabra de esposa
la alcanza tanto que, aun hoy,
el pensamiento la cobra,
habiendo sido un tirano   2760
tan Eneas de su honra
que la dejó hasta la espada.
Enváinese aquí su hoja,
que yo la desnudaré
antes que acabe la historia.   2765
Deste, pues, mal dado nudo,
que ni ata ni aprisiona,
o matrimonio o delito,
si bien todo es una cosa,
nací yo tan parecida   2770
que fui un retrato, una copia,
ya que en la hermosura no,
en la dicha y en las obras.
Y así no habré menester
decir que, poco dichosa   2775
heredera de fortunas,
corrí con ella una propia.
Lo más que podré decirte

scoundrel, whose name can't cross my lips because it is unknown to them, although his character informs my own; and thus, as the product of his desire, I regret now not being born pagan so that I could madly convince myself that he was one of those gods who, transformed into a shower of gold, a swan, or a bull, are lamented by Danae, Leda, and Europa. While I thought that by citing dastardly tales I would merely lengthen my speech, I see now that I have foreshadowed how my mother, swept away in the game of love, was more beautiful than any other woman and as unlucky as all of them. She was so completely duped by that foolish old ruse of a secret wedding vow that she relives it even today; and her betrayer was such an Aeneas to her honour that he even left her a sword. Its blade will remain sheathed for now, but I shall reveal it before my story is over. From this poorly tied knot, which neither binds nor imprisons, from this marriage, from this crime – for it's all the same thing – I was born, so similar to my mother that I was her living portrait, her double, if not in loveliness then in luck and circumstances. And so it goes without saying that my stormy fate drove me to shipwreck. The most I can tell you about myself is the

de mí es el dueño que roba
los trofeos de mi honor,   2780
los despojos de mi honra:
Astolfo — ¡Ay de mí!, al nombrarle
se encoleriza y se enoja
el corazón, propio efeto
de que enemigo se nombra — ,   2785
Astolfo fue el dueño ingrato
que, olvidado de las glorias
— porque en un pasado amor
se olvida hasta la memoria — ,
vino a Polonia, llamado   2790
de su conquista famosa,
a casarse con Estrella,
que fue de mi ocaso antorcha.
¿Quién creerá que, habiendo sido
una estrella quien conforma   2795
dos amantes, sea una Estrella
la que los divida agora?
Yo, ofendida, yo, burlada,
quedé triste, quedé loca,
quedé muerta, quedé yo,   2800
que es decir que quedó toda
la confusión del infierno
cifrada en mi Babilonia;
y declarándome muda,
porque hay penas y congojas   2805
que las dicen los afectos
mucho mejor que la boca,
dije mis penas callando;
hasta que una vez a solas,
Violante, mi madre, ¡ay cielos!,   2810
rompió la prisión, y en tropa
del pecho salieron juntas,
tropezando unas con otras.
No me embaracé en decirlas;
que, en sabiendo una persona   2815
que a quien sus flaquezas cuenta
ha sido cómplice en otras,
parece que ya le hace
la salva y le desahoga;
que a veces el mal ejemplo   2820
sirve de algo. En fin, piadosa

name of the lord who steals the prizes of my honour, the spoils of my reputation: Aistulf. Oh, miserable me! At the mention of his name my heart fills with anger and choler, a natural reaction to an allusion to the enemy. Aistulf was the ungrateful lord who, forgetful of love's delight – for in a past love, even memories are forgotten – came to Poland, lured by conquest, to marry Stella, his sunrise and my sunset. Who would guess that lovers brought together by stellar design would now be separated by Stella's design? Humiliated and mocked, I was left feeling sad, demented, dead; I was left with myself, and I raged with the confusion of hell and the chaos of Babel. And refusing to talk about it, because some suffering and anguish is better left to feelings than to words, I spoke my sufferings in silence until one day, when I was alone with my mother Viola – Oh, heavens! – she broke them free of their prison, and they all poured out together, tripping over one another in their haste. I was not ashamed to relate them, for when a person confesses his faults to someone he knows has similar faults, it seems as though he feels free and uninhibited in doing so, for there are times when a bad example does some good. In any case, my mother listened

oyó mis quejas, y quiso
consolarme con las propias:
juez que ha sido delincuente,
¡qué fácilmente perdona!   2825
Y escarmentando en sí misma
– que por dejar a la ociosa
libertad, al tiempo fácil,
el remedio de su honra,
no le tuvo en mis desdichas – ,   2830
por mejor consejo toma
que le siga y que le obligue
con finezas prodigiosas
a la deuda de mi honor;
y, para que a menos costa   2835
fuese, quiso mi fortuna
que en traje de hombre me ponga.
Descolgó una antigua espada,
que es ésta que ciño – agora
es tiempo que se desnude,   2840
como prometí, la hoja – ,
pues, confiada en sus señas,
me dijo: «Parte a Polonia,
y procura que te vean
ese acero que te adorna   2845
los más nobles, que en alguno
podrá ser que hallen piadosa
acogida tus fortunas
y consuelo tus congojas.»
Llegué a Polonia en efeto…   2850
Pasemos, pues que no importa
el decirlo, y ya se sabe,
que un bruto que se desboca
me llevó a tu cueva, adonde
tú de mirarme te asombras.   2855
Pasemos que allí Clotaldo
de mi parte se apasiona;
que pide mi vida al Rey;
que el Rey mi vida le otorga;
que, informado de quién soy,   2860
me persuade a que me ponga
mi propio traje y que sirva
a Estrella, donde, ingeniosa,

dutifully to my laments and tried to console me with her own. How easily a guilty judge forgives! And having learned from her own experience – whereby, having entrusted the remedy of her dishonour to idle liberty and lenient time, she now had no way to remedy my own misfortunes – she considered it best that I go after him and oblige him, with overpowering arguments, to pay the debt of my honour; and to make it easier, fortune suggested dressing me in the clothes of a man. She took down an old sword, this one you see me wearing – now's the time to unsheathe its blade as I promised – for my mother, trusting in its design, said to me: "Make your way to Poland, Rossaura, and do your best to have the nobles there see you wearing this sword, for in one of them your fortune may find a merciful welcome and your anguish, consolation." Thus I arrived in Poland. Let's pass quickly over details that are unimportant or already known: that a bucking beast brought me to your cave, where you were astonished to see me; that Clothold took pity on me, asked the king to spare my life, and the king granted his request; that Clothold, informed of my identity, persuaded me to wear my normal clothes and enter the service of Stella, where I ingeniously thwarted

estorbé el amor de Astolfo
y el ser Estrella su esposa.   2865
Pasemos que aquí me viste
otra vez confuso, y otra,
con el traje de mujer,
confundiste entrambas formas;
y vamos a que Clotaldo,   2870
persuadido a que le importa
que se casen y que reinen
Astolfo y Estrella hermosa,
contra mi honor me aconseja
que la pretensión deponga.   2875
Yo, viendo que tú, ¡oh valiente
Segismundo! – a quien hoy toca
la venganza, pues el cielo
quiere que la cárcel rompas
desa rústica prisión,   2880
donde ha sido tu persona
al sentimiento una fiera,
al sufrimiento una roca – ,
las armas contra tu patria
y contra tu padre tomas,   2885
vengo a ayudarte, mezclando
entre las galas costosas
de Dïana, los arneses
de Palas, vistiendo agora
ya la tela y ya el acero,   2890
q[ue] entrambos juntos me adornan.
¡Ea, pues, fuerte caudillo!
A los dos juntos importa
impedir y deshacer
estas concertadas bodas: 2895
a mí porque no se case
el que mi esposo se nombra;
y a ti porque, estando juntos
sus dos estados, no pongan
con más poder y más fuerza   2900
en duda nuestra vitoria.
Mujer, vengo a persuadirte
el remedio de mi honra;
y varón, vengo a alentarte
a que cobres tu corona.   2905
Mujer, vengo a enternecerte

Aistulf's courtship and prevented Stella from becoming his wife; and that there, in the palace, you were again baffled at the sight of me, this time dressed as a woman, my past and present appearances confused in your mind. Let's turn our attention to how Clothold, convinced that Aistulf should marry the lovely Stella and rule jointly with her, advised me, in an affront to my honour, to end my crusade. But now that, O valiant Sigismund, your turn at vengeance has arrived, for Heaven has allowed you to break free of the confines of that crude prison, where your temperament was a savage to sorrow and a rock to suffering; now that you are taking up arms against your fatherland and against your father, I am here to offer my help, combining the rich garments of Diana and the armament of Pallas, dressed in cloth as well as steel, for I am suited to both. Let's move quickly, then, brave chief, for we both have an interest in preventing and annulling this arranged marriage: I, to stop the man who would be my husband from marrying another; you, to nullify the threat posed by the strength and power that their countries, once united, would represent. As a woman, I come to move you to the cause of my honour; as a man, I come to encourage you to recover your crown. As a woman, I come to request your

cuando a tus plantas me ponga;
y varón, vengo a servirte
cuando a tus gentes socorra.
Mujer, vengo a que me valgas   2910
en mi agravio y mi congoja;
y varón, vengo a valerte
con mi acero y mi persona.
Y así, piensa que si hoy
como a mujer me enamoras,   2915
como varón te daré
la muerte en defensa honrosa
de mi honor; porque he de ser
en su conquista, amorosa
mujer para darte quejas,   2920
varón para ganar honras.

SEGISMUNDO. (*Aparte.* ¡Cielos, si es verdad que sueño,
suspendedme la memoria,
que no es posible que quepan
en un sueño tantas cosas!   2925
¡Válgame Dios! ¡Quién supiera,
o saber salir de todas,
o no pensar en ninguna!
¿Quién vio penas tan dudosas?
Si soñé aquella grandeza   2930
en que me vi, ¿cómo agora
esta mujer me refiere
unas señas tan notorias?
Luego fue verdad, no sueño;
y si fue verdad, que es otra   2935
confusión, y no menor,
¿cómo mi vida le nombra
sueño? Pues ¿tan parecidas
a los sueños son las glorias
que las verdaderas son   2940
tenidas por mentirosas
y las fingidas por ciertas?
¿Tan poco hay de unas a otras
que hay cuestión sobre saber
si lo que se ve y se goza   2945
es mentira o es verdad?
¿Tan semejante es la copia
al original que hay duda
en saber si es ella propia?

sympathy by throwing myself at your feet; as a man, I come to serve you by aiding your soldiers. As a woman, I come to request your support in my dishonour and anguish; as a man, I come to support you with my sword and my character. And finally, consider that if you see me now as a woman and try to seduce me, I will become a man and slay you in legitimate defence of my honour; for to recover it I must act as a lovesick woman in complaining and as a man in accruing fame.

SIGISMUND.   *(Aside.)* Heavens, if I'm really dreaming, then restrain my memory, for it's impossible for a dream to have so many twists and turns. God help me! Who could escape them all or avoid thinking about any of them? Who ever heard of such enigmatic torments? If that splendour in which I found myself was a dream, how is it that this woman can now describe it to me in such vivid detail? So it was real, not a dream. But if it was real, then it's no less confusing, for why does my life call it a dream? Are delights so akin to dreams that the real ones are taken for lies and the fake ones for genuine? Is there so little difference between one and the other that it's debatable whether what's seen and enjoyed is real or made up? Is the copy so close to the original that the mind doubts which is

Pues si es así, y ha de verse   2950
desvanecida entre sombras
la grandeza y el poder,
la majestad y la pompa,
sepamos aprovechar
este rato que nos toca,   2955
pues sólo se goza en ella
lo que entre sueños se goza.
Rosaura está en mi poder,
su hermosura el alma adora;
gocemos, pues, la ocasión: 2960
el amor las leyes rompa
del valor y confianza
con que a mis plantas se postra.
Esto es sueño; y pues lo es,
soñemos dichas agora,   2965
que después serán pesares.
Mas, con mis razones propias,
vuelvo a convencerme a mí.
Si es sueño, si es vanagloria,
¿quién, por vanagloria humana,   2970
pierde una divina gloria?
¿Qué pasado bien no es sueño?
¿Quién tuvo dichas heroicas
que entre sí no diga, cuando
las revuelve en su memoria,   2975
«sin duda que fue soñado
cuanto vi»? Pues si esto toca
mi desengaño, si sé
que es el gusto llama hermosa
que le convierte en cenizas   2980
cualquiera viento que sopla,
acudamos a lo eterno,
que es la fama vividora
donde ni duermen las dichas,
ni las grandezas reposan.   2985
Rosaura está sin honor:
más a un príncipe le toca
el dar honor que quitarle.
¡Vive Dios, que de su honra
he de ser conquistador   2990
antes que de mi corona!

which? If so, and all grandiosity and power, all majesty and splendour will eventually fade into shadow, then we must take advantage of this moment while we can, for it affords us delights that are found only in dreams. Rossaura is in my power; my soul longs for her loveliness. Let's enjoy, then, the moment and allow love to violate the understanding of bravery and trust with which she kneels before me. This is a dream, and that being the case, let's dream of delights now, for they will become sorrows later. And yet I can use the same argument to convince myself differently. If it's a dream, a show, who would risk losing divine glory for the sake of human ego? What past pleasure is not a dream? Who has never thought, in looking back on his most heroic escapades, "I'm sure this was all a dream"? If this is my epiphany, if I know pleasure is a lovely flame that will be reduced to ash by the first breeze that blows, then we must hearken to the eternal, or fame everlasting, where joy never sleeps and grandeur never rests. Rossaura is without honour, and it is more fitting for a prince to give honour than to take it away. By God, I must recover her honour before my own crown!

	Huyamos de la ocasión,	
	que es muy fuerte). ¡Al arma toca,	
	que hoy he de dar la batalla	
	antes que las negras sombras	2995
	sepulten los rayos de oro	
	entre verdinegras ondas!	
ROSAURA.	Señor, ¿pues así te ausentas?	
	¿Pues ni una palabra sola	
	no te debe mi cuidado,	3000
	no merece mi congoja?	
	¿Cómo es posible, señor,	
	que ni me mires ni oigas?	
	¿Aun no me vuelves el rostro?	
SEGISMUNDO.	Rosaura, al honor le importa,	3005
	por ser piadoso contigo,	
	ser crüel contigo agora.	
	No te responde mi voz,	
	por que mi honor te responda;	
	no te hablo, porque quiero	3010
	que te hablen por mí mis obras;	
	ni te miro, porque es fuerza,	
	en pena tan rigurosa,	
	que no mire tu hermosura	
	quien ha de mirar tu honra.	3015

(Vanse.)

ROSAURA.	(*Aparte.* ¿Qué enigmas, cielos, son éstas?	
	Después de tanto pesar,	
	¿aún me queda que dudar	
	con equívocas respuestas?	

(Sale CLARÍN.)

CLARÍN.	Señora, ¿es hora de verte?	3020
ROSAURA.	¡Ay, Clarín! ¿Dónde has estado?	
CLARÍN.	En una torre encerrado,	
	brujuleando mi muerte,	
	si me da, o no me da;	
	y a figura que me diera,	3025
	pasante quínola fuera	
	mi vida; que estuve ya	
	para dar un estallido.	
ROSAURA.	¿Por qué?	

We must overcome the temptation of this moment.
[To a SOLDIER.] Sound the call to arms, for today I shall begin battle before dark shadows bury the sun's golden rays in waves of greenish black!

ROSSAURA. My lord, are you going to turn away just like that? My problems and anguish don't merit a single word from you in reply? How can you ignore me so completely? You won't even show me your face?

SIGISMUND. Rossaura, honour demands, in order to be merciful, that I be cruel to you now. My voice is silent so that my honour may respond; I don't speak to you because I want my actions to speak for me; I don't look at you because it's essential, when you're so helpless, that he who is to look after your honour not look upon your beauty.

(Exit SIGISMUND and SOLDIERS.)

ROSSAURA. What enigmatic talk is this, heavens? After so much sorrow, must I still put up with equivocal replies!

(Enter BUGLE.)

BUGLE. My lady, do you have a minute?
ROSSAURA. Oh, Bugle! Where have you been?
BUGLE. Locked away in a tower wondering when death might appear in the cards for me, for they could have zapped me at any moment.
ROSSAURA. Why?

CLARÍN.	Porque sé el secreto
	de quién eres, y en efeto, 3030
	(Dentro, cajas.)
	Clotaldo... Pero ¿qué ruido
	es éste?
ROSAURA.	¿Qué puede ser?
CLARÍN.	Que del palacio sitiado
	sale un escuadrón armado
	a resistir y vencer 3035
	el del fiero Segismundo.
ROSAURA.	Pues ¿cómo cobarde estoy
	y ya a su lado no soy
	un escándalo del mundo,
	cuando ya tanta crueldad 3040
	cierra sin orden ni ley?

(Vase.)

DENTRO UNOS.	¡Viva nuestro invicto Rey!
DENTRO OTROS.	¡Viva nuestra libertad!
CLARÍN.	La libertad y el Rey vivan;
	vivan muy en hora buena, 3045
	que a mí nada me da pena,
	como en cuenta me reciban;
	que yo, apartado este día
	en tan grande confusión,
	hago el papel de Nerón, 3050
	que de nada se dolía.
	Si bien me quiero doler
	de algo, y ha de ser de mí.
	Escondido, desde aquí
	toda la fiesta he de ver. 3055
	El sitio es oculto y fuerte
	entre estas peñas. Pues ya
	la muerte no me hallará,
	dos higas para la muerte.

(Escóndese CLARÍN. Suena ruido de armas. Salen el REY, CLOTALDO y ASTOLFO, huyendo.)

BASILIO.	¿Hay más infelice rey? 3060
	¿Hay padre más perseguido?

BUGLE.	Because I know the secret of your identity. You see, Clothold *(Offstage, the drums of war are heard.)*... but what's all that racket?
ROSSAURA.	What could it be?
BUGLE.	An armed squadron is spilling out of the besieged palace in hopes of resisting and defeating the one commanded by the fierce Sigismund.
ROSSAURA.	Well how can I stand here like a coward when so much cruelty is being unleashed in defiance of order and law? I must rush to his side and astonish the world. *(Exit.)*
SOLDIERS.	*(Offstage, one group.)* Long live our invincible king! *(Offstage, another group.)* Long live our freedom!
BUGLE.	I say, long live freedom *and* the king! Let them live with my blessing, for as long as they look out for me, I have no problem with anything. And now, amid such confusion, I shall be as pitiless as Nero as he watched Rome burn. Though if I have to take pity on something, it might as well be me. If I hide, I can watch the whole party from here among the crags. It's a safe place where death won't find me, so to hell with death! *(He [makes an obscene gesture, directed at Death, and] hides.)*

(The sound of war intensifies. Enter the king, CLOTHOLD, and AISTULF, in retreat.)

VASILY.	Has there ever been an unluckier king? Has there ever been a more persecuted father?

CLOTALDO.	Ya tu ejército vencido
	baja sin tino ni ley.
ASTOLFO.	Los traidores vencedores
	quedan.
BASILIO.	En batallas tales, 3065
	los que vencen son leales,
	los vencidos, los traidores.
	Huyamos, Clotaldo, pues,
	del crüel, del inhumano
	rigor de un hijo tirano. 3070

(Disparan dentro, y cae CLARÍN, herido, de donde está.)

CLARÍN.	¡Válgame el cielo!
ASTOLFO.	¿Quién es
	este infelice soldado
	que a nuestros pies ha caído
	en sangre todo teñido?
CLARÍN.	Soy un hombre desdichado 3075
	que, por quererme guardar
	de la muerte, la busqué.
	Huyendo della, topé
	con ella, pues no hay lugar
	para la muerte secreto; 3080
	de donde claro se arguye
	de quien más su efeto huye
	es quien se llega a su efeto.
	Por eso tornad, tornad
	a la lid sangrienta luego; 3085
	que entre las armas y el fuego
	hay mayor seguridad
	que en el monte más guardado;
	que no hay seguro camino
	a la fuerza del destino 3090
	y a la inclemencia del hado.
	Y así, aunque a libraros vais
	de la muerte con hüir,
	mirad que vais a morir,
	si está de Dios que muráis. 3095

(Cae dentro.)

BASILIO.	Mirad que vais a morir,
	si está de Dios que muráis.

CLOTHOLD.	Your army, now defeated, retreats in disorder.
AISTULF.	The traitors have become victors.
VASILY.	In battles such as this, loyalty belongs to the winners and treachery to the defeated. We must flee, Clothold, from the cruel and inhuman severity of a tyrannical son.

(A shot is heard offstage, and BUGLE falls wounded from his hiding place.)

BUGLE.	Heaven help me!
AISTULF.	Who is this unlucky soldier fallen at our feet, drenched in blood?
BUGLE.	Just an unfortunate man who, in trying to run from death, ran right into her, for there's no hiding place she can't find. Which goes to show that he who most tries to flee her reach is the one who will fall within her reach. So return, return to the bloody fighting immediately, for you're safer amid arms and open fire than on the most remote mountaintop, and there's no sure way past destiny's power and fate's inclemency. And thus, although you aim to free yourselves from death by fleeing, consider that, if it's God's will that you die, then you shall die. *(He falls dead offstage.)*
VASILY.	Consider that, if it's God's will that you die, then you shall

¡Qué bien, ay cielos, persuade
nuestro error, nuestra ignorancia,
a mayor conocimiento   3100
este cadáver que habla
por la boca de una herida,
siendo el humor que desata
sangrienta lengua que enseña
que son diligencias vanas   3105
del hombre cuantas dispone
contra mayor fuerza y causa;
pues yo, por librar de muertes
y sediciones mi patria,
vine a entregarla a los mismos   3110
de quien pretendí librarla!

CLOTALDO.   Aunque el hado, señor, sabe
todos los caminos y halla
a quien busca entre lo espeso
de dos peñas, no es cristiana   3115
determinación decir
que no hay reparo a su saña.
Sí hay, que el prudente varón
vitoria del hado alcanza.
Y si no estás reservado   3120
de la pena y la desgracia,
haz por donde te reserves.

ASTOLFO.   Clotaldo, señor, te habla
como prudente varón
que madura edad alcanza;   3125
yo, como joven valiente.
Entre las espesas ramas
dese monte está un caballo,
veloz aborto del aura;
huye en él, que yo entretanto   3130
te guardaré las espaldas.

BASILIO.   Si está de Dios que yo muera,
o si la muerte me aguarda
aquí, hoy la quiero buscar,
esperando cara a cara.   3135

(Tocan al arma, y sale SEGISMUNDO y toda la compañía.)

SEGISMUNDO. En lo intrincado del monte,
entre sus espesas ramas,

die. How easily, O heavens, we are brought from error and ignorance to greater understanding by this corpse that speaks through the mouth of an open wound, which, like a bloody tongue, teaches us that all of man's attempts to cheat fate are in vain! And thus I, in attempting to save my fatherland from sedition and death, have in the end turned it over to the very people from whom I was attempting to save it.

CLOTHOLD. Although fate, my lord, sees all and is capable of finding its target among the darkest crags, it's not a Christian sentiment to say that there's no way around its wrath. There is, for the prudent man can triumph over fate; and now, unless you desire more suffering and tragedy, you must find a place where you can protect yourself.

AISTULF. My lord, Clothold speaks with the wisdom of old age, and I with the valour of youth. Over there in the thicket is a horse, swift miscarriage of the wind; use it to flee, and I shall guard your back.

VASILY. If it's God's will that I die or if death awaits me here, today I shall seek her out and await her face to face.

(The call to arms is sounded, and SIGISMUND enters accompanied by his SOLDIERS.)

SIGISMUND. Among the crags and thickets of the mountain hides the king.

el Rey se esconde. Seguilde,
no quede en sus cumbres planta
que no examine el cuidado,   3140
tronco a tronco y rama a rama.

CLOTALDO.   ¡Huye, señor!

BASILIO.   ¿Para qué?

ASTOLFO.   ¿Qué intentas?

BASILIO.   ¡Astolfo, aparta!

CLOTALDO.   ¿Qué intentas?

BASILIO.   Hacer, Clotaldo,
un remedio que me falta.   3145
Si a mí buscándome vas,
ya estoy, príncipe, a tus plantas.
Sea dellas blanca alfombra
esta nieve de mis canas.
Pisa mi cerviz, y huella   3150
mi corona; postra, arrastra
mi decoro y mi respeto;
toma de mi honor venganza;
sírvete de mí cautivo;
y, tras prevenciones tantas,   3155
cumpla el hado su homenaje,
cumpla el cielo su palabra.

SEGISMUNDO.   Corte ilustre de Polonia,
que de admiraciones tantas
sois testigos, atended,   3160
que vuestro príncipe os habla.
Lo que está determinado
del cielo, y en azul tabla
Dios con el dedo escribió,
de quien son cifras y estampas   3165
tantos papeles azules
que adornan letras doradas,
nunca engaña, nunca miente;
porque quien miente y engaña
es quien, para usar mal dellas,   3170
las penetra y las alcanza.
Mi padre, que está presente,
por excusarse a la saña
de mi condición, me hizo
un bruto, una fiera humana;   3175
de suerte que, cuando yo

Seek him out; let no shrub on the summit go unexamined, trunk by trunk and branch by branch!

CLOTHOLD. *[To the king.]* Flee, my lord!

VASILY. To what end?

AISTULF. What do you intend to do?

VASILY. Step aside, Aistulf.

CLOTHOLD. What do you intend to do?

VASILY. Something that must be done, Clothold. *[To SIGISMUND.]* If I'm the one you're looking for, you have me at your mercy, my prince. Use my grey hairs as a mat for your feet; trample my neck and tread upon my crown; humiliate me and drag my good name through the mud; take your vengeance on my honour, and treat me as your captive. After so many attempts to circumvent it, let fate claim its reward; let the stars keep their word.

SIGISMUND. Illustrious Court of Poland, witness to so many amazing events, listen carefully, for your prince wishes to address you. What is determined by Heaven and written by God's finger on the azure tablet – of which the numerous blue leaves adorned in gold letters are the signs and annotations – never lies or deceives; the lies and deceptions come from the one who, wishing to manipulate the information, undertakes to decipher it. My father, who is present among us, in order to avoid the wrath of my character, turned me into a brute, a human beast; thus, whereas my gallant nobility,

por mi nobleza gallarda,
por mi sangre generosa,
por mi condición bizarra,
hubiera nacido dócil   3180
y humilde, sólo bastara
tal género de vivir,
tal linaje de crianza,
a hacer fieras mis costumbres:
¡qué buen modo de estorbarlas!   3185
Si a cualquier hombre dijesen:
«alguna fiera inhumana
te dará muerte», ¿escogiera
buen remedio en despertalla
cuando estuviese durmiendo?   3190
Si dijeran: «esta espada
que traes ceñida ha de ser
quien te dé la muerte», vana
diligencia de evitarlo
fuera entonces desnudarla   3195
y ponérsela a los pechos.
Si dijesen: «golfos de agua
han de ser tu sepultura
en monumentos de plata»,
mal hiciera en darse al mar,   3200
cuando soberbio levanta
rizados montes de nieve,
de cristal crespas montañas.
Lo mismo le ha sucedido
que a quien, porque le amenaza   3205
una fiera, la despierta;
que a quien, temiendo una espada
la desnuda; y que a quien mueve
las ondas de una borrasca.
Y cuando fuera – escuchadme –   3210
dormida fiera mi saña,
templada espada mi furia,
mi rigor quieta bonanza,
la fortuna no se vence
con injusticia y venganza;   3215
porque antes se incita más.
Y así, quien vencer aguarda
a su fortuna, ha de ser

genteel lineage, and generous nature should have made me
congenial and humble, my living conditions and upbringing
were sufficient to cultivate a ferocious disposition. What a
way to cheat fate! If any man were told, "One day you will
be killed by an inhuman beast," would it be a good solution
for him to wake one up while it was sleeping? If he were
told, "That sword you're wearing will one day be the death
of you," to take it out and point it at his chest would prove a
futile remedy. If he were told, "Your grave will lie beneath
walls of water and bear tombstones of silvery waves," he
would be foolish to set sail just when the defiant sea was
whipping up frothy mountains of glass. My father has ended
up just like the one who, threatened by a beast, woke it up;
like the one who, fearful of the sword, unsheathed it; and
like the one who stirred up the waves of a tempest. But even
if – and listen well – my wrath were a dormant beast, my
fury a temperate sword, and my severity a calm sea, fortune
could not be overcome through injustice and vengeance,
for such measures only make matters worse. And thus,
whoever wishes to overcome his fortune must do so through

con prudencia y con templanza.
No antes de venir el daño   3220
se reserva ni se guarda
quien le previene; que, aunque
puede humilde – cosa es clara –
reservarse dél, no es
sino después que se halla   3225
en la ocasión, porque aquesta
no hay camino de estorbarla.
Sirva de ejemplo este raro
espectáculo, esta extraña
admiración, este horror,   3230
este prodigio; pues nada
es más que llegar a ver,
con prevenciones tan varias,
rendido a mis pies a un padre,
y atropellado a un monarca.   3235
Sentencia del cielo fue.
Por más que quiso estorbarla
él, no pudo; y podré yo,
que soy menor en las canas,
en el valor y en la ciencia,   3240
vencerla. Señor, levanta;
dame tu mano, que ya
que el cielo te desengaña
de que has errado en el modo
de vencerle, humilde aguarda   3245
mi cuello a que tú te vengues.
Rendido estoy a tus plantas.

BASILIO.   Hijo, que tan noble acción
otra vez en mis entrañas
te engendra, príncipe eres: 3250
a ti el laurel y la palma
se te deben; tú venciste;
corónente tus hazañas.

TODOS.   ¡Viva Segismundo, viva!

SEGISMUNDO.   Pues que ya vencer aguarda   3255
mi valor grandes vitorias,
hoy ha de ser la más alta
vencerme a mí. Astolfo dé
la mano luego a Rosaura,

prudence and temperance. He who foresees a danger can't remove himself from its path; yes, he can take a few humble measures to guard against it, but not until the moment is upon him, for there's no way of forestalling its arrival. Of this there's no better proof than this extraordinary spectacle, this bizarre event, horrible and monstrous to behold. Just look and you'll see, despite all efforts to the contrary, a father vanquished at my foot, a monarch grovelling in defeat. This was Heaven's judgment; no matter how he tried to prevent it, he was unable. And I – inferior to him in years, valour, and knowledge – shall succeed where he failed. Rise, my lord, and give me your hand; now that the stars have shown you the error in your attempts to overcome them, my neck humbly awaits your vengeance. I am at your mercy.

VASILY.

My son, you are prince, for such a noble action remoulds you from my flesh; the laurel and the palm are yours. You have triumphed; your deeds shall be your crown.

ALL.

Long live Sigismund! Long live Sigismund!

[Enter ROSSAURA.]

SIGISMUND.

[Observing ROSSAURA.] My valour promises great victories, and today the greatest of all will be my victory over myself. Aistulf, promise your hand to Rossaura immediately, for you

pues sabe que de su honor   3260
es deuda y yo he de cobrarla.

ASTOLFO.   Aunque es verdad que la debo
obligaciones, repara
que ella no sabe quién es;
y es bajeza y es infamia   3265
casarme yo con mujer...

CLOTALDO.   No prosigas, tente, aguarda;
porque Rosaura es tan noble
como tú, Astolfo, y mi espada
lo defenderá en el campo;   3270
que es mi hija, y esto basta.

ASTOLFO.   ¿Qué dices?

CLOTALDO.   Que yo, hasta verla
casada, noble y honrada,
no la quise descubrir.
La historia desto es muy larga;   3275
pero, en fin, es hija mía.

ASTOLFO.   Pues siendo así, mi palabra
cumpliré.

SEGISMUNDO. Pues, porque Estrella
no quede desconsolada,
viendo que príncipe pierde   3280
de tanto valor y fama,
de mi propia mano, yo
con esposo he de casarla
que en méritos y fortuna,
si no le excede, le iguala.   3285
Dame la mano.

ESTRELLA.   Yo gano
en merecer dicha tanta.

SEGISMUNDO. A Clotaldo, que leal
sirvió a mi padre, le aguardan
mis brazos con las mercedes   3290
que él pidiere que le haga.

SOLDADO 1. Si así a quien no te ha servido
honras, a mí, que fui causa
del alboroto del reino
y de la torre en que estabas   3295
te saqué, ¿qué me darás?

SEGISMUNDO. La torre; y porque no salgas
della nunca hasta morir,

know that you're a debtor to her honour, and I intend to make you pay.

AISTULF. Although it's true I owe her something, bear in mind that she doesn't know who her father is; and it would be a low and infamous deed for someone like me to marry a woman who...

CLOTHOLD. Do not go on; hold your tongue and listen. Rossaura is just as noble as you, Aistulf, and I will argue her case with my sword if I have to. She is my daughter, and that's all you need to know.

AISTULF. What are you saying?

CLOTHOLD. Until I saw her promised in noble marriage and her honour avenged, I didn't want to reveal her identity. It's a very long story, but the point is that she's my daughter.

AISTULF. Well, that being the case, I'll honour my word.

SIGISMUND. And now, so Stella won't feel left out, given that she's lost a prince of such merit and reputation, by my own hand I shall wed her to a man who is, in distinction and good fortune, if not greater than Aistulf, at least his equal. Give me your hand, my lady.

STELLA. I'm honoured to be worthy of such joy.

SIGISMUND. To Clothold, who served my father loyally, I offer my warm embrace together with any favours that he might ask of me.

SOLDIER 1. If that's how you reward someone who never served you, what do I get for inciting the uprising in the kingdom and for freeing you from the tower in which you were imprisoned?

SIGISMUND. The tower. And so that you'll never emerge until you die,

	has de estar allí con guardas;	
	que el traidor no es menester	3300
	siendo la traición pasada.	
BASILIO.	Tu ingenio a todos admira.	
ASTOLFO.	¡Qué condición tan mudada!	
ROSAURA.	¡Qué discreto y qué prudente!	
SEGISMUNDO.	¿Qué os admira, qué os espanta,	3305
	si fue mi maestro un sueño	
	y estoy temiendo, en mis ansias,	
	que he de despertar y hallarme	
	otra vez en mi cerrada	
	prisión? Y cuando no sea,	3310
	el soñarlo sólo basta;	
	pues así llegué a saber	
	que toda la dicha humana,	
	en fin, pasa como sueño.	
	Y quiero hoy aprovecharla	3315
	el tiempo que me durare,	
	pidiendo de nuestras faltas	
	perdón, pues de pechos nobles	
	es tan propio el perdonarlas.	3319

you'll be under the constant watch of the guards, for traitors are of no use once their treachery has passed.

VASILY. Your ingenuity amazes us all.

AISTULF. What a change of character!

ROSSAURA. What discretion, what prudence!

SIGISMUND. Whence comes your amazement, your shock, given that my teacher was a dream? I still fear, deep down inside, that I'll wake up and find myself locked away again in my dark prison. And if that doesn't happen, it's enough to dream it so, for that's how I came to realize that all human happiness is, in the end, as ephemeral as a dream. So I'd like to take advantage of this happy moment while I can... *[To the audience.]* ...and ask you to overlook our flaws, for forgiveness comes naturally to noble souls.

GLOSSARY

Note: I firmly believe that all these terms will be comprehensible in performance in the contexts in which I have translated them. For directors who disagree, I offer in brackets acceptable substitutions of the most obscure entries.

Aeneas. Trojan hero of Virgil's epic poem, the *Aeneid,* he was the son of Anchises and Aphrodite. He escaped the sack of Troy and wandered for seven years before settling in Italy. Book 4 of the *Aeneid* recounts how he stops in Carthage (near present-day Tunis), where the queen, Dido, falls in love with him; but he is convinced by the gods to abandon her in order to pursue his destiny as the founder of Rome. He leaves behind a sword, and the queen, overwhelmed by grief, stabs herself with it and hurls herself onto a funeral pyre.

Atlas. In Greek mythology, a Titan condemned by Zeus to support the heavens upon his shoulders. Calderón often refers to him as a metaphor for those who support the elderly. [Atlases → pillars]

Aurora. Roman personification of the dawn who came to be identified with the Greek goddess Eos. Aurora is seen as a lovely woman who flies across the sky announcing the arrival of the sun. According to one myth, her tears cause the dew as she flies across the sky weeping for one of her sons, who was killed. [Dawn]

Babylonia. Ancient empire of Mesopotamia in the Euphrates River valley with its capital at Babylon. It flourished under Hammurabi and Nebuchadnezzar II but declined after 562 BC and fell to the Persians in 539. In Calderón, a symbol of chaos through its associations with the Tower of Babel.

Bellona. Roman goddess of war, popular among Roman soldiers. Her attribute is the sword and she is depicted wearing a helmet and armed with a spear and a torch. She accompanied Mars in battle, and was variously given as his wife, sister or daughter; but Calderón identifies her with the sun, meant to represent the king. ["act as Bellona" → "fight with ferocity"]

Danae. In Greek mythology, the daughter of Acrisius. An oracle warned her father that Danae's son would someday kill him, so Acrisius shut Danae in a bronze room, away from all male company. However, Zeus conceived a passion for her and came to her through the roof in the form of a shower of gold that poured down into her lap; as a result she had a son, Perseus, who eventually fulfilled the prophecy by killing Acrisius. ["Danae, Leda, Europa" → "those who fell for such ruses"]

Diana. In Roman mythology, the virgin goddess of hunting and childbirth, traditionally associated with the moon and identified with the Greek Artemis. Calderón seems to want to contrast her to the warlike Pallas, perhaps because of the nurturing qualities associated with midwives, but both her virginity and her role as huntress blur the opposition. In the Zaragoza branch of the play's textual transmission, "Venus" appears in place of "Diana" at this point in the manuscript. [Venus]

Dropsy. Medical condition, known in modern times as oedema, that is characterized by abnormal accumulation of fluid in the body tissues or in the body cavities causing swelling or distension of the affected parts. In the Renaissance it was thought to be caused by excess drinking, so that further intake of liquids was considered life threatening. ["suffer from the dropsy" → "be insatiable"]

Euclid. Greek mathematician of the third century BC who applied the deductive principles of logic to geometry, thereby deriving statements from clearly defined axioms. Calderón's reference to him is an example of *antonomasia*, that is, the use of a proper name to denote, par excellence, a member of a group (in this case, mathematicians). [mathematician]

Europa. In Greek mythology, a Phoenician princess who inflamed the desire of Zeus. He appeared to her in the form of a beautiful white bull and encountered her at the seashore. By appearing to be very tame, he coaxed her to climb onto his back and then swam off with her across the sea to Crete. The so-called *Rape of Europa* is a favourite motif of Renaissance poetry and iconography. [For substitutions, see **Danae**.]

Flora. Roman goddess of the blossoming flowers of spring. [Springtime.]

Halberd. Weapon of the 15th and 16th centuries that came to replace the lance in combat; it had an axe-like blade and a steel spike mounted on the end of a long shaft. Halberds are still brandished today by the Swiss Guard at the Vatican. [halberd-brandishing → well-armed]

Henbane. Poisonous Eurasian plant *(Hyoscyamus niger)* having an unpleasant odour, sticky leaves, and funnel-shaped greenish-yellow flowers. Its effects are similar to those of belladonna, which causes deep sleep, delirium, euphoria, and hallucinations. In addition to both these drugs, the cocktail the prince is made to drink in act 2 contains opium, creating a super-potent narcotic capable of inducing borderline hysteria and schizophrenia.

Hippogriff. Fabulous beast popularized in Ariosto's *Orlando furioso* (1532). The hippogriff has the body and hindquarters of a horse and the wings, claws, and head of a griffin (itself a mythological monster with the head, wings, and talons of an eagle and the body of a lion). As the very first word in the Spanish version of the play, the hippogriff alludes to the swiftness of the horse that has just thrown Rossaura; more importantly, it is a central metaphor that represents the half-man, half-beast nature of Sigismund and foreshadows the chaos and confusion into which the country is about to plunge. See Introduction, section 4 for a discussion. [chimera]

Icarus. In Greek mythology, the son of Daedalus who, in escaping from Crete on artificial wings made for him by his father, flew so close to the sun that the wax with which his wings were fastened melted, and he fell to his death in the Aegean Sea. Bugle refers to him in allusion to the servant thrown off the balcony by Sigismund. [little Icarus → the servant]

Leda. In Greek mythology, queen of Sparta who, seduced by Zeus in the form of a swan, laid an egg from which hatched the twins Castor and Pollux. [For substitutions, see **Danae**.]

Lysippus. Greek sculptor, head of the school of Argos and Sicyon in the time of Alexander the Great (fourth century BC). His works are said to have numbered 1500, some of them colossal, but nothing of his own hand is known to have survived. Calderón may have been familiar with him through Alexander's famous edict that no one carve him in stone but Lysippus. [Michelangelo]

Nero. Emperor of Rome (54–68), whose cruelty and recklessness provoked widespread revolts and ultimately led to his suicide. He was widely synonymous with tyranny in the Renaissance, and Bugle's allusion springs from a long tradition that blamed him (probably unjustly) for intentionally starting the disastrous fire of AD 64 and then calmly playing music as the city burned. Cf. Shakespeare: "Plantagenet, I will – and like thee, Nero, / Play on the lute, beholding the towns burn" (*1 Henry VI* 1.6.73–74).

New Calendar. The Gregorian Calendar, which replaced the Julian Calendar throughout Catholic Europe, by mandate of Pope Gregory XIII, in 1582. (Its implementation was resisted in Protestant Europe until the eighteenth century and in Eastern Orthodox countries until the twentieth.) When the reform was implemented, ten days were taken out of October so that the fourteenth followed the fourth. This caused great confusion, of which people apparently took advantage in order to cut out fasting days from religious celebrations. In the passage in question, Bugle is in the opposite situation because he fasts and never feasts.

Pallas. Title of the goddess Athena (Pallas Athena) who, according to some accounts, was the daughter of the Titan Pallas. In Greek mythology, Pallas Athena was a virgin goddess of wisdom, war, the arts, industry, justice, and skill; but Calderón alludes to her primarily in reference to her role in war. [Pallas Athena]

Phaethon. In Greek mythology, the son of the sun god Helios. He induced his father to allow him to drive the chariot of the sun across the heavens for one day. The horses, feeling their reins held by a weaker hand, ran wildly off their course and came close to the earth, threatening to burn it. Zeus noticed the danger and destroyed Phaethon with a thunderbolt. In Calderón (who wrote a play titled *Hijo del Sol, Faetón*), he is a symbol of rash arrogance. [ill-fated leader]

Seneca, Lucius Annaeus. *c.* 4 BC to AD 65. Known as "the Younger." Roman Stoic philosopher, writer, and tutor of Nero. His works include treatises on rhetoric and governance and numerous plays that influenced Renaissance drama. Born in what is now Spain (the Roman province Hispania), he was a favourite of classical Spanish authors including Calderón.

Shawm. Medieval wind instrument, forerunner of the modern oboe. [oboe]

Syncopate. In grammar, to shorten a word by omitting a sound, letter, or syllable from the middle. Thus, to "syncopate the light of day" would mean to obliterate the sun. [truncate]

Thales. Greek thinker (*c.* 624–546 BC) traditionally considered the first Western philosopher and a founder of geometry and abstract astronomy. He maintained that matter is composed of water and, most important in the context of *Life's a Dream*, accurately predicted a solar eclipse in 585 BC. Calderón's reference to him is another instance of antonomasia (see entry for *Euclid*), in this case meaning astrologer. [astrologer]

Timanthes. A celebrated Greek painter at Sicyon who flourished around 400 BC and whose masterpiece was a famous picture of the sacrifice of Iphigenia. He seems to have represented classical painting par excellence for Calderón. [Leonardo]